# Monkey Game De

## Beginner's Guide

Create monetized 2D games deployable to almost any platform

**Michael Hartlef**

BIRMINGHAM - MUMBAI

# Monkey Game Development
## Beginner's Guide

First published: April 2012

Production Reference: 1130412

Published by Packt Publishing Ltd.
Livery Place
35 Livery Street
Birmingham B3 2PB, UK.

ISBN 978-1-84969-203-8

www.packtpub.com

Cover Image by J.Blaminsky (jarek@jblaminsky.com)

# Credits

**Author**
Michael Hartlef

**Reviewers**
Nikolas Kolm

Meri Morganov

**Acquisition Editor**
Kartikey Pandey

**Lead Technical Editor**
Shreerang Deshpande

**Technical Editors**
Apoorva Bolar

Arun Nadar

Priyanka S

**Copy Editor**
Brandt D'Mello

**Project Coordinator**
Alka Nayak

**Proofreader**
Aaron Nash

**Indexer**
Hemangini Bari

**Graphics**
Manu Joseph

**Production Coordinator**
Melwyn D'Sa

**Cover Work**
Melwyn D'Sa

# About the Author

**Michael Hartlef** has been into game development for a long long time, starting in 1984, at the early age of 18, with this great hobby called developing computer games, on the Commodore C64. After developing for this machine, he has worked on most other well-known computers, such as the Amiga 1000 and 500, the Atari 1024 STFm, and of course various PCs. These days it is mostly his iMac that he uses.

Over the years, he has become very knowledgeable about general and specific concepts for developing games and has worked on a large range of game development tools/ programming languages, such as thinBasic, Delphi, 3D GameStudio, Blitz3D, BlitzMax, DarkBasic Pro, App Game Kit (AGK), Corona SDK, and of course, Monkey! Besides working on games, Michael has developed various add-ons for tools such as command library extensions and programming editors.

During the day, Michael works for a utility company where he maintains the billing system (SAP IS-U). Michael is also the founder of an independent game developer startup called Whitesky Games (http://www.whiteskygames.com). There, he spends a lot of his spare time working on game development tools (IndeED), add-ons and games for friends and clients, and his own projects.

First, I'd like to thank my wonderful wife Katherine and my great son Marc Justin for having so much patience with me during the time of writing this book and giving me all the support I needed. Without you guys, I would not have made it. I love you!

Also, I would like to thank the people at PacktPub for giving me the opportunity to write this book, which has been a great experience in my life. Next, I send a big thank you to Jayant Varma from Oz Apps, who hinted to me that PacktPub was looking for an author for this book. Also, I want to thank Lee Bardsley from GameLab3D for being my friend and talk buddy.

And finally, a big thank you goes to Mark Sibly, the creator of Monkey, for providing such an awesome tool for the people and me.

# About the Reviewers

**Nikolas Kolm** has been active as a Level Designer, World Builder, and Interactive Storyteller for a long time, in capacities ranging from community Mod projects, to student work, to indie production. During this time, he has gathered a lot of experience in different editors and production settings, most commonly the Unreal Editor, the NWN2 Toolset, and the Dragon Age Toolset as well as Game Maker, and recently, Unity 3D.

During his time along with the Mod team responsible for a persistent world server for Neverwinter Nights 2, Nikolas was responsible for the creation of interesting areas and levels for players to traverse and live in, which needed to adhere to a common theme with the rest of the world, and also had to offer challenges for groups of players out for an adventure. This included setting up encounters with enemies, setting up the ambient effects, creating dialogue for scripted encounters, and ensuring that the area supported the environmental storytelling of the module.

While working on the indie title AVOID, as Lead Game Designer, Niko also had to fill in as Level Designer from time to time, which allowed him to practice his skills with the Unity editor. It also allowed him to work in a leadership capacity with a team of over 30 other team members, to experience a complete production cycle.

His unique background, living in Japan, traveling the world, and studying many cultures and history, has given him a wealth of experience from which to draw when designing believable characters, dramatic encounters, and immersive worlds.

**Meri Morganov** has been playing video games for most of her life and has always wondered what the magic behind them was. She took game programming courses at the Art Institute of Vancouver to learn more on the topic and worked with big student groups to make games. From high-level scripting to low-level programming, she worked hard to learn the art of the trade.

After college she has been working on indie projects with friends and small companies. She loves working in teams and staying in close contact with her teammates to get the job done right. Unity3D and Visual Studio have been her favorite tools to use.

> I'd like to thank my teachers and friends who made it possible for me to learn such a great skill.

# www.PacktPub.com

## Support files, eBooks, discount offers and more

You might want to visit www.PacktPub.com for support files and downloads related to your book.

Did you know that Packt offers eBook versions of every book published, with PDF and ePub files available? You can upgrade to the eBook version at www.PacktPub.com and as a print book customer, you are entitled to a discount on the eBook copy. Get in touch with us at service@packtpub.com for more details.

At www.PacktPub.com, you can also read a collection of free technical articles, sign up for a range of free newsletters and receive exclusive discounts and offers on Packt books and eBooks.

http://PacktLib.PacktPub.com

Do you need instant solutions to your IT questions? PacktLib is Packt's online digital book library. Here, you can access, read and search across Packt's entire library of books.

## Why Subscribe?

- ◆ Fully searchable across every book published by Packt
- ◆ Copy and paste, print and bookmark content
- ◆ On demand and accessible via web browser

## Free Access for Packt account holders

If you have an account with Packt at www.PacktPub.com, you can use this to access PacktLib today and view nine entirely free books. Simply use your login credentials for immediate access.

# Table of Contents

# Preface

Welcome to *Monkey Game Development Beginner's Guide*. This book will teach you (as a step-by-step guide) how to develop 2D games with Monkey. With eight sample games included, the book covers a great range of the toolset and important game development techniques. You will also learn how to deploy your games to mobile platforms, such as iOS, Android, and other platforms, such as OSX and Windows.

When you are done studying this book, the knowledge you have gained about creating 2D games with Monkey will have you transformed from being a beginner-level game developer to experienced creator of your virtual dreams. So what are you waiting for? Start reading and create some Monkey-powered games!

## What this book covers

*Chapter 1, Monkey Huh?,* takes you on a fast-paced tour of what Monkey is, which tools are included, what games you can create with it, and which programming features Monkey provides for you, in general.

*Chapter 2, Getting to Know your Monkey—a Trip to the Zoo*, will show you the first steps in working with the Monk editor and creating your very first Monkey script. The next step is to develop a PONG clone with Monkey and to learn the basic structure of a Monkey script. Running your game inside the browser is the final goal for this chapter.

*Chapter 3, Game #2, Rocket Commander*, teaches you how to develop a Missile Command clone. During its development, you will learn more about how to render drawing primitives, read mouse input, handle different game objects with their own game logics in separate files, and use basic circle-to-circle collision detection. Exporting your game to HTML5 will round up this chapter.

*Chapter 4*, *Game #3*, *Comet Crusher*, is the first chapter where we will make extensive use of an external game framework called fantomEngine. It will allow us to develop our game even faster, because we don't need to develop our own basic methods for rendering and updating objects anymore. During the development of an Asteroids clone, you will learn how to use the framework, display images, load and save a high-score list, and use timers and automatic object updating events. At the end of the chapter, you will export your game to the FLASH platform.

*Chapter 5*, *Game #4*, *Chain Reaction*, covers the development of a typical casual puzzle game called Chain Reaction. You will utilize features of the fantomEngine even further, learn how to use touch input, scale content depending on the devices screen size, and optimize your collision detection. Playing sounds, transition objects, using typical mobile device events, and exporting your game to the Android platform are covered in this chapter, too.

*Chapter 6*, *Game #5*, *Balls Out!*, will cover game development for the iOS mobile platform and a typical hardware feature of mobile devices called the accelerometer. During the development of a Breakout-inspired game called Balls Out!, you will learn how to use tilt movement to control your game, how to create and use particle emitters, and store data in a different container objects called stacks.

*Chapter 7*, *Game #6*, *At The Docks*, which covers the development of a Sokoban clone, will show you how to read joystick input for your XNA game and covers another collision detection method. It shows you how to load game levels that are stored in text files.

*Chapter 8*, *Game #7*, *Air Dogs 1942*, brings you to the development of Air Dogs 1942, a typical WWII-based arcade shooter. We will focus on creating a nice single player computer AI to control the enemy planes. The final goal will be to deploy your game to the OSX and Windows desktop platforms.

*Chapter 9*, *Game #8*, *Treasure Chest*, is a mix of everything we have learned so far, put together, to create a Bejewled clone called Treasure chest.

*Chapter 10*, *Making Some Money for Bananas*, will show you how to sign, prepare your apps, and load them up to different markets, such as the the Apple App store or the Android market. Making money from your games is the goal of this chapter. For this, it will cover how to use external features such as implementing advertising in your mobile game, too. You will also learn what kinds of markets exist for your apps.

# Who this book is for

Do you want to quickly create games deployable to all the major desktop and mobile platforms? If so, look no further. You will learn how to utilize the highly versatile Monkey programming language/toolset to create 2D games, deployable almost anywhere. Only very basic knowledge of Monkey is required, so if you are a total beginner, it will help if you have studied the samples that come with Monkey.

# Conventions

In this book, you will find several headings appearing frequently.

To give clear instructions of how to complete a procedure or task, we use:

## Time for action – heading

1. Action 1
2. Action 2
3. Action 3

Instructions often need some extra explanation so that they make sense, so they are followed with:

## What just happened?

This heading explains the working of tasks or instructions that you have just completed.

You will also find some other learning aids in the book, including:

## Have a go hero – heading

These set practical challenges and give you ideas for experimenting with what you have learned.

You will also find a number of styles of text that distinguish between different kinds of information. Here are some examples of these styles, and an explanation of their meaning.

Code words in text are shown as follows: "The source code file, `fantomEngine.monkey` is included with this book."

A block of code is set as follows:

```
    g.SaveHighScore()
    Return 0
Endif
```

When we wish to draw your attention to a particular part of a code block, the relevant lines or items are set in bold:

```
Field layerBackground:ftLayer
Field layerGame:ftLayer
Field layerClouds:ftLayer
Field layerInfo:ftLayer
Field layerTitle:ftLayer
```

**New terms** and **important words** are shown in bold. Words that you see on the screen, in menus or dialog boxes for example, appear in the text like this: "clicking the **Next** button moves you to the next screen".

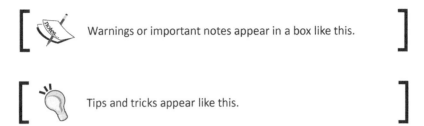

Warnings or important notes appear in a box like this.

Tips and tricks appear like this.

# Reader feedback

Feedback from our readers is always welcome. Let us know what you think about this book—what you liked or may have disliked. Reader feedback is important for us to develop titles that you really get the most out of.

To send us general feedback, simply send an e-mail to feedback@packtpub.com, and mention the book title through the subject of your message.

If there is a topic that you have expertise in and you are interested in either writing or contributing to a book, see our author guide on www.packtpub.com/authors.

# Customer support

Now that you are the proud owner of a Packt book, we have a number of things to help you to get the most from your purchase.

## Downloading the example code

You can download the example code files for all Packt books you have purchased from your account at http://www.packtpub.com. If you purchased this book elsewhere, you can visit http://www.packtpub.com/support and register to have the files e-mailed directly to you.

# Errata

Although we have taken every care to ensure the accuracy of our content, mistakes do happen. If you find a mistake in one of our books—maybe a mistake in the text or the code—we would be grateful if you would report this to us. By doing so, you can save other readers from frustration and help us improve subsequent versions of this book. If you find any errata, please report them by visiting http://www.packtpub.com/support, selecting your book, clicking on the **errata submission form** link, and entering the details of your errata. Once your errata are verified, your submission will be accepted and the errata will be uploaded to our website, or added to any list of existing errata, under the Errata section of that title.

# Piracy

Piracy of copyright material on the Internet is an ongoing problem across all media. At Packt, we take the protection of our copyright and licenses very seriously. If you come across any illegal copies of our works, in any form, on the Internet, please provide us with the location address or website name immediately so that we can pursue a remedy.

Please contact us at copyright@packtpub.com with a link to the suspected pirated material.

We appreciate your help in protecting our authors, and our ability to bring you valuable content.

# Questions

You can contact us at questions@packtpub.com if you are having a problem with any aspect of the book, and we will do our best to address it.

# 1
# Monkey—Huh?

*Monkey is a high-level programming language developed by Mark Sibly, the creator of the very popular* **Blitz Basic** *range of programming languages. If you happen to know Blitz Basic, Blitz3D, or BlitzMax, then you know where Monkey is coming from. Its main purpose is to provide you with a helpful tool to create 2D games, but of course, if you are creative, you will be able to create other kinds of apps and programs with it, too. For example, interactive books could a very good playing field for Monkey.*

*The Monkey programming language is strongly inspired by BASIC and JAVA. BASIC, in particular, is known to be a beginner's programming language. So naturally, Monkey is easy to learn and you can get up and running very fast; just as with most of the BASIC dialects. But it doesn't have to stop there. Monkey is also very extendable through third-party, or your own, Monkey source code and also native code running on each platform.*

*In this chapter, we will learn what Monkey is in general, how the toolset behind it works, and what kind of general features Monkey provides you with. We won't go into these things in great detail, but just give an overview. We also will have some playtime with games that were created with Monkey. So, if you happen to know all this already, it is safe for you to skip this little chapter and head right on to Chapter 2, Getting to Know Your Monkey—a Trip to the Zoo. If not, then keep on reading and you will learn a little about Monkey's background.*

# Game development for the rest of us

Since you are reading this book, we can safely assume that you have got the bug that makes a lot of people want to become a great and successful game developer. We have all played these awesome games and read stories about individuals who became wealthy overnight by selling their games on markets such as the Apple AppStore. And you want that too, right? We all do, and there is nothing wrong with that. Go for it! The way to get there was very difficult and long, in the past. For example, not long ago, learning Objective-C and using Xcode was the only way to create a game for the iPhone. Objective-C is not easy to learn if you are a complete beginner when it comes to programming. And a lot of people will tell you to study C and C++ in general before you head into Objective-C. Some people will tell you to study the BASIC language at first. You can imagine that it will take some time to study all this, never mind studying the techniques that are relevant to game development!

Now, with Monkey and various other game creation tools, this process has become much easier and quicker than before. A programming language that is based on a BASIC dialect is easy to learn and the features of Monkey will help you bring your dream of becoming a game developer to life.

# Cross-platform development

Ahh, the magic term... cross-platform development! It is the current hype thing. Because before the era of smart phones and tablets, the Windows platform, OSX and Linux were basically the only markets, where an individual game developer could publish games to. Game consoles were accessible only to huge game development companies with a lot of financial background.

Even these days, it is almost impossible to publish a game for an individual on some platforms. But new markets have arisen and new development tools such as Monkey are available now. Today it is more and more important to target several platforms with your game.

Why miss out on the money that can be made and the extra exposure for your game? There are so many markets to cater to, such as Apple AppStore, Android Market, and others, that it would be silly to throw away the opportunity to publish on them and rake in the extra cash. So, a cross-platform development tool such as Monkey is worth its weight in gold, and you will realize this very soon.

# Compiler or translator?

Under the hood, Monkey is a translator. That means it will translate your program, which is written in the Monkey programming language, into source code for the supported target languages. And because of this, your program will be able to run on various platforms, such as iOS, Android, XNA, OSX, and Windows.

After Monkey has translated your program into source code for a certain target platform, it will then utilize native tools and **SDKs (Software Development Kits)** on these platforms to finish the compilation and linking process. For this, you will need to install various tools and SDKs. For example, you need to install Xcode and the iOS SDK to create iPhone apps. Or, to create a Flash app, you need to install the Flex Actionscript compiler.

The following illustration shows the process of creating an application with Monkey:

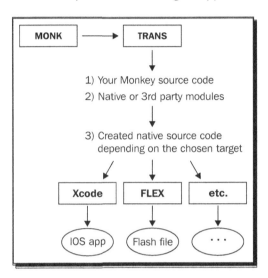

Don't worry about installing any of these SDKs and other tools for now. We will go through this together. Your default installation of Monkey can always export to HTML5 . To play HTML5 games, the only tool you need to have installed is a current version of an HTML5-compatible browser, such as FireFox, Safari, Chrome, or Internet Explorer.

# The Monkey toolbox

Every good toolman has a good toolbox. Monkey's toolbox is small but well-equipped. It is basically a combination of two tools and some accessories. The first tool is TRANS, the source code translator. It is responsible for transforming/translating your Monkey source code into code, which can be compiled for each target platform. Basically, you feed it with one programming language and it spills out your code in a different programming language.

The second tool is Monk, the in-built source code editor for Monkey. You can also use other code editors as well, but we will work with Monk in this book, and it wouldn't hurt for you to do the same. A great benefit  is that your Monkey installation includes all the source code for the tools, modules, and other stuff. So, if you happen to own a license for BlitzMAX (another programming language) and know what you are doing with it, then you could add features to Monk yourself or change it according to your needs.

The same thing goes for TRANS; you could change it as per your needs. The good thing is that you don't need another programming language. TRANS is self-compiling.

The accessories are Monkey's source code modules. They provide you with all the needed functionality for your games. We will learn more about this module, later on.

## Time for action – installing Monkey

I guess it is time for the first action. If you haven't already installed Monkey, then you should do so now.

Head over to the Monkey website at `http://www.monkeycoder.co.nz` and grab your copy of Monkey. This book is based on the full version, so you should get that. Of course, you have to buy it first, but you won't regret this investment. And keep in mind that it is only a one-time investment. Other game creation tools are only available through subscription price models which can become very costly later on. It is not so with Monkey; you buy it once, and then you never have to pay for it again.

Ok, let's go and get it:

1. Go to `http://www.monkeycoder.co.nz`.

2. After you buy Monkey and sign up your user account on the website, download the latest full version from your user account.

3. Unpack the ZIP file to a location you want to run Monkey from.

   That wasn't much to do, was it? Like everything in Monkey, it is very easy to handle, even the first installation. But oh, we forget something. Something major.

4. Start Monk, to see the glorious development environment of Monkey.

## Please welcome... Monk

Yes, here it is. Monk. Monkey's very own code editor.

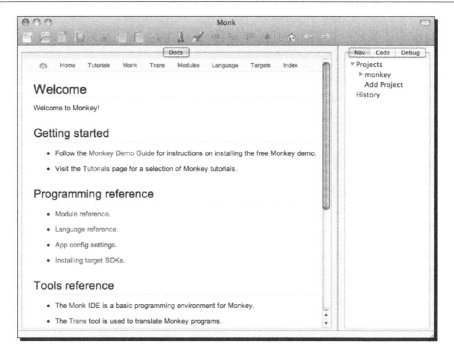

This is the place where most of the magic will happen. The magic you will create—your own games. Your own awesome games. You still want to do it, right? Ok, then let's carry on.

When it comes to writing your Monkey code, you won't need anything else. There are other source code editors you could use to code your games with, but this book will utilize Monk for all the coding action.

How Monk works and which tools it provides you with, for your development, will be explained in *Chapter 2, Getting to Know your Monkey— a Trip to the Zoo*.

# MSERVER—Monkey's own web server

Since Version 39, Monkey has been shipped with its own HTML server. This was necessary as certain operations required some security rights for actions such as writing the app state within an HTML app. When **MServer** starts, you will see a window such as the following:

Later on, when you let an HTML5 game run via Monk, MSERVER will provide you with useful information for certain actions of the game.

## *What just happened?*

Installing Monkey is easy, right? And please note, you can copy the extracted folder to any location you want. The settings file for Monk is called `monk.yourComputerName.ini` and is located in the root folder of the Monkey installation. If you move the Monkey folder to a new location on your harddrive, you might want to delete it or alter the content in this file depending on the new location of Monkey.

# Let's have a little playtime

Now that you have this task out of the way, close Monk again. Why? Because we should first see what kinds of games you could create, and then get familiar with Monkey and its feature set.

Game developers should always play other computer games, not only to have fun but also to study them. When you play a game, try to analyze how it could be done; how a certain feature affects gameplay. Or look at the technical aspects of a game, such as what kind of graphic effects a game uses, how the game rewards the player, and so on. You can get so much information out of a game, that it really can help you become a better game developer and designer.

And to get a better picture of Monkey's abilities, you should take the time now to play some games that have already been created with Monkey. As two of Monkey's target platforms are HTML5 and Flash, we can do this inside your browser.

Just make sure you have installed Internet Explorer 9, Firefox 4, Safari, or Google's Chrome browser. Chrome seems to feature the best performance when it comes to HTML5, but it is up to your personal preference.

Ok, head again to Monkey's website, and from there into the apps section. Have a look and play the first game we want to try.

## Time for action – playing Pirate TriPeaks

Pirate TriPeaks is a solitaire kind of card game. You can find it at `http://www.monkeycoder.co.nz/Community/topics.php?forum=1059&app_id=59`.

The gameplay is easy, features nice animations of its graphics, and has some good sound effects. You have to click on matching cards to have them removed onto the open stack on the right. Also, you can click on a hidden card on the left stack to have it flip over and be visible on the right stack. The round ends once all cards from the left side are gone or in the event of removing all cards lying out in the open.

Play a few rounds and try to see what kind of gameplay or visual features make Pirate TriPeaks special.

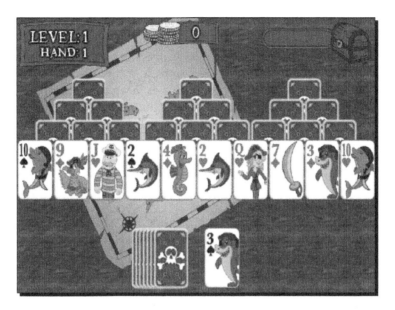

## What just happened

Did you notice a few things? For example, the spinning card animation when you click on a card and it flips down onto the stack. Or the coin animation, when you removed one of the three pyramids? Or the sound effects? All these little extras are the eye and ear candy that can separate one game from another. Here is a short list of features:

- Spinning card animation
- Flipping card animation
- Sound effects
- Coins falling from the top when a pyramid is removed
- Playable with just the mouse or a finger on a mobile device

As a game developer, and also game designer, you should always play other people's games. Not only to have fun, but also to take inspiration from other games for your own one. Try to analyze them—what they did wrong in your opinion and also what they did great.

# Time for action – playing Surviball

Next stop, Surviball. You can find this awesome game at `http://www.monkeycoder.`
`co.nz/Community/topics.php?forum=1048&app_id=48`.

This game kind of looks a bit like the old Marble Madness. Your goal there is to move a
marble through a parcour filled with obstacles, ramps, and enemies. In Surviball, you have
to direct a marble over a difficult course filled with tiles that give your marble a good speed
boost, when sometimes that is not what you need at that very moment.

When you play Surviball, try to pay attention to the controls and the graphical effects.

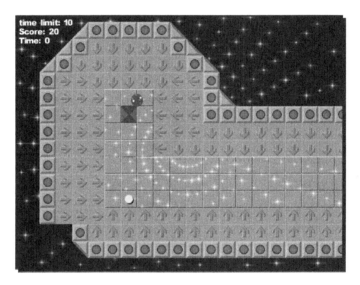

## What just happened?

Ok, what did you notice? Maybe this rotating start effect, which is pretty simple to archive
but visually very intense. Or the control scheme. By pressing the cursor keys on your
keyboard, the marble speeds up. So you have to take the current speed into account when it
comes to directing your marble in the required direction. Another thing is that the play field
is assembled by a lot of repeating small tiles, each with a different functionality. Also, there is
a timer, which gives the player some pressure to reach the goal in the given time frame.

Again, let's list some of the features of Surviball that we have discovered:

- ◆ Rotation star effect
- ◆ Indirect control scheme of the marble
- ◆ Playfield assembled via small tiles with different functionality
- ◆ Game timer

## Playing to have fun, playing to study

Like we have seen already, when you play other developers' games, you should study them. Look at how graphics are used, how the control scheme is set up, and so on. Find out how the player gets rewarded and what makes the player go on and play further.

Of course, have fun with the games, but also analyze them to learn how things could be done. Take inspiration from them and also take the motivation you get from this for your own projects. There is nothing wrong with taking existing ideas and reusing them. Why reinvent the wheel when someone is already driving the car with it! I don't mean shamelessly copy other games, but take a proven concept, enhance it, and put your own stamp on it.

# So let's go for something big? No!

Ok, so you want to create the next Diablo game, or another Star Craft. Do yourself a favor and take a step back; better, take 10 steps. Each of these games was created by an army of people. We are not talking about five to 10 people. Multiply these figures by 10 or 20 and the result will give you a good estimate of how many people are working on titles like the ones I have mentioned.

The games we have just played were created by individuals. They did the graphics, the sound effects, and the coding, all on their own. So when you start game development, set a small goal. The most important aspect for a game developer is to finish projects. Go for something that you can finish easily and in a short period of time. There are thousands of wannabe game developers out there who have never had something released in their whole career. You will definitely agree that someone who has never finished a game project can't call themselves a game developer.

## The alternative

So instead of the next AAA title, we will first work together on the small projects. Starting with *Chapter 2*, *Getting to Know your Monkey—a Trip to the Zoo*, we will work on projects that you will be able to finish in a short period of time. We will look together at some classic games and will recreate them. Along the way, you will learn your tools and techniques that you'll need when you create games on your own.

The rewards and motivation from finishing a project are immense and will make you want more and more. So let's take some small steps first. Learn how to walk before you learn how to run.

## *What just happened?*

Enough with all this game playing and having fun. Game development is also work. Sometimes it is fun work, but also sometimes dry and tough. But Monkey supports you with a great feature set in its arsenal, and you should now have a little study time in addition to this book. So it's not about what you can do for your Monkey, it's now about what your Monkey can do for you. After all, you shelled out quite a bit of cash and you should get something worthwhile back for it!

## Time for action – read the manual

There will be a time when you will be participating in some online communities, mostly regarding game development. And of course, you will ask questions. Sometimes they will be good ones, but also sometimes questions about things that you could have figured out on your own. If other people see this, it could happen that you will get told to read the manual/instructions first before asking. Do yourself a huge favor and do just that, as it is rule number one. For every tool you use, read the instructions first. It can be dry and boring sometimes, but don't skip that task. It might come back to you, if you don't. When it comes to Monkey, it ships with a good-sized documentation. Monkey's creator and some helpers took quite some time to create the documentation. You will find information about Monkey's language, the specific modules of Monkey, and also two nice little tutorials to get you started. You will find all this when you open Monk and click on the **Docs** tab of the coding area.

When you are done with this, come back to this book and we will go over what you have seen. So go... now

## *What just happened ?*

Wow!... the documentation for Monkey is quite a book (when printed)! You can get a lot of information out of it. It describes Monkey's features pretty well. But what are those features?

# The Trans tool and the supported target platforms

The **Trans** tool translates your monkey source code into the native source code for a specific platform. Thanks to Monkey, there are already quite a few platforms you can choose from.

## HTML5

Without having installed any platform SDKs and tools, such as Xcode and so on, Monkey can create HTML5 apps right out of the box. If your goal is only to create games for websites, then you won't need anything else besides a HTML5-compatible browser to develop your games. An HTML5 game is always a combination of an HTML file and a Javascript file where your game logic rests. All of your Monkey code is translated to Javascript code. Together with a calling HTML file, you can play this code directly in your browser or put it onto a web server to play it online.

## FLASH

To create FLASH games, you need to have another tool installed—FLEX. We will go through this process later on in the book, so don't worry about how to install FLEX. In the process of creating a FLASH game, TRANS translates your Monkey source code into ACTIONSCRIPT code. ACTIONSCRIPT is the programming language behind FLASH apps/games. Then, after TRANS is done, FLEX compiles the created ACTIONSCRIPT code into a FLASH file. The created FLASH file can then be loaded onto a web server and can be played from there. FLASH games created with Monkey tend to perform a little faster than HTML5 apps, but that can change. To play FLASH apps/games, all you need is a browser with a FLASH player plugin installed in it.

## iOS

Of course, iOS is supported. iOS is the iPhone/iPod/iPad platform, and for this, you need to have Xcode with the iOS SDK installed. Again, we will install that together later. If you want to create an iOS app, TRANS translates your Monkey code into C++ code. Then Monk will  execute XCODE, which will compile your code into an iOS application. The resulting app can then be played inside the Xcode simulator. To test your game on an actual device, you need to sign up for a separate iOS developer account at Apple. There you can create the certificates needed to have an app installed on a device.

## Android

The second mobile platform supported is Android. To create Android apps, you need to install the Android SDK, which we will also do together, later on. TRANS will translate your Monkey code into JAVA code. Then, the compiler of the Android SDK will create an application that you can either test on the Android simulator or on an actual device. To test an app on a device, you don't need to sign up for a Google developer account. You need to do this only when you want to sell your game on the Android market.

## XNA

Behind XNA are actually three platforms: XNA for Windows desktop, for Mobile Phone 7, and for the XBOX 360. Again, you need to install an SDK for it, the Windows XNA SDK. Monkey's TRANS tool will translate your source code into C#, and then Visual Studio C# will create an application that can run on one of the mentioned XNA platforms.

## GLFW

Just like XNA is basically three platforms, GLFW is two platforms. It depends on which development platform you compile your game with, OSX or Windows. For OSX, you need Xcode installed, and for Windows you need Visual Studio C++. So you actually have two platforms for the Windows desktop. Again, TRANS will translate your code into C++ source code, and the platform-corresponding SDK tools will compile that generated C++ code into an executable.

# The Monkey standard modules

Modules are a huge part of the concept of Monkey. Besides the general language features, other commands are added to Monkey, via modules. They are written in Monkey code and maybe native code (C++, JavaScript, and so on). These modules either provide new commands and/or interface with commands from external native code, so you can use them in your game. In the following text, we will see what they are good for. It won't be a detailed explanation of how they work; only what you can do with them.

For more information on modules, please look into the Monkey documentation within the *Module Reference* section.

## Lang

The **lang** module adds basic features to Monkey, such as `Print`, different data type-related handling functions, and one of the most important features, objects—the base for Monkey's class implementation. Here is a short code example:

```
Function Main()
    Print ("Hello World")
End
```

## Lists

If you know the concept of linked lists, this module provides something that will be familiar to you. If not, Wikipedia has a good explanation at `http://en.wikipedia.org/wiki/Linked_list`.

A **list** is a data container that lets you store something, from the same type of object as a node, inside memory. The list supports easy addition and removing from objects. You can iterate through the list of nodes in each direction. Another nice feature of a list is that you can convert it to an array of strings. To find a specific node inside the list, you need to iterate through the list, node-by-node, till you find the one you need.

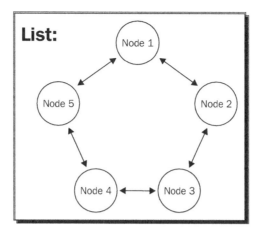

Here is a small code example for a list in Monkey, without further explanation:

```
Function Main()
    'create a new list
    Local myList:=New StringList

    'add some data
    myList.AddLast "first entry"
    myList.AddLast "second entry"
    myList.AddLast "third entry"

    'iterate through a list with an EachIn loop
    For Local item:=Eachin myList
            Print item
    Next
End
```

## Map

A map data container is similar to a list, as it is built from nodes too, and you can iterate through them. And node of a map is a pair of a value object and a key object. This key can only exist once. With it, you can retrieve the corresponding value very fast. If you need to find elements of a data container very fast, choose a map over a list.

The following image shows how map nodes have a relationship with each other. In a list, there is always a pre and post node from a current one. In a map, nodes have a loose relationship with each other. That means that you CAN iterate through a map, like you can with a list, but the real strength comes from searching nodes with the corresponding keys. So when you add a node to a map, this node will be placed inside a pool of nodes.

That is shown in the following screenshot with with **Node 6**. Knowing their keys, you can retrieve the corresponding data very very fast.

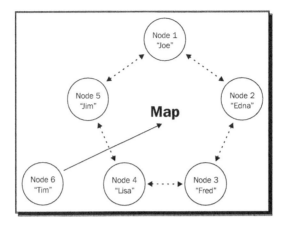

Here is a small code example with no further explanation:

```
Function Main()
    'Define a string map with a string key
    Local myMap:= New StringMap<String>

    'insert entries
    myMap.Insert("First","First entry")
    myMap.Insert("Second","Second entry")
    myMap.Insert("Third","Third entry")
    'Print all entries
    Print (myMap.Get("Third"))
    Print (myMap.Get("First"))
    Print (myMap.Get("Second"))
End
```

# Math

Almost each game needs something to be calculated. The **Math** module provides a good set of mathematical functions for your game developing needs. Here is a nice example where the Sin function is used:

```
Function Main()
    Local pi:Float
    pi = 3.14159265
    Print (Sin(pi))
End
```

# Random

Since our game should not always run in the same way as the last time we played it, we need some randomness in it. The random module provides functions just for that—to retrieve random numbers. The following code is a little example of how to retrieve a random number:

```
Function Main()
    'Retrieve a random number and print it inside the console
    Local r:Float = Rnd(10,100)
    Print (r)
End
```

# Set

A set stores objects. It is like a shoebox that you can store your toy cars in. Like lists and maps, you can iterate through them. The difference from a list is that the objects in a set can only exist once in it. No matter how many times you add an object to it, the set will contain it only once. So it is good to keep track of a number of objects.

In the next example, you will see that the same entries won't be stored inside the set:

```
Function Main()
    'create a new set
    Local mySet:=New StringSet
    'Add entries
    mySet.Insert("First")
    mySet.Insert("Second")
    mySet.Insert("Second")
    mySet.Insert("Second")
    mySet.Insert("Third")
    'Print all entries in the set
    For Local s:= Eachin mySet
            Print (s)
    Next
End
```

## Stack

Monkey provides a few ways to store data. The last module in this category is **Stack**. Imagine a stack of books. Basically, you can store them by placing one book on top of another (**Push**). If you want to take away one, you take it back from the top (**Pop**). Of course, you can squish a book in between the stack (`Insert`) or remove one from in between (`Remove`). And like all data storing features, you can iterate through a Stack in all directions.

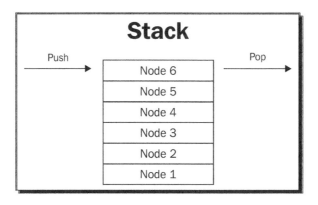

Here is a small example for the usage of Stacks:

```
Function Main()
    'create a new stack
    Local myStack:=New Stack<String>
    'Add entries
    myStack.Push("First")
    myStack.Push("Second")
    myStack.Push("Third")
    'Print all entries in the set
    For Local s:= Eachin myStack
            Print (s)
    Next
End
```

# Mojo – The 2D framework/modules

Monkey ships with a 2D framework module called Mojo. It provides all the meat (functionality) for each supported target platform. From handling graphics, to sound over input and device events, Mojo provides everything a good 2D game needs.

## App

The app module provides some basic functions to load strings from the device and store/retrieve an application's state. Also, you can control the update rate for your `render` process with it and make it react to certain events, such as `onResume`, `onSuspend`, and others.

## Audio

Ding dong!... Bang!...Wooosh! Almost all games have some kind of sound effect, and the audio module is Mojo's one-stop-shop for that. Load and play sound effects or total music for your background.

## Graphics

Ladies and gents...please have a look at...the engine! The graphics module is responsible for loading and rendering images, drawing all kinds of graphical shapes, such as lines, rectangles, and circles, and also text. How else could you tell the player what to do next? Without this module, there is no output in Monkey. So this is a very important part of Monkey.

## Input

When it comes to mouse input, violently hitting the keyboard, touching softly the screen of your mobile device, or tilting it wildly in every possible direction, the **Input** module is the way to go to retrieve information about how the user interacts with a game and its controls.

# Monkey is extendable

One of Monkey's greatest features is that you can easily extend it. And the good thing is that you don't have to wait till Blitz Research does that for you. You are not bound to what the creator of Monkey will implement.

## Your own modules

If you have Monkey code that you will use all the time and in every project you work on, then it is time for a module. Study how the native modules of Monkey implement new commands and functionalities.

## Native source code

Another great thing is that you can add and link to external native code, import that code, and make some external declarations. It is very easy to do.

## Third-party modules

Slowly, there are more and more third-party modules being developed for Monkey. Just to name a few, the following modules add some pretty interesting and valuable features:

◆ fling—A physaxe 2D implementation that will add nice physics to your games

◆ diddy—A great library of mixed functions

◆ mnet—A network module to add access to server-based network connections

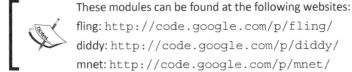

These modules can be found at the following websites:

fling: `http://code.google.com/p/fling/`

diddy: `http://code.google.com/p/diddy/`

mnet: `http://code.google.com/p/mnet/`

You will find links to these modules and other modules inside the module registry section of Monkey's website. You can find this section at `http://www.monkeycoder.co.nz/Community/modules.php`.

## Your own targets

The final feature you have with Monkey is that you can add your own target platforms, but, for this, you would need good knowledge of Monkey's internal structure and extensive knowledge to code for this platform. We definitely won't cover this topic further in this book. Say someone is working on a target for the Nintendo DS; you can find more about this at:

`http://www.monkeycoder.co.nz/Community/posts.php?topic=652#5053.`

## Your game is easily portable

The last feature, which you're going to love, is that you don't have to code differently when it comes to making your game run on different platforms. Your Monkey code stays the same; the difference lies inside the created source code on each platform.

# Summary

Wow! A lot to read and not much to do. Ok, you got some playtime here but also some good information. Let us revise what we have learned so far and looked at in this chapter:

- We learned where Monkey comes from
- We found out that Monkey translates your code into the native language of each platform
- To find out what kind of games Monkey can create, we played a few
- We studied the key features of the games we played
- Of course, we installed Monkey on our computer
- And, most importantly we learned about Monkey's feature set in general

So what's next? Do you agree that we can now dive into the inner caves of Monkey, bring out some fine functionality, and create your first game? Yes? You should answer more loudly! YES! Ok, so let's get rolling with the next chapter!

# 2
# Getting to Know your Monkey—a Trip to the Zoo

*Phew, there was a lot of dry and general information in the first chapter! As I told you, you could have skipped the chapter if you already knew about all that it covered. Anyway, it is time now to become a little bit more practical, and so we should get down to business.*

Assuming that you already have Monkey installed on your machine, we will work together through some Monkey game development basics. We won't go through every Monkey command as it is shipped with good documentation. There is no need to repeat everything again, here. Anyway, I am right behind you!

So, in this chapter, we will learn the following:

- ◆ How to load a script
- ◆ About projects and how we can create one
- ◆ The basic structure of a simple game
- ◆ How to draw circles and rectangles
- ◆ How to read keyboard input
- ◆ How to print messages to the browser window
- ◆ How to export your game to HTML5 and run it inside a browser

Quite some stuff, isn't it? Hopefully the page limit for this chapter will be enough for it. So let's get on with it!

At first, we will experiment with Monk a little bit, by creating a project. Then, you will write your first lines of Monkey code, a typical *Hello World* app. And of course how to save your code and reopen it at a later point.

Of course, you will have to create your first little game, PONGO—a very simple one, but a game in all its glory. You want be a game developer, right? So you've got to do what a game developer has to do. Together, we will recreate one of the first video games in history, Pong. Never heard about it? As always, look at this Wikipedia page to get an idea about Pong: `http://en.wikipedia.org/wiki/Pong`.

As a game developer, you have to start small, and this game is the perfect ground to build up your development skills with Monkey.

After we are finished with the development of the little game, you can call yourself a Monkey programmer! You don't think so? Yes you are! You learned to walk, and now we will learn how to run. And as they say, *practice makes perfect*. The best way to learn is by creating some nice little games. So let's get down to business, shall we?

# Call the Monk and start praying—the Monkey IDE

We are just kidding here; there are no religious activities planned in this chapter. Even though sometimes you will find yourself praying that a new piece of code you have created works like it should.

Ok, if you haven't installed Monkey already, then it is time to do that now. We have covered this part in *Chapter 1*, *Monkey–Huh?*, already.

## Why learn about Monk?

Monk is the code editor/IDE that ships with Monkey. It is the first place that you will fire up when you start using Monkey. So, it is important to know your first main tool, if you want to develop games with Monkey.

## Starting up Monk

It's time now to start Monk. You will do this by double-clicking on the **Monk.app** icon on OSX or start `Monk.exe` in Windows.

# Monk's user interface

Monk's user interface is divided into three sections:

- ◆ The toolbar
- ◆ The code editor area
- ◆ The info box

## The toolbar

All functions of Monk can be called through keyboard shortcuts and through the main menu. Some functions are also reachable through the toolbar.

## The code editor area

The code editor in Monk supports syntax highlighting and automatic casing of the basic commands in the Monkey programming language. Sadly, it doesn't highlight and auto-case the commands from the modules, which is something that could help tremendously. But, the usual suspects are all there—copy, cut, paste, search and replace, Block in and out denting, goto line, and Find in Files will get you a long way before you ask for more.

## The info box

The info box is your navigation system, when it comes to Monkey coding. You can open your code files, and also the files included with Monkey, from the **Nav** tree view:

In the **bananas** section of the **Nav** tree view, you will find all the sample scripts that ship with Monkey. Shortly, we will go there and start a sample script from there.

The next tab header is the **Code** tree view. It contains all function and method headers of the included classes in the currently visible code file.

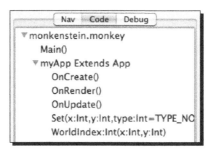

The last **Debug** tab is a relic from Monk's origins, being the native editor for BlitzMax. There, it has a built-in debugger, something that Monkey lacks at the moment. So, please just ignore that tab.

Ok, now let's do something. How about opening one of the sample scripts?

# Time for action – opening a sample script

Opening an existing script can be done through several methods. One is through the toolbar. Follow the given steps:

**1.** Click on the **Open** icon in the toolbar:

Next, you will see a file dialog where you can select a `.Monkey` file to be opened.

**2.** Navigate, within the dialog, into the `bananas` folder of Monkey's main directory. There, you have subfolders from some authors of sample scripts.

**3.** Head to the `mak` folder, and from within that, to the `firepaint` folder. Inside, you will find the `firepaint.Monkey` file.

**4.** Select it and click on the **Open** button in the **File** dialog. Voila! Monk just opened the selected script:

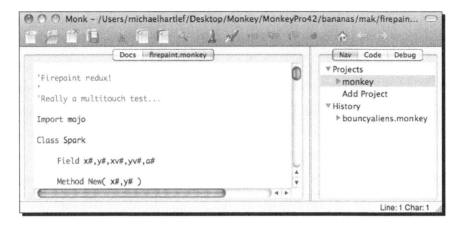

**5.** Of course, there are other ways to open a script. For example, you can double-click on a filename inside the **Nav** tree view.

## What just happened?

You have opened your first Monkey script. Good job! Please note how the GUI has changed. In the top of Monk, you see the file path of your currently visible script. Also, for each script you open or create, Monk creates a new tab inside the code area. In our example, this tab is named **firepaint.Monkey**. If you have several scripts open at once, you can switch between them by clicking on the tab header or press *Ctrl* + the left/right key on Windows or *cmd* + the left/right key on OSX.

# Where is my navi?

Games are not usually coded with just 10-20 lines. We talk here about at least a few hundred lines of code. And to help you navigate through your code more easily, Monk supports the **Code** tab in the info box on the right. To practice navigation in a script file a little, here is the next task.

## Time for action – navigating to the Main() function

Every Monkey game needs a **Main()** function. To find it, select the **Code** tab in the info box. There you find two parent nodes. Try to find **Main()** in one of them. Found it? Good. Click on it. You will see that the code area changed and the cursor jumped to the top line of the definition of the **Main()** function:

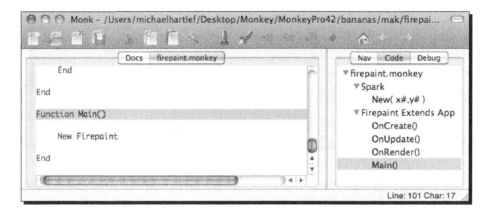

### What just happened?

Navigating through a script is very easy. Search for the item you want to jump to inside the **Code** tab of the info box and click on it. The content of the code tab always reflects the changes inside the code area!

# Save... save... save!

One of the first and most important rules of software development is *save your code, save it a lot*. Remember this and live by it. There is nothing worse than a hard drive failure or a power outage after an hour of coding.

## Time for action – saving a script

To save a script, here are some things you have to do:

1.  Open an empty script by pressing *Ctrl + N* in Windows or *cmd + N* on OSX. Monkey will open a fresh and empty code area for you.

2.  Next, type anything inside it, just anything.

3.  Now, save your script. For this, you should use your mouse and the menu. Click on **File | Save as**. A dialog opens where you can set the filename and location to save your script to.

4.  Do this and click on **Save**.

## What just happened?

You have saved your first script. Most likely, it isn't even close to a run-worthy script, but you have learned how to save your creation. Did you notice how the caption of the tab for the code area changed? And also the title bar of Monk's window? They now reflect the name you gave your script when you saved it.

# Projects—bringing in some organization

When you look at the **Nav** tab of the info box, it's nice that you can browse through the folders of Monkey and open scripts from there. Good news is near; you can do this with your own code too. That is why Monk supports projects. They become new entries under the initial tree view inside the **Nav** tab.

## Time for action – creating a project

Let's assume that we want to turn the FirePaint example into a project. For this, you have to create a new project first. Follow the ensuing steps:

1.  Click on **File | Project Manager**, in the menu. A new dialog will open.

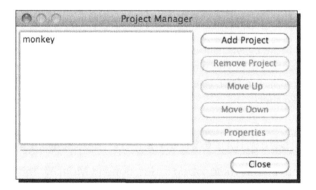

2.  There, you will first see the **Monkey** project. To create a new one, click on **Add Project**.

3. In the following dialog, you need to give your project a name. For now, My firepaint project should be fine. Also select the folder where the previous sample script was loaded from. After you do this, the top of the dialog should look a little like this:

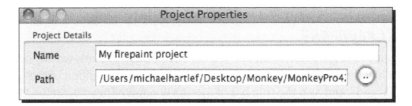

The bottom of the dialog with fields including sub-version controls is not functional and is probably a relic from Monk's origins of being the BlitzMAX IDE.

4. Now, click on **OK** to create your project.

## What just happened?

In the first dialog, there is now a new line with the project title. If you select this line, you could either change the properties of your project or remove it completely. You can close this dialog for now. Another thing you will notice is that, in the info box on the **Nav** tab, there is now a new project entry with the name you have given before. Browse through this entry and open the scripts from there by double-clicking on the script name. Convenient, isn't it? Yes, it is. And the cool thing is that this now stays there, even if you close Monk. At the next start of Monk, your new project entry is still there.

# The Monkey programming language

To create games with Monkey, you should know a little bit about its programming language and its features. We won't cover the whole manual here, but will go through some of the most important parts of it. But first, you should write your first script. *Without any practice, you say?* Right, just like that!

## Time for action – Monkey's Hello World

Here is a version of the famous *Hello World* script, done in Monkey. You have to start somewhere. You will learn what the starting point of every Monkey app looks like, the Main() function, and how to print some text to the browser. Ok, let's go!

1. Start with a single line comment that describes the app.

```
'Monkeys Hello World
```

2. Next is the function header for the `Main()` function, the piece of code that will be called at the start of the app. Every function starts with the keyword `Function`, then its name, followed by opening and closing parentheses.

```
Function Main()
```

3. Now, it's time to print the famous text *Hello World*. For this, Monkey provides the `Print` command. And don't forget to indent the code through the menu or just by pressing the *Tab* key once.

```
    Print ("Hello World")
```

4. Every function needs to be closed. In Monkey, we do this with the `End` command.

```
End
```

5. Now, save your script. The name and folder are not important.

6. Build and run the script by clicking on the tilted rocket in the toolbar.

## What just happened?

Drum roll please.... tadaaaa! You have coded your first Monkey script and just ran it inside the browser. If everything is correct, you will have seen a plain (white) background and then the text **Hello World** printed on it.

# Running your first script in a browser

To start this script, press *Ctrl + R* for Windows or *cmd + R* for OSX, to build and run the script. For this, select **HTML5** as the target platform. You should see something similar to the following screenshot:

Cool, isn't it? And you did this all yourself.

# Our first little game... PONGO

It's time that you develop your first little game. A small game, but a game for sure. Do you remember a game called PONG? If not, here again is a Wikipedia link that describes PONG: `http://en.wikipedia.org/wiki/Pong`.

Your game PONGO will be a single-player game. The opponent will be controlled by the computer. As it is pretty brainless, it will actually have two paddles to work with. Unfair, but who said life is fair?

The paddle for the player will be controlled by pressing the up and down keys on the keyboard. The goal of the game is to reach 10 points. You get a point once the opponent is not able to play the ball back.

So what features does the game have?

- You need to read the keyboard to control the paddle
- You need to draw a circle for the ball
- You need to draw rectangles for the paddles
- You need to check if the ball collides with the paddles and react to it
- You need to print some messages on the screen to inform the player about the state of the game

## Time for action – the basic structure of your game

We will now build the basic structure for every game. Follow the given steps:

1. Your first command in Pongo, and in every game, should be the `Strict` command, so that Monkey will keep us on track regarding giving identifiers the right type.

   ```
   Strict
   ```

2. Next should be some comments that describe the script somehow.

   ```
   #rem
     Script:    Pongo.Monkey
     Description:  Sample script from chapter #2 of the book "Monkey
     Game Development Beginners guide" by PacktPub
     Author:    Michael Hartlef
   #end
   ```

3. Because we want to use the Monkey built-in framework `mojo`, we have to import it.

   ```
   Import mojo
   ```

4. Now, we need to create the `pongo` class that extends from `mojo`'s app class. We will include empty `OnCreate`, `OnUpdate`, and `OnRender` methods that we will fill later on.

```
Class pongo Extends App
 Method OnCreate:Int()
  SetUpdateRate(60)        .
  Return True
 End
 Method OnUpdate:Int()
  Return True
 End
 Method OnRender:Int()
  Return True
 End
End

Function Main:Int()
 New pongo
 Return True
End
```

5. The last thing a basic Monkey script needs is the Main function. It is the starting point of every Monkey script.

```
Function Main:Int()
  New pongo    'This creates a new running instance from our class
  Return True
End
```

6. Save the script now, under a name of your choice.

7. To use a pre-build file for the next steps, you can load up the file `S2038_02_02.Monkey` and let it run by pressing *Ctrl + R* on Windows or *cmd + R* on OSX. After you have selected the HTML5 platform target and Trans has created a HTML5 project, it should start your HTML5-compatible browser and display a blank canvas, most likely in white.

This basic structure can be reused with every game you start. Only the class name should be changed from `pongo` to something that fits your game.

# Pongo's data structure

Each game needs to store data. We have talked about variables and stuff like that. For this, we will include some field variables in our pongo class:

## Time for action – adding some data fields

1. One of the elements of Pongo is the paddle, so we need to add fields to store its X and Y position at the beginning of the class definition. To add data fields we need to extend the pongo class.

```
Class pongo Extends App
Field pX:Float = 630.0    'X pos on the right side of the canvas
Field pY:Float = 240.0    'Y pos in the middle of the canvas
```

2. Next will be the data fields for the ball. X/Y position and its X/Y speed.

```
Field pX:Float = 240.0    'Y pos in the middle of the canvas
Field bX:Float = 320.0    'X pos of the ball in the middle of
canvas
Field bY:Float = 240.0    'Y pos in the middle of the canvas
Field bdX:Float = 3.5     'X speed of the ball
Field bdY:Float = 1.5     'Y speed of the ball
```

3. For both enemy paddles, we need to add their data fields for the X/Y positions and the Y speed. We will use 1-dimension arrays for this.

```
Field bdY_Float = 1.5     'Y speed of the ball
Field eX:Float[] = [5.0, 55.0]     'X pos of both paddles
Field eY:Float[] = [240.0, 240.0]   'Y pos of both paddles
Field edY:Float[] = [-10.0, 5.0]    'Y speed of both paddles
```

4. The last thing to add are some fields to store—the game score, the mode the game is in, and a helper field for printing some text info.

```
Field edY:Float[] = [-10.0, 5.0]    'Y speed of both paddles
Field pPoints:Int = 0     'Player points
Field ePoints:Int = 0     'Enemy points
Field gameMode:Int = 0    'Gamemode 0=Start game, 1=Game,
2=GameOver
Field modeMessage:Int = 0    '0=Message can be printed
Method OnCreate:Int()
```

5. It's time to save your script again and test it, to see if you made any mistakes. For going further with a pre-built script, you can use the Pongo_02.Monkey file.

Now that we have all the data fields in place, we can see that we will create the methods of our class, which will render the actual game.

## Time for action – rendering the game field

Which elements will be rendered in the game?

◆ The player paddle

◆ Enemy paddle #1

◆ Enemy paddle #2

◆ The ball

◆ A wall at the top

◆ A wall at the bottom

◆ A middle line

The last three elements can be grouped together as a background. So let us do just that:

**1.** Now, insert the drawing routines for the background graphics. Between the OnUpdate method and the OnRender method, create a new method called DrawPlayField.

```
Method OnUpdate:Int()
   Return True
End

Method DrawPlayField:Int()
  'Draw the top wall with a rectangle
  DrawRect(0,0,640,5)
  'Botton wall
  DrawRect(0,475,640,5)
   'Middle line, 13 pieces, each 10 pixel long
  For Local i:= 5 To 465 Step 20
    DrawRect(318,i,4,10)
  Next
  Return True
End

Method OnRender:Int()
```

**2.** We need to modify the `OnRender` method now, so that the new `DrawPlayField` method can be called.

```
Method OnRender:Int()
    Cls      'Clear the canvas each frame
    DrawPlayField()    'this call draws the background
    Return True
End
```

**3.** Like before, save your script and test it, to see if it runs fine. For going further with a pre-built script, you can use the `Pongo_03.Monkey` file. You should now see a screen that looks as follows:

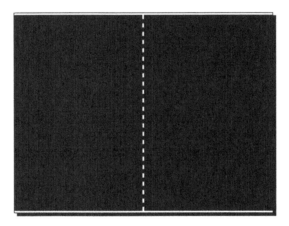

## Time for action – drawing the ball and the paddles

The next thing we want to draw is the ball and the paddles. Follow the ensuing steps:

**1.** For this, we will add a single `DrawCircle` command and some `DrawRect` commands to the `OnRender` method.

```
Method OnRender:Int()
    Cls    'Clear the canvas each frame
    DrawPlayField()    'Draw the play field
    DrawRect(pX, pY-30, 5, 60)    'Draw the player paddle
    DrawRect(eX[0], eY[0]-30, 5, 60)    'Draw the enemy paddle #1
    DrawRect(eX[1], eY[1]-30, 5, 60)    'Draw the enemy paddle #2
    DrawCircle(bX, bY, 5)    'Draw the ball with a radius of 5
    Return True
```

**2.** Better "save" than sorry. So, you should save this script under a name of your choice and test it again.

**3.** For the rest of the process, you can use the pre-built script `Pongo_04.Monkey`. Does your game look like this now?

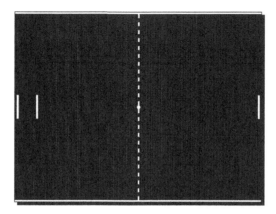

Visually, we are 99 percent done. What's missing is the printing of the game score and a message about the game state. We will get to this soon.

The next thing we will add is the movement of the paddles and the ball.

# Time for action – player paddle movement

First, we will create a new method called `ControlPlayer`.

**1.** This method will check for keyboard input and move the player paddle according to it. Add this method to the `pongo` class.

```
Method ControlPlayer:Int()
```

**2.** When the player presses the up key, we are moving the player paddle by 5 pixels, upwards.

```
If KeyDown(KEY_UP) Then        'check if UP key is pressed
    pY -= 5.0        'subtract 5 pixel from Y position
```

As the paddle should stop at the top, we check if its Y position is less than 25 pixels away (paddle height is equal to 50 pixel) and set its Y position back to 25 pixels.

```
    If pY < 25.0 Then pY = 25.0   'Check against top wall
Endif:Now we check if the DOWN key is pressed and move the
paddle accordingly. Again, we check if it reaches the bottom wall.
    If KeyDown(KEY_DOWN) Then   'Check if DOWN key is pressed
        pY += 5.0        'Add 5 pixels to Y position
        If pY > 455.0 Then pY = 455.0   'Check against bottom
wall
    Endif
```

**3.** Now, close the method.

```
    Return True
End
```

**4.** To actually be able to control the paddle, we need to call up the `ControlPlayer` method. You need to do this during the `OnUpdate` event. We could call it from there, but we need to implement the game mode logic, soon. So, we will create an `UpdateGame` method that will be called by itself from the `OnUpdate` method.

**5.** Create the `UpdateGame` method that calls the `ControlPlayer` method:

```
Method UpdateGame:Int()
    ControlPlayer()    'Control the player up an down
    Return True
End
```

**6.** Next, call `UpdateGame` from within the `OnUpdate` event:

```
Method OnUpdate:Int()
    UpdateGame()
    Return True
```

**7.** This is a good time to save again. For further progress, you can load up the pre-made script called `Pongo_05.Monkey`.

Slowly, we are getting some animation into the game. Next will be the enemy paddles.

## Time for action – moving the enemy paddles

Computer-controlled movements, or the so-called **Artificial Intelligence (AI)**, are sometimes very hard to create. But for a start, we will keep it very simple. And simple will be the key here. Our computer-controlled movement will look like this. One paddle will move with a speed of 10 pixels up and down, the other with a speed of 5 pixels in the opposite direction.

**1.** For this, you need to create a new method, called `ControlEnemies`.

```
Method ControlEnemies:Int()
```

**2.** Next, we update the paddles' Y positions. As we have two paddles to control, we will use a FOR loop for this, so we don't have to repeat the code. Remember that arrays in Monkey are zero-based.

```
For Local ep:Int = 0 to 1
    eY[ep] += edY[ep]    'Update the paddles Y position
```

**3.** Next, we will check if a paddle reaches the top wall.

```
If eY[ep] < 25.0 Then    'Check if paddles reaches top
wall
    eY[ep] = 25.0
    edY[ep] *= -1       'Revers its Y speed
Endif
```

**4.** Now, we will check if a paddle reaches the bottom wall.

```
If eY[ep] > 455.0 Then    'Check if paddles reaches bottom
wall
    eY[ep] = 455.0
    edY[ep] *= -1       'Revers its Y speed
Endif
```

**5.** Close the FOR loop and the method.

```
    Next
    Return True
End
```

**6.** To actually get the enemy paddles moving, we need to call our new method from within the UpdateGame method.

```
ControlPlayer()
ControlEnemies()    'Control the enemy
Return True
```

**7.** Again, and like always, it is a good time to save your changes. For further progress, you can load up the file Pongo_06.Monkey.

Cool! All paddles are moving. Now only the ball is missing. Let's get rollin'!

## Time for action – moving the ball

Moving the ball is as simple as moving the paddles, as you will see.

**1.** For updating the ball's position, you need to create a new method called UpdateBall. At first, we will update the ball's X and Y position:

```
Method UpdateBall:Int()
    bX += bdX    'Add the X speed of the ball to its X position
    bY += bdY    'Add the Y speed of the ball to its Y position
```

We could end here, but then the ball would not bounce of the walls and would just disappear in nowhere land.

**2.** Add a check if the ball hits the top wall and reacts to it.

```
If bY < 10.0 then
    bY = 10.0        'Set the Y position back to 10.0
    bdY *= -1        'Inverse the balls Y speed
Endif
```

**3.** Next, check if the ball hits the bottom wall and, again, reacts to it.

```
If bY > 470.0 then
    bY = 470.0        'Set the Y position back to 470.0
    bdY *= -1         'Inverse the balls Y speed
Endif
```

**4.** Now, check against the left wall. If it hits it, add a point to the player's points.

```
If bX < 5.0 then
    bX = 5.0         'Set the X position back to 5.0
    bdX *= -1        'Inverse the balls X speed
    pPoints += 1     'Add 1 to the player's points
```

**5.** As a score was made, check if the victory conditions of 10 points are reached. If yes, set the gameMode to GameOver. After that, close the If statement.

```
If pPoints >= 10 then gameMode = 2
Print (ePoints + ":" + pPoints)
Endif
```

**6.** The last thing in this method will be the check against the right wall. Again, if it hits, add a point to the enemy's points.

```
If bX > 635.0 then
    bX = 635.0    'Set the X position back to 635.0
    bdX *= -1         'Inverse the balls X speed
    ePoints += 1      'Add 1 to the enemies points
```

**7.** The enemy made a score, so check if the victory conditions of 10 points have been reached. If yes, set the gameMode to GameOver. After that, close the If statement. And close the method.

```
If ePoints >= 10 then gameMode = 2
Print (ePoints + ":" + pPoints)
Endif
End
```

**8.** This was one of our biggest methods so far. All we need to do now is to add a call to `UpdateBall` into the `UpdateGame` method.

```
ControlEnemies()     'Control the enemy
UpdateBall()         'Update the ball's position
Return True
```

**9.** Phew! We are getting there. Save your game now and test it. The ball should bounce off the walls now, and if it hits the left or right wall, you should see a message with the current score printed.

If you need a pre-made source file for the next steps, `Pongo_07.Monkey` can help you there.

# Time for action – controlling the ball with the player's paddle

It's nice to see the ball bounce off the walls, but in a game of Pongo, you need to be able to control the ball with your paddle. So we will implement this now. Follow the given steps:

**1.** Let's start with the player paddle. We need a new method that checks the collision of the ball with the player's paddle. Create a new method called `CheckPaddleCollP`. Please note the return type is Boolean.

```
Method CheckPaddleCollP:Bool()
```

**2.** Next, we want to check if the ball is close to the paddle regarding its X position.

```
If bX > 625.0 Then
```

**3.** The next check will be if the ball's Y position is between minus 25 pixels and plus 25 pixels from the paddel's Y position. If yes, then return `True` from this method.

```
If ((bY >= pY-25.0) and (bY <= pY+25.0)) Then
    Return True
Endif
```

**4.** Now, close off the first `If` check, return `False`, because the ball didn't hit the paddle, and then close the method.

```
    Endif
    Return False
End
```

**5.** Ok, now we need to call `CheckPaddleCollP` from somewhere. We implement it inside the `UpdateGame` method. We make an `If` check against `CheckPaddleCollP`, if it is `True` and also if the ball's X speed is positive. That means it goes from left to right.

```
    UpdateBall()        'Update the ball's position
    If CheckPaddleCollP() = True And bdX > 0 Then
```

**6.** If the paddle got hit, then first we inverse its X speed and bounce it back.

```
    BdX *= -1
```

**7.** Next, we want to check where it hit the paddle exactly. In the top area, the ball should bounce upwards. In the lower area, it should bounce downwards. And in the middle, it should bounce back straight. At the end, we will close the former `If` check.

```
        If ((bY - pY) > 7) Then bdY = 1.5
        If ((bY - pY) < -7) Then bdY = -1.5
        If ((bY - pY) <= 7) And ((bY - pY) >= -7 Then bdY = 0
    Endif
```

Ok, save here and test the code again. You are able to play back the ball. For the next step, you can load up the file `Pongo_08.Monkey`, if you need to.

## Time for action – letting the enemy paddles fight back

It isn't fair that only the player can push the ball back. The enemy needs this ability too. For sure, you can imagine it already; we will build a method first that will check and report back a collision of the ball with the enemy paddles:

**1.** Create a new method with the name `CheckPaddleCollE`, but this time with the return type of an integer.

```
    Method CheckPaddleCollE:Int()
```

**2.** Again, we first want to check if the ball is close to the paddles. As there are two of them, we will do this inside a `FOR` loop and set the index for the paddle arrays.

```
        For Local ep:Int = 0 To 1
            If (bX > (eX[ep]-5)) And (bX < (eX[ep]+5)) Then
```

**3.** Next, we check again if the ball's Y position is within +25/-25 pixels of the paddle's Y position. If it is, then return the index of the paddle.

```
If ((bY >= eY[ep]-25.0) And (bY <= eY[ep]+25.0)) Then
    Return ep
Endif
```

**4.** Now, close off the first `If` check and the `FOR` loop. Then, return `-1`, so we can see that no paddle was hit if the check was negative. Then close the method.

```
    Endif
  Next
  Return -1
End
```

**5.** Again, we will modify the `UpdateGame` method to check and react to the enemy paddles and a possible collision with the ball.

```
    If ((bY -pY) <= 7) And ((bY -pY) >= -7 Then bdY = 0
Endif
'Next assign the possible index
Local ep:Int = CheckPaddleCollE()
```

**6.** If there was a collision, `ep` contains the enemy paddle index now. So we check if `ep` is greater than `-1` and also if the ball moves from right to left.

```
If ep >=0 And bdX < 0 Then
```

**7.** We know now that a collision happened. We will determine where the ball hit the enemy paddle and change its Y speed accordingly. Of course, we will inverse its X speed first.

```
If ((bY - eY[ep]) > 7) Then bdY = 1.5
If ((bY - eY[ep]) < -7) Then bdY = -1.5
If ((bY - eY[ep]) <= 7) And ((bY - eY[ep])>= -7)
Then bdY= 0
```

**8.** All we need to do now is close off the `IF` check.

```
    Endif
```

Cool, we now have enemy paddles that play the ball back. If they hit the ball.

Save again, under a name that you choose, and test your code. For the next step, you might load up `Pongo_09.Monkey`, which reflects all the coding we have done so far.

# Time for action – acting on the different game modes

The last thing to add is the need to act to the game modes. We have three modes:

- 0=Start of game
- 1=Gameplay
- 2=GameOver

We want to direct and inform the player about what mode the game is in and how they can start it. Then if the victory conditions are achieved, we want to give a visual response.

**1.** The first mode is bound to a new method that we will create now. Create a new method called StartGame.

```
Method StartGame:Int()
```

**2.** We want to print a message only once; that is why we need the field modeMessage. If it is 0, then we can print this message. If we don't use such an approach, the message will be printed every time we call this method.

```
If modeMEssage = 0 Then
```

**3.** Now set messageMode to 1 and print a message:

```
    modeMessage = 1
    Print ("Press P to start the game")
Endif
```

**4.** In this method, we will also check if the P key was hit and set messageMode and gameMode accordingly.

```
If KeyHit(KEY_P) Then
    modeMessage = 0
    gameMode = 1       'mode = Game playing
Endif
```

**5.** Close off the method now.

```
    Return True
End
```

The method for gameMode = 1 exists already; it's the UpdateGame method we have created and modified before.

For gameMode = 2, we will need another method that informs the player about the end of the game and who the winner is.

**6.** Create a new method called `GameOver`.

```
Method GameOver_Int()
```

**7.** Again, we will print some messages now, and we want to do this only once. Remember this method will be called at each frame as long we are in this game mode. So we check against `modeMessage = 0` now.

```
If modeMessage = 0 Then
```

**8.** Now, set `modeMessage` to 1 and print an info message that the game has ended.

```
modeMessage = 1
Print ("G A M E   O V E R")
```

**9.** Depending on who has more points, we will inform the player who won the game. For this, we will check if `ePoints` is equal to or greater than 10.

```
If ePoint >= 10 Then
    Print ("Don't cry, the computer won! Next time try
    harder.")
Else
    Print ("Congratulations, you won! It must be your
    lucky day.")
Endif
```

**10.** We want to inform the player now about what they can do next and close off this `IF` check.

```
    Print ("Press P to restart the game")
Endif
```

**11.** As the player has the ability to restart the game, we will check now whether the P key was hit. Then, we will set the `gameMode` variable accordingly and also some position variables.

```
If KeyHit(KEY_P) Then
    ePoints = 0
    pPoints = 0
    Print (ePoints + ":" + pPoints)
    pY = 240.0            'player paddle Y pos
    bX = 320.0            'ball Y pos
    bY = 240.0            'ball Y pos
    bdX = 3.5             'ball X speed
    bdY = 1.5             'ball Y speed
    eY[0] = 240.0         'enemy paddle 1 Y pos
    eY[1] = 240.0         'enemy paddle 2 Y pos
    modeMessage = 0
```

```
            gameMode = 1
        Endif
```

12. Close off this method now.

```
        Return True
    End
```

13. Not much is left to building our game. We have built the last two methods for the missing game modes and now call them when we need to. For this, we need to replace the OnUpdate method.

```
    Method OnUpdate:Int()
```

14. To check which mode the game is in, we will use a Select statement this time and call the different methods according to the value of the field gameMode.

```
        Select gameMode
            Case 0
                StartGame()
            Case 1
                UpdateGame()
            Case 2
                GameOver()
        End
```

15. Close off our new OnUpdate method, now.

```
        Return True
    End
```

16. Save the game one last time and test it. For sure, the enemy paddles are not very competitive, but it will be a good practice for you to enhance this. If you want to compare your code to a final version, load up Pongo_final.Monkey.

## What just happened?

Yeah, you can be proud of yourself. You have coded your first little game. It has everything a good game needs—good data structure, separate render and update methods, even collision detection, and a very simple computer AI.

## Have a go hero – enhancing the computer AI

It will be good practice for you if you try to make the enemy paddles react more intelligently. Try to do this, perhaps as follows:

- Maybe they should react on the Y speed of the ball somehow
- Make the start of the ball more random
- Give it a try and don't be afraid to change this. Just remember... save your code!

# Exporting your game as an HTML5 website

Everytime you let your code run by pressing *Ctrl + R* on Windows or *cmd + R* on OSX, you have built all the files that are needed to run your code from a web server. In the folder of your project, Monkey has created a `build` folder. Inside this folder, you will find an HTML5 folder with all translated HTML5 and JavaScript files and a data folder containing your resources.

If you want to run your game from a web space, all you need to do is copy and transfer all the content of the HTML5 folder to your web space. The web address for your game could look like this: `http://www.yourdomain.com/MonkeyGame.html`.

Remember that to play HTML5 games on your browser, you need one that supports HTML5!

# One more thing... comment your code!

Well, we are not at a presentation show of the next big thing from a fruity computer company, but this is very important! As you might have noticed already, we have commented the code in Pongo a lot. Some will say that you only need to add comments to your code when you show it to other people. Other people say that it will also help you to understand your own code, later on.

Imagine finishing a piece of code, and then after several months, having to look at it again and make important changes or fix a nasty bug. Without comments, it could become very difficult to do, even for yourself on your own code. A well-commented source code is much easier to understand.

And remember the two different methods to comment code in Monkey:

- Single-line comments, such as:

  ```
  'This is a single line comment
  ```

- And multi-line comments, such as:

  ```
  #rem
    This is
    a multi line
    comment!
  #end
  ```

So, make it a habit to comment your code. One day you will thank yourself for it!

# Summary

We covered quite a few Monkey basics here and also programmed our first little game, Pongo. So what did we learn about exactly in this chapter?

- We opened Monk, the code editor, and learned how to create a project. This is something you will use very often, later on.

- While we created our first script, we learned how to print messages into the browser during the development of our first game, Pongo.

- We learned how to read input from the keyboard and draw basic shapes, such as circles and rectangles.

- In Pongo, we created a very simple computer AI and used a simple algorithm to check for collisions.

Now you know quite a few things about Monkey. But do yourself a favour; also study the documentation of Monkey, and study the sample scripts in the `bananas` folder. They are a fountain of information.

Next stop, next game!

# 3
# Game #2, Rocket Commander

*Every game developer should know about* **Missile Command**. *You don't? Well, the game we will create in this chapter Rocket Commander, is based on the classic* **ATARI** *hit game Missile Command. It is a single–player arcade game. In Rocket Commander, you are in control of the* **AEDS (Arial Earth Defence Squadron**) *and so have two powerful rocket launchers at your command. The enemy will try to destroy our beloved cities with their bombs and rockets, which will fall from the sky. You have to use your missiles and destroy the incoming weapons before they destroy the cities and cause total mayhem.*

*First, have a look at the original game at* `http://en.wikipedia.org/wiki/Missile_Command`*.*

*Missile Command was a huge hit. It was mainly controlled with three buttons for the missile launching bases and a trackball for aiming your shots. Using the mouse to control this game is perfect. But, under HTML5, you can only use the left mouse button, you might say. That is right, but we can still use keys to shoot the rockets.*

In this chapter, we will learn the following:

- How to draw more primitives, such as lines and dots
- How to print text on the screen
- How to make use of functions
- Reading the coordinates and button clicks of a mouse
- Randomly generating numbers
- Basic circle-collision detection

Again, we will use the primitives that Monkey provides, since there is no need to create any media for this game. We will create the basic structure of the game at first. Next, we will create the data structures to hold the game data, such as game score, numbers of rockets left, and so on.

As a first test, you will build the game interface. This means drawing the cities and rockets. The next step will be to implement the ability to read the mouse state.

To actually fire the rockets, we have to implement the rocket data and handle updating it in every frame.

As we need something to shoot at, we need the enemy to throw down some bombs. You will create their data structures and spawn these deadly things on the screen!

Finally, we need to check if our rockets have destroyed something, or worse, the enemy has hit the cities. So, we will learn how to check for a collision.

When the game is completed, it will resemble the following screenshot:

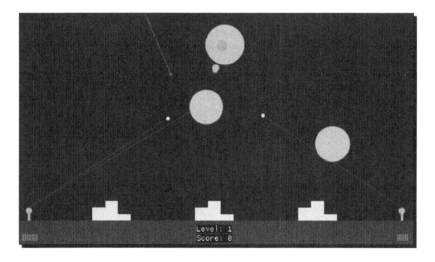

Are you ready to rumble? Ok! Let's get rolling!

# The game objects

Each game is made of some objects. These can be images, or sounds, but also complex structures, such as a game character and its abilities. In our game, we have a few objects, as follows:

- The cities we have to defend
- The rocket launchers that will fire our rockets

- The rockets themselves
- The bombs that will fall down on our precious cities and try to destroy them
- Explosions that will show up once a rocket bursts into pieces (the particle clouds from these explosions will be the real harm to the bombs; if they collide with an explosion cloud, the bombs will be destroyed)

There are few more elements/objects to the game, such as the game UI (score, background, and so on), but we will concentrate on the ones just listed. Each object will be built with a separate class.

# The basic file structure

In the game, we will have a mix of classes and functions. Each class will be hosted in a separate file, so we will need to import them. Once your projects become bigger and bigger, you will love it when you can organize your code neatly in separate files.

## Time for action – building the basic file structure of the game

Let's begin with the basic game structure:

1. Open an empty script and save it under the file name `RocketCommander.monkey`, in a folder of your choice.

2. The first line in this new script will tell Monkey to compile your script in `STRICT` mode.

   ```
   Strict
   ```

3. Now, add some comments about the script.

   ```
   #rem
   Script:  RocketCommander.monkey
   Description: Sample script from chapter #3 of the book
       "Monkey Game Development Beginners guide" by PacktPub
   Author:   Michael Hartlef
   #end
   ```

4. This time we won't import **mojo**, but another file, in which we'll import all the classes and other files. This file will be created soon, under the name `gameClasses.monkey`.

   ```
   Import gameClasses
   ```

**5.** And finally in this file, we need the `main` function. Without it, Monkey will complain when you try to build it.

```
Function Main:Int()
```

**6.** Inside the `main` function, we will create a new instance of the main class, called `RocketCommander`, and store it inside a global variable called `game`, which again will be created very soon in another file.

```
game = New RocketCommander
```

**7.** Now, close the function.

```
   Return True
End
```

**8.** Ok, that is all for this file. Save it.

You might close it for now, but when you want to run the game later, this is the file you want to build from.

As you can see, this is quite an unusual approach, as we have used identifiers and objects which don't exist at the moment. But, you will create them very soon! First, we start with creating the file to import all the classes, functions, and data definitions.

**9.** Create an empty file and save it in the same folder as the first one, with the name `gameClasses.monkey`.

**10.** In this empty script, tell Monkey to use the `Strict` mode again (for this file and importing the mojo framework).

```
Strict
Import mojo
```

**11.** In this file, we will also import our other files that include all the classes, functions, and global definitions. Add an `Import` command for the next file we will create.

```
Import mainClass
```

**12.** Now save the `gameClasses.monkey` file and close it for now.

The next file we will create is called `mainClass.monkey`. This will store our main class, `RocketCommander`.

**13.** Create a new empty script and save it under the name `mainClass.monkey`.

**14.** Tell Monkey to activate the `Strict` mode in this file and import the previously created file `gameClasses.monkey`.

```
Strict
Import gameClasses
```

**15.** As we have mentioned a variable called `game` before, we will add its definition to this file now. Remember, `game` holds the instance of the class `RocketCommander`.

```
Global game:RocketCommander
```

**16.** Now, we create the actual `RocketCommander` class, which of course extends from mojo's `App` class.

```
Class RocketCommander Extends App
```

As usual, we will add the `OnCreate`, `OnUpdate`, and `OnRender` methods.

**17.** Let's start with the `OnCreate` method. Remember that it will always have to contain a `SetUpdateRate` statement.

```
Method OnCreate:Int()
   SetUpdateRate(60)  'Set update rate to 60 fps
   Return True
End
```

**18.** Next, we will add the `OnUpdate` and `OnRender` methods.

```
Method OnUpdate:Int()
   Return True
End


Method OnRender:Int()
   Return True
End
```

**19.** It is time to close this class.

```
   Return True
End
```

**20.** Save the file and close it for now.

## What just happened?

We have created three files for now. The `RocketCommander.monkey` file holds the `Main` function and is the one that has to be built when you want to compile the game. The `gameClasses.monkey` file imports all other files where we actually defined the game. It's also the only file we will import in all other files. And last but not least, we have created our `mainClass.monkey` file, which will hold the main class called `RocketCommander`.

You could try to build and run the game now. If Monkey does not report any problems, you should see just a white screen in the browser. So let's get closer to something visible.

# Hold that data—RocketCommander's data structure

In every game, you also need to store some data. As the main objects will be created with their own classes, the RocketCommander class will have some definitions that store the state of the game, canvas sizes, and stuff like that.

## Time for action – creating the general data structure of the game

If you don't have the mainClass.monkey file opened already, then please do so. We need to add to it now.

In RocketCommander, we will also use a finite-state, machine approach for the OnUpdate and OnRender methods.

**1.** Add the game states as constants into the RocketCommander class.

```
Class RocketCommander Extends App
    Const gmMenu:Int = 1  'This mode shows the start menu
    Const gmPlay:Int = 2  'This mode shows the game playing
    Const gmGameOver:Int = 3 'This mode shows the game over message
```

**2.** Below the constants, add two fields to store the size of the canvas.

```
Field cWidth:Int   'X size of the canvas
Field cHeight:Int 'Y size of the canvas
```

**3.** Next will be a variable that stores the game mode. It will also be set to the initial mode.

```
Field gameMode:Int = gmMenu
```

**4.** To store the game score, we need another field, called score. Easy, isn't it?

```
Field score:Int = 0
```

**5.** The final fields in the data section will be a field for the level number, and a field to store the total number of destroyed bombs.

```
Field levelNumber:Int = 0
Field totalBombsDestroyed:Int = 0
Method OnCreate:Int()
```

**6.** Now, save the mainClass.monkey file.

## *What just happened?*

That's all for the general data section of `RocketCommander`. As we will use classes for the different objects in the game, these classes will have their own data structures. So there is simply no need to add more fields to the `RocketCommander` class.

# Detailing the Update process

In both events of the `RocketCommander` class, `OnUpdate` and `OnRender`, we will use a **finite state machine (FSM)** approach.

If you don't know what a finite state machine is, here is a link to a nice explanation:

`http://en.wikipedia.org/wiki/Finite-state_machine.`

An FSM does different things at anyone time, depending on which mode it is in. Consider the `OnUpdate` method of a Monkey game. Let's say the mode is the 'start' of a new game. Through IF checks or SELECT statements, you would call different methods or functions, as compared to when the mode was set to 'play' the game.

And in our case, depending on our variable `gameMode`, we will call different methods. It is one way of controlling and also structuring code. So, spice it up a little!

## Time for action – detailing the Update process

We have have three game modes. Two of them, `gmMenu` and `gmGameOver`, are modes where some kind of menu or text is displayed. The third mode, `gmPlay`, is for rendering and updating the actual game play.

1. Add a `Select` statement to the `OnUpdate` method.

   ```
   Method OnUpdate:Int()
      Select gameMode
   ```

2. Depending on whether `gameMode` is `gmMenu` or `gmOver`, we will call a new method `UpdateMenu`.

   ```
   Case gmMenu, gmGameOver
      UpdateMenu()
   ```

3. When `gameMode` is equal to `gmPlay`, call another new method called `UpdateGame`.

   ```
   Case gmPlay
      UpdateGame()
   ```

**4.** Close the `Select` statement.

```
    End
End
```

**5.** Now, add the bodies of the formerly mentioned methods, `UpdateMenu` and `UpdateGame`. Inside `UpdateMenu`, we will also add an IF statement to act differently, depending on the game mode.

```
Method UpdateMenu:Int()
  If gameMode = gmMenu
   'we will add code here later
  Else
   'Code that runs when gameMode = gmGameOver
  Endif
  Return True
End

Method UpdateGame:Int()
  Return True
End
```

## What just happened?

As you can imagine, the preceding code is still far from being ready to run, as we have no objects so far. But once we add them, you will see the action easily. We have just laid out the logic for the `Update` process.

# Detailing the Render process

Just like with the `OnUpdate` event, we need to put more detail into the `OnRender` event.

## Time for action – detailing the Render event

Ok, let's start with detailing the `OnRender` method.

**1.** First, before we render anything, we will clear the screen with a nice blue color.

```
Method OnRender:Int()
  Cls(0, 0, 50)
```

**2.** Next, we will call different render methods, depending on the mode the game is in.

```
Select gameMode
 Case gmMenu, gmGameOver
  RenderGame()
```

```
      RenderMenu()
    Case gmPlay
      RenderGame()
    End
    Return True
  End
```

3. Add the `RenderMenu` method. Inside, we will draw different text, depending on the mode the game is in.

```
Method RenderMenu:Int()
  Local cd:Int = Rnd(0,100)
  If gameMode = gmMenu
    SetColor(255-cd,0,0)
    Local s1:String = "*** Rocket Commander ***"
    DrawText(s1, cWidth/2, cHeight/2 - 48, 0.5, 0.0)
    SetColor(255,255,255)
    Local s2:String = "Press P to start the game"
    DrawText(s2, cWidth/2, cHeight/2, 0.5, 0.0)
    Local s3:String = "Press A Or S To fire the rockets"
    DrawText(s3, cWidth/2, cHeight/2 + 48, 0.5, 0.0)
  Else
    SetColor(255-cd, 0, 0)
    Local s1:String = "*** GAME OVER ***"
    DrawText(s1, cWidth/2, cHeight/2 - 24, 0.5, 0.0)
    SetColor(255,255,255)
    Local s2:String = "Press R to restart the game"
    DrawText(s2, cWidth/2, cHeight/2 + 24, 0.5, 0.0)
    Return True
  Endif
  Return True
End
```

4. Add the body of the `RenderGame` method. We will fill it with details later.

```
Method RenderGame:Int()
  Return True
End
```

It's better to be safe than sorry. Save the file, so your changes are not destroyed if your computer shuts down for any reason.

## What just happened?

As you can see, we have slowly acquired the skeleton of our game. Of course, no objects so far, but the basic structure is almost set.

# Enhancing the OnCreate event

We detailed the OnUpdate event and the OnRender event. What is left is the OnCreate event of our RocketCommander class.

## Time for action – detailing the OnCreate process

The OnCreate method is the only method we can set into stone now. Cool!

1.  Set UpdateRate to 60 frames per second.

    ```
    Method OnCreate:Int()
      SetUpdateRate(60)
    ```

2.  Now, read the dimensions of the canvas, your visible area. You will store this information inside the previously defined variables.

    ```
    cWidth = DeviceWidth()
    cHeight = DeviceHeight()
    ```

3.  Before the method is closed, we will call a new method called SetupGame. In this method, we will set up the starting values of a new game. Putting this inside a method will enable us to call this part again, once the game is over.

    ```
    SetupGame()
    Return True
    End
    ```

4.  Now, create a new method called SetupGame. Some previously defined variable will be used and set to values appropriate for a new game.

    ```
    Method SetupGame:Int()
      totalBombsDestroyed = 0
      levelNumber = 1
      score = 0
    ```

5.  Later on, we will add some more stuff, but for now, we leave it like that. Close the method.

    ```
    Return True
    End
    ```

## What just happened?

Again, save the file. It is a good time to build the RocketCommander.monkey file to see if you have any errors inside your code. If you run the code, you should see a nice dark blue empty screen.

# Let's build some cities

Rome wasn't built in a day, they say, but you can be sure you that we will build our cities within an hour—and that's, if you are slow! So get the shovel out and start digging!

## Time for action – building some cities

For each of the objects in `RocketCommander`, we will build an individual class, in its own file. So, let's just do that.

**1.** Create a new empty script and save it under the name `cityClass.monkey`.

**2.** Add the usual `Strict` statement to it and import our `gameClasses.monkey` file.
```
Strict
Import gameClasses
```

**3.** Create a global list that stores all instances of the city class.
```
Global cities := New List<city>
```

Besides the methods of an object, we will create some functions that we can use from within the `mainClass` file; for example, a function to render all the cities in one batch. These helper functions are wrappers for code, which we could have stored inside the `mainClass.monkey` file. But, we want to keep things nice and neat. So let's create them here.

The first wrapper function will be the one that renders all cities in one call on the canvas.

**4.** Create a new function called `RenderCities`.
```
Function RenderCities:Int()
```

**5.** Now, loop through our list of cities.
```
For Local city := Eachin cities
```

**6.** Inside the loop, we will call a method of the `city` class, which we will implement soon. This `Render` method will render that particular city.
```
  city.Render()
```

**7.** Now, close the FOR loop, and also close the function in the usual way.
```
Next
Return True
End
```

Next will be a function to create a new city. As a function parameter, it will have its horizontal (x) position in pixels. As all cities sit always at the same height, we don't need to add another parameter for this.

**8.** Create a new function header called `CreateCity`.

```
Function CreateCity:Int(xpos:Float)
```

**9.** Create a local instance of the city class.

```
Local c:city = New city
```

**10.** To initialize the properties of a new city, we will call its `Init` method, which we will add soon. As a parameter, we will give the x position.

```
c.Init(xpos)
```

**11.** Now, add this city to the list of cities and close the function.

```
    cities.AddLast(c)
    Return True
End
```

Even if a function basically wraps only one line of code, it makes sense from a higher level of view. The next function clears the list of cities. A list in Monkey is a one-line statement. Let's assume that we want to use a different way of storing cities, such as in an array, for example. Then, we would only need to change the wrapper function, but the call in the `main` class could stay the same.

**12.** Add a function called `RemoveCities`.

```
Function RemoveCities:Int()
```

**13.** Call the `Clear` method of the cities list to empty it. Then close off the function.

```
    cities.Clear()
    Return True
End
```

The same goes for the next function, used to determine the number of cities stored inside the cities list.

**14.** Create a new function called `GetCityCount`.

```
Function GetCityCount:Int()
```

**15.** Instead of returning TRUE, we will return the result of the `Count` method of the cities list. Then close the function.

```
    Return cities.Count()
End
```

Enough of these wrapper functions! It is time to build our actual city class.

**16.** Create a new class called `city`, which is not extended from any other class.

```
Class city
```

**17.** Add two fields to store the $x$ and $y$ positions of the city.

```
Field x:Float = 0.0   'x pos of a city
Field y:Float = 0.0   'y pos of a city
```

**18.** Add the previously mentioned method called `Init`, to initialize a new city.

```
Method Init:Int(xpos:Float)
```

**19.** Set its fields, giving an x position and a height, which is calculated as the canvas height minus `40`. Then close this method.

```
x = xpos
y = game.cHeight - 40.0
Return True
End
```

Now, we will create a method that draws a city on the canvas. You will notice that all the objects in the game have mostly the same methods. The difference will be in the details of each method.

**20.** Add a method called `Render`.

```
Method Render:Int()
```

**21.** Set the drawing color to a bright yellow.

```
SetColor(255,255,0)
```

**22.** Draw the city as three rectangles and their $x$ and $y$ positions on the canvas.

```
DrawRect(x - 30, y - 20, 20, 20)
DrawRect(x - 10, y - 30, 20, 30)
DrawRect(x + 10, y - 10, 20, 10)
```

**23.** Close this method, and the `city` class.

```
    Return True
  End
End
```

That's it for the `city` class. No other functions and/or methods are needed. Just make sure that you have saved the file.

## What just happened?

Here we are. We didn't build Rome, but we can now build small little cities for our game. Each city has the methods `Render` and `Init`. As cities are not dynamic objects, and we don't need to check for collisions, you won't need an `Update` or `CollisionCheck` method for them. We have also built wrapper functions that will do the dirty work for us when it comes to rendering all the cities at once, or deleting all the cities that are remaining.

# Implementing the city class into the game

Now that we have a class that deals with our cities, we should implement it into the game and finally see something on the screen when we run the game.

## Time for action – changing the gameClasses file

The first thing you need to do is add a new object to the `gameClasses.monkey` file.

1. Open the `gameClasses.monkey` file.

2. Add an `Import` statement for the `cityClass.monkey` file.

   ```
   Import mainClass
   Import cityClass
   ```

3. Save the file and close it.

## What just happened?

We have added an `Import` statement for our new `cityClass.monkey` file to the `gameClasses.monkey` file. As we only import `gameClasses.monkey` in all of our scripts, the new class will be automatically visible in them, and so will all the other objects we create later on too.

## Modifying the RocketCommander class

Ok, now comes the actual fun part. First, we want to to create some cities in our game. For this, we have created the `CreateCity` function. To set up the game objects at the beginning of a game, inside the `RocketCommander` class, there is a method called `SetupGame`. So, let's modify it.

# Time for action – spawning some cities in the game

To spawn some cities, follow the ensuing steps:

1. Open the `mainClass.monkey` file, if you haven't done so already.

2. Inside the `SetupGame` method, to create three cities, we will use a FOR loop.

```
score = 0
'Create 3 cities
For Local i:Int = 1 To 3
```

3. Call the `CreateCity` function. The `x` position will be at one-fourth of the canvas width. After that, close the FOR loop.

```
    CreateCity((cWidth/4) * i)
  Next
```

## What just happened?

We told our script to create three cities once the game starts.

# Rendering the ground and the cities

As we actually want to see the cities in the game, we need to add something to ensure it happens.

# Time for action – rendering the cities

To render cities, follow the ensuing steps:

1. To render the ground, we will draw a bluish rectangle.

```
Method RenderGame:Int()
  SetColor(0, 0, 150)
  DrawRect(0, cHeight-40, cWidth, 40)
```

2. To render all cities at once, call the function `RenderCities`.

```
  RenderCities()
  Return True
End
```

## What just happened?

Now, the hard work of creating classes and wrapper functions pays off. It is very easy to implement an object and draw it. Of course, we could have used all the rendering code here, instead of the `city` class. But this way we can make changes behind the scenes and the `mainClass.monkey` file doesn't have to be changed.

Save the file and let it run. You should see now a nice blue ground and three yellow cities on top of it. One of them should look like the following image:

Cool! The next thing we will add are the rocket launchers. You want to fire some ammunition, don't you? So here we go!

# Get the launchers ready!

The rocket launchers are essential to our game. Without them, we can't fire some deadly rockets to destroy the bombs that will rain on our beloved cities. And again, like all important objects of our game, we will create a new class in its own file for the launchers.

## Time for action – implementing the rocket launchers

As you will see yourself, quite a few things look similar to the `city` class definition and its wrapper functions. However, the launchers are different objects, and so we need different methods and functions for them. Not every step of code is explained now, as some is the same as for the `city` class.

1. Create an empty script and save it under the name `launcherClass.monkey`.

2. At the beginning of the script, tell Monkey to switch into `Strict` mode and import the `gameClasses.monkey` file.

   ```
   Strict
   Import gameClasses
   ```

3. Create a new list that stores all instances of the `launcher` class.

   ```
   Global launchers := New List<launcher>
   ```

Launchers will have to be updated for each frame, so we will have a new wrapper function to call the corresponding method for all existing launchers.

**4.** Create a wrapper function called `UpdateLaunchers`. In it, we will loop through the launcher's list and call their `Update` method.

```
Function UpdateLaunchers:Int()
  'Loop through the list of launchers
  For Local launcher := Eachin launchers
    'Call the Update method of each launcher
    launcher.Update()
  Next
  Return True
End
```

The same goes here with drawing the launchers to the canvas.

**5.** Add a function called `RenderLaunchers`. In it, we will loop through the launcher's list to call their `Render` method.

```
Function RenderLaunchers:Int()
  For Local launcher := Eachin launchers
    launcher.Render()
  Next
  Return True
End
```

**6.** At some point, we will want to know how many rockets are left totally in the game. So, create a new function called `GetTotalRocketcount`. In this function, we will add up all the rockets from each launcher found.

```
Function GetTotalRocketcount:Int()
  Local rc:Int = 0  'Var to store the total amount of rockets
  'Loop through the list of launchers
  For Local launcher := Eachin launchers
    'Add the rocket count to the global var rc
    rc += launcher.cRockets
  Next
  Return rc  'Return back the number of rockets found.
End
```

To add rockets to to each launcher, we will build another function that does just that.

**7.** Add a function called `AddLauncherRockets`. As a parameter, it will take the amount, which then will be added to a launcher inside the loop.

```
Function AddLauncherRockets:Int(ramount:Int)
  For Local launcher := Eachin launchers
    launcher.cRockets += ramount 'Add rockets to the launcher
  Next
  Return True
End
```

Now, we will add a function to actually create a rocket launcher.

**8.** The function you will now add will get the name `CreateLauncher`. As parameters, it will have the x position of the launcher, the keyboard key that triggers a shot, and the number of rockets it has initially.

```
Function CreateLauncher:Int(xpos:Float, triggerkey:Int,
rcount:Int)
  Local l:launcher = New launcher 'Create a new launcher
  l.Init(xpos, triggerkey, rcount) 'Initialize it
  launchers.AddLast(l) 'Add the launcher to the launchers list
  Return True
End
```

The last wrapper function we will add is to remove all existing launchers.

**9.** Add a function called `RemoveLaunchers`. In it, we will call the `Clear` method of the launchers list.

```
Function RemoveLaunchers:Int()
  launchers.Clear()
  Return True
End
```

Phew! Again, quite a few wrapper functions! But now it is time for the actual `launcher` class.

**10.** Create a new class called `launcher`.

```
Class launcher
```

**11.** It will feature four fields for the position, the rocket count, and a trigger key.

```
Field x:Float = 0.0    'x pos of a launcher
Field y:Float = 0.0    'y pos of a launcher
Field cRockets:Int = 0  'Rocket count
Field triggerKey:Int = 0 'Trigger key to shoot
```

To initialize a launcher, the class has an `Init` method.

**12.** Add a method called `Init`, parameters for the x position, the trigger key, and the count of rockets.

```
Method Init:Int(xpos:Float, trigkey:Int, rcount:Int)
  x = xpos        'Set the x position
  y = game.cHeight - 40.0  'Calculate the y position
  cRockets = rcount   'Set the rocket count
  triggerKey = trigkey 'Set the trigger key
  Return True
End
```

Updating a launcher means checking if the trigger key was pressed and then launching a rocket at the target.

**13.** To update a launcher, add the `Update` method.

```
Method Update:Int()
```

**14.** Check if the trigger key was hit and that there are still rockets left.

```
If KeyHit(triggerKey) And cRockets > 0 Then
```

**15.** The next function call is one that doesn't exist at the moment. `CreateRocket` will be featured in the next class that we add. Still, add it as a comment.

```
'CreateRocket(MouseX(), MouseY(), Self.x )
```

**16.** Reduce the rocket count and close off the IF check and the method.

```
    cRockets -= 1
  Endif
  Return True
End
```

Again, as with the `city` class, we have a `render` method here too. After all, we need to render the launchers, right?

**17.** Add a `Render` method.

```
Method Render:Int()
```

**18.** First, we set the color to turquoise. Then, we draw a circle for the launcher head and a rectangle for the launcher base.

```
SetColor(0, 255, 255)
DrawCircle(x, y - 15, 5)
DrawRect(x-2, y - 15, 4, 15)
```

**19.** Next, we will draw some markers for the remaining rockets. Start with setting the color to white.

```
SetColor(255, 255, 255)
```

**20.** Next, we will calculate the local `xdiff` variable that will be an offset, to draw the rocket markers.

```
Local xdiff:Int = cRockets*3 / 2
```

**21.** Now, check if some rockets are left.

```
    If cRockets > 0 Then
```

**22.** For each rocket, we will draw a small line beneath the launcher.

```
        For Local i:Int = 1 To cRockets
          DrawLine(x + i*3 - xdiff, y+20, x + i*3 - xdiff, y + 30)
        Next
    Endif
```

**23.** Close the method and the class.

```
        Return True
    End
End
```

We're done! The launcher class is ready to be implemented.

## What just happened?

Now we have the device to fire our rockets. Sadly there aren't any rockets to fire, but we will get there. But what have we done? We built a class for a launcher with its own `Init`, `Update`, and `Render` methods. Also, we created some wrapper functions that will help us to act on several launchers at once. The class is ready to be implemented; the only thing we have to change later on is a small line in the `Update` method, so that it becomes active:

```
CreateRocket(MouseX(), MouseY(), Self.x )
```

## Implementing the launcher class into the game

Without implementing the `launcher` class now into the game, we won't be able to fire just one rocket. So, what are you waiting for?

## Time for action – changing the gameClasses file again

The first thing you need to do is to add a new object to the `gameClasses.monkey` file.

**1.** Open the `gameClasses.monkey` file.

**2.** Add an `Import` statement for the `launcherClass.monkey` file.

```
Import cityClass
Import launcherClass
```

**3.** Save the file and close it.

### What just happened?

You have just added the `launcher` class to the game, and it can be used now.

## Modifying the RocketCommander class

As we want to create a launcher in our game, we need to modify the main class, `RocketCommander`. To add them, we have created the `CreateLauncher` function. Remember, when you want to set up objects, the perfect place is the `SetupGame` method. Let's modify it.

## Time for action – creating some launchers in the game

To create launchers follow the ensuing steps:

**1.** Open the `mainClass.monkey` file.

**2.** Inside the `SetupGame` method, add the left launcher by calling `CreateLauncher`. Its x position is `30` pixels and it has the *A* key as a trigger and `15` rockets to start with.

```
Next
CreateLauncher(30.0, KEY_A, 15)
```

**3.** Add the right launcher using a different x position and *S* as the trigger key, but also specify that there are `15` rockets.

```
CreateLauncher(cWidth - 30.0, KEY_S, 15)
```

### What just happened?

You told the game to create two rocket launchers at the beginning of the game. Easy, isn't it? Creating those classes pays off now.

# Updating the rocket launchers

In each frame, we want to check if one of the trigger keys was hit and then fire a rocket.

## Time for action – updating the launchers

To update all the launchers at once, call the function `UpdateLaunchers`, inside the `UpdateGame` method.

```
Method UpdateGame()
  UpdateLaunchers()
  Return True
```

## What just happened?

The call of `UpdateLaunchers` in the game will check if their trigger keys were hit in each of existing rocket launchers, and then will fire a rocket.

## Enhancing the UpdateMenu method

Now that we have the `city` and the `launcher` classes implemented, we can also finish the `UpdateMenu` method.

## Time for action – modifying the menu update process

1. Head to the `UpdateMenu` method and add the following lines:
```
If gameMode = gmMenu
  'we will add code here later
```

2. Check if the *P* key was hit.
```
If KeyHit(KEY_P) Then
```

3. Set game mode to `gmPlay`, and also seed the random number generator with the current time (in milliseconds) from when this game is active.
```
    gameMode = gmPlay
    'Set random number generator
    Seed = Millisecs()
  Endif
Else
  'Code that runs when gameMode = gmGameOver
```

4. Check if the *R* key is hit after one game is over.
```
If KeyHit(KEY_R) Then
```

**5.** Remove all cities and rocket launchers.

```
RemoveCities()
RemoveLaunchers()
```

**6.** Set up the game again, and set the game mode to `gmPlay`.

```
      SetupGame()
      gameMode = gmPlay
    Endif
  Endif
  Return True
End
```

## What just happened?

Good, now we can leave this part of code and forget about it. We can start the game now or restart it.

# Rendering our precious rocket launchers

Just like the cities, we want to see our launchers in the game. That is why we need to enhance the `RenderGame` method.

## Time for action – rendering the launchers

To render all the launchers at once, call the function `RenderLaunchers`.

```
RenderCities()
RenderLaunchers()
Return True
```

## What just happened?

With just a few calls, we have implemented the `launcher` class into the game and created, updated, and rendered each launcher.

Again, save the file and let it run. You should see two nice rocket launchers in your game. One of them would look like the following image. You will notice that there are also little lines for each rocket. Press *A* or *S*, and you will see them being removed, one by one.

Cool! The next thing we will add are the rocket launchers. You want to fire some ammunition, don't you? So here we go!

# Fire! Blast them to pieces!

Slowly, the game comes together. We have our cities, which we must defend, and two rocket launchers that will fire our rockets. Wait, rockets? I guess we'll use the ones we will create now.

## Time for action – implementing some rockets

Surely you know what you have to do now. Like all the other main objects we have created so far, each rocket will have its own class, which is located in its own file.

*1.*  Create a new file and save it under the name `rocketClass.monkey`.

*2.*  Start the script with the usual mumbo jumbo: `Strict` mode, importing `gameClasses`, and a global `rockets` list definition.

```
Strict
Import gameClasses
Global rockets := New List<rocket>
```

Just like with cities and launchers, we will have some wrapper functions. Let's start with the function to update all rockets.

*3.*  Create the `UpdateRockets` function. There we loop through the `rockets` list and call the `Update` method of each rocket we find.

```
Function UpdateRockets:Int()
  For Local rocket := Eachin rockets
    rocket.Update()
  Next
  Return True
End
```

The same goes for drawing the rockets on the canvas.

*4.*  Add the function `RenderRockets`. Again, it loops through all rockets and calls the `Render` method.

```
Function RenderRockets:Int()
  For Local rocket := Eachin rockets
    rocket.Render()
  Next
  Return True
End
```

To create a rocket, we will have the `CreateRocket` function.

**5.** The parameters of the `CreateRocket` function will be the mouse position and the starting `x` position.

```
Function CreateRocket:Int(mx:Int, my:Int, xp:Int)
  Local r:rocket = New rocket 'Create a new rocket
  r.Init(mx, my, xp)      'Initialize the rocket
  rockets.AddLast(r)      'Add the rocket to the rockets list
  Return True
End
```

And, to remove all existing rockets, we have the `RemoveRockets` function.

**6.** Implement a function called `RemoveRockets`. In it, we call the `Clear` method of the rockets list.

```
Function RemoveRockets:Int()
  rockets.Clear()
  Return True
End
```

The last function we need is one that calculates the distance between two coordinates. We need this to determine speed factors and also for our collision checks later on.

**7.** Create a function called `GetDistance`. The parameters are two pairs of `X` and `Y` position variables.

```
Function GetDistance:Float( x1:Float, y1:Float, x2:Float, y2:Float
)
  Local diffx:Float, diffy:Float 'to store the difference
  diffx = x1 - x2       'Calculate the X difference
  diffy = y1 - y2       'Calculate the Y difference
  'Return the square root of the sum of divX^2 plus divY^2
  Return Sqrt((diffx * diffx) + (diffy * diffy))
End
```

That's all for the wrapper functions. Save the file now. Next stop, the `rocket` class!

**8.** Create a new class called `rocket`.

```
Class rocket
```

Now, we will create some data fields to help with animating the rocket.

**9.** First add fields to store the starting position.

```
Field sx:Float = 0.0  'x start pos
Field sy:Float = 0.0  'y start pos
```

**10.** Next, we need fields to store the target position.

```
Field tx:Float = 0.0  'x target pos
Field ty:Float = 0.0  'y target pos
```

**11.** The following fields will store the current position.

```
Field cx:Float = 0.0  'x current pos
Field cy:Float = 0.0  'y current pos
```

**12.** And finally, we add some fields to help with calculating the rocket movement.

```
Field dx:Float = 0.0     'x difference
Field dy:Float = 0.0     'y difference
Field speed:Float = 0.0  'speed factor
```

Ok, we have created the data fields for each rocket. Let's implement some methods.

**13.** Create the `Init` method. The parameters are the target position and the starting $x$ position.

```
Method Init:Int(rx:Float, ry:Float, xp:Int)
```

**14.** Next, we will set the starting position. $x$ is given by the method parameter and $y$ is calculated.

```
sx = xp
sy = game.cHeight - 60.0
```

**15.** Again, we will store some parameters—the rocket's target position.

```
tx = rx
ty = ry
```

**16.** Now, we set the current position to the starting position.

```
cx = sx
cy = sy
```

**17.** To determine difference between the $x$ and $y$ starting position and target, we calculate these by a simple subtraction formula.

```
dx = tx - sx
dy = ty - sy
```

**18.** Lastly, we calculate the speed of the rocket by determining the distance in pixels and dividing it by 4. Then, close the method.

```
speed = GetDistance(sx, sy, tx, ty)/4.0
Return True
End
```

In each frame, we will need to calculate the new position of a rocket. For this, we need an `Update` method.

**19.** Add a method called `Update`.

```
Method Update:Int()
```

**20.** Calculate the current position by dividing the difference between $x$ and $y$ by the speed factor.

```
cx += dx/speed
cy += dy/speed
```

**21.** Rockets travel upwards, so to check if they have reached their target, you need to check if the current $Y$ position is less than the target $Y$ position.

```
If cy < ty Then
```

**22.** If the target position is reached, remove the rocket from the `rockets` list. After that, close the IF check, and the method.

```
    rockets.Remove(Self)
  Endif
  Return True
End
```

Just like cities and launchers, we want to render a rocket.

**23.** Create the `Render` method.

```
Method Render:Int()
```

**24.** Draw a grey trail behind the rocket with the `DrawLine` statement.

```
SetColor(70, 70, 70)
DrawLine(sx, sy, cx, cy)
```

**25.** Now, draw the rocket head with a random color, and as a circle.

```
Local cd:Int = Rnd(0, 50) 'Determine a random color factor
SetColor(255-cd, 255-cd, 255-cd)
DrawCircle(cx, cy, 3)
```

**26.** Close the method and the class.

```
      Return True
   End
End
```

## What just happened?

That was quick, right? We have a class for our rockets now. We can create them easily and update them through a simple call of a function. Once they reach their target, they destroy themselves.

## Implementing the rocket class into the game

To be able to finally shoot something, we will now add the rocket class to the game.

## Time for action – modifying the gameClasses file

To modify the gameClasses file, follow the ensuing steps:

**1.** Open the gameClasses.monkey file.

**2.** Add an Import statement for the rocketClass.monkey file.

```
Import launcherClass
Import rocketClass
```

**3.** Save the file and close it.

## What just happened?

By adding this Import statement, the rocket class can be used to create neat, deadly little missiles.

## Modifying the launcher class

Remember, to actually fire a rocket, each launcher has some code inside its Update method. So, you need to add some code there.

# Time for action – modifying the launcher class

To modify the `launcher` class, follow the ensuing steps:

1. Open the `launcherClass.monkey` file.

2. Modify the `Update` method and add a `CreateRocket` call there. The parameters are the mouse coordinates and the `X` position of the launcher.

```
Method Update:Int()
    If KeyHit(triggerKey) And cRockets > 0 Then
        CreateRocket(MouseX(), MouseY(), Self.x )
        cRockets -= 1
```

## What just happened?

We have just activated the functionality that will create a rocket when you hit a trigger key.

## Updating the rockets

As the game progresses, each rocket should move closer to its target position and check if it has been reached. We can do that with the `UpdateRockets` function.

# Time for action – updating the rockets

Add a call to the function `UpdateRockets`, inside the `UpdateGame` method.

```
Method UpdateGame()
    UpdateLaunchers()
    UpdateRockets()
    Return True
```

## What just happened?

That was quick, right? We have a class for our rockets now. We can create them easily and update them through a simple call of a function. Once they reach their target, they destroy themselves.

## Rendering our furious rockets

To render all active rockets, we need to change the `RenderGame` method.

## Time for action – rendering the rockets

Implement a call to the function `RenderRockets`, inside the `RenderGame` method.

```
RenderLaunchers()
RenderRockets()
Return True
```

### What just happened?

One call inside the `RenderGame` function, and all rockets that exist are drawn to the canvas. Save the file and let it run. Press *A* or *S* and you will see rockets flying to your mouse position, as long as some rockets are remaining.

# And it goes BOOM!... Explosions

Once a rocket reaches its target destination, it just disappears in a moment. But we need something else—an explosion! One that will grow over time. For this, we need a new class. Let's create it.

## Time for action – implementing explosions

To implement explosions follow the ensuing steps:

1.  Create a new script and save it under the name `explosionClass.monkey`.

2.  Again, switch into `Strict` mode, import `gameClasses`, and create a global list called `explosions`, to store each explosion created in it.

    ```
    Strict
    Import gameClasses
    Global explosions := New List<explosion>
    ```

    Just like with the other objects before, we need some wrapper functions, which we can implement into the `RocketCommander` class. Only the names of the functions are different, so you already now how they work.

3.  Implement functions to create, update, render, and remove explosions.

    ```
    Function UpdateExplosions:Int()
      For Local explosion := Eachin explosions
        explosion.Update()
      Next
      Return True
    End
    ```

```
Function RenderExplosions:Int()
  For Local explosion := Eachin explosions
    explosion.Render()
  Next
  Return True
End
```

```
Function RemoveExplosions:Int()
  explosions.Clear()
  Return True
End
```

```
Function CreateExplosion:Int(x:Float, y:Float)
  Local e:explosion = New explosion
  e.Init(x, y)
  explosions.AddLast(e)
  Return True
End
```

Now, we will add the actual `explosion` class.

**4.** Add a new class called `explosion`.

```
Class explosion
```

**5.** To store the position of an explosion, we need the usual fields.

```
Field x:Float = 0.0   'x pos of an explosion
Field y:Float = 0.0   'y pos of an explosion
```

**6.** As an explosion is a circle, we need fields to store the radius.

```
Field cr:Float = 2.0   'current radius
Field tr:Float = 40.0   'target radius
```

**7.** The last field will be a score modifier, which will be used when a bomb collides with the explosion and we get points for it.

```
Field score:Int = 100   'Points for destroying a bomb
```

Now, let's add some methods so that the class is functional.

**8.** Add methods to initialize, render, and update an explosion.

```
Method Init:Int(xp:Float,yp:Float)
  x = xp
  y = yp
```

```
      Return True
   End

   Method Update:Int()
      cr += 0.25     'Raise the radius
      'Check if target radius is reached
      If cr > tr Then
         explosions.Remove(Self)
      Endif
      Return True
   End

   Method Render:Int()
      Local cd:Int = Rnd(0,100)
      SetColor(255-cd, 155+cd, 0)
      DrawCircle(x, y, cr)
      Return True
   End
End
```

## What just happened?

We have created a class that deals with explosions. The explanation to implement it was very short as we did similar things with cities, launchers, and rockets, before. There is no need to repeat everything again.

## Implementing the explosion class into the game

Let us implement the explosion class into the game.

## Time for action – modifying the gameClasses file

To modify the gameClasses file, follow the ensuing steps:

1. Open the gameClasses.monkey file.

2. Add an Import statement for the explosionClass.monkey file.

   ```
   Import rocketClass
   Import explosionClass
   ```

3. Save the file and close it.

## *What just happened?*

You have added the `explosion` class to the game, so that it can be used later on.

## Modifying the rocket class

Once a rocket reaches its target position, a new explosion has to be created there. We need to add some code inside the rocket class' `Update` method.

## Time for action – modifying the rocket class

To modify the `rocket` class, we will follow the ensuing steps:

1. Open the `rocketClass.monkey` file.

2. Modify the `Update` method and add a `CreateExplosion` call there. The parameters are the current X and Y positions of the rocket.

```
If cy < ty Then
   CreateExplosion(Self.cx, Selfish)
   rockets.Remove(Self)
Endif
```

3. Save the file.

## *What just happened?*

We have modified the `rocket` class to create a new explosion once the rocket reaches its target position.

## Updating the explosions

An explosion will grow in size over time, before it disappears. For this, we have created a function called `UpdateExplosions`.

## Time for action – updating the explosions

Add a call to the function `UpdateExplosions`, inside the `UpdateGame` method.

```
Method UpdateGame()
   UpdateLaunchers()
   UpdateRockets()
   UpdateExplosions
   Return True
```

## What just happened?

With that call to `UpdateExplosions`, the game will update created explosions automatically.

## Rendering beautiful explosions

If you want to render all active explosions, we need to change the `RenderGame` method.

## Time for action – rendering the explosions

Add a call to the function `RenderExplosions`, inside the `RenderGame` method.

```
RenderLaunchers()
RenderRockets()
RenderExplosions
Return True
```

## What just happened?

With just a few new statements, we implemented the `explosion` class inside the game. When you run the game now, you will see neat explosions, once the rocket reaches its target position.

## Don't fear the enemy—bombs

Without the enemy bombs, there would be nothing to defend our cities from, and there would be no game. So, let's create some nice bombs. It is the last class we will create for the game.

## Time for action – creating the bomb class

To create the `bomb` class, we will follow the ensuing steps:

1. Open an empty script and save it under the name `bombClass.monkey`.

2. As always, switch into `Strict` mode, import `gameClasses`, and create a global list that holds all instances of the `bomb` class.

```
Strict
Import gameClasses
Global bombs := New List<bomb>
```

For one last time, we will add a few wrapper functions, which we then can add to the `mainClass.monkey` file, later on.

**3.** Add functions to create, update, render, remove, and count bombs.

```
Function UpdateBombs:Int()
  For Local bomb := Eachin bombs
    bomb.Update()
  Next
  Return True
End

Function RenderBombs:Int()
  For Local bomb := Eachin bombs
    bomb.Render()
  Next
  Return True
End

Function CreateBomb:Int()
  Local b:bomb = New bomb
  b.Init()
  bombs.AddLast(b)
  Return True
End

Function RemoveBombs:Int()
  bombs.Clear()
  Return True
End

Function GetBombsCount:Int()
  Return bombs.Count()
End
```

Now, define the actual bomb class.

**4.** Create a class called bomb.

```
Class bomb
```

Add the data fields for a bomb.

**5.** Add fields to store the start, target, and current positions.

```
Field sx:Float = 0.0   'x start pos
Field sy:Float = 0.0   'y start pos
Field tx:Float = 0.0   'x target pos
Field ty:Float = 0.0   'y target pos
```

```
Field cx:Float = 0.0   'x current pos
Field cy:Float = 0.0   'y current pos
```

**6.** The last fields will be needed to store the difference between $x$ and $y$, and the speed factor.

```
Field dx:Float = 0.0   'x difference
Field dy:Float = 0.0   'y difference
Field speed:Float = 0.0   'speed factor
```

Now, let's add the usual methods to the class.

**7.** Implement a method to initialize a bomb, called `Init`.

```
Method Init:Int()
```

**8.** Set its starting position. The $x$ value is determined randomly.

```
sx = Rnd(5.0, (game.cWidth - 5.0))
sy = 0.0
```

**9.** Determine the $x$ position of the target. Depending on whether there are no rockets left, the bomb will automatically target the first city that is remaining.

```
If GetTotalRocketcount() > 0 Then
  'Get random target x position
  tx = Rnd(5.0, (game.cWidth - 5.0))
Else
  'Get target x position of first city
  Local c:city = game.cities.First()
  tx = c.x
Endif
ty = game.cHeight - 40.0
```

**10.** Set the current position to the starting one.

```
cx = sx
cy = sy
```

**11.** Calculate the difference between the starting and target $x$ and $y$ positions.

```
dx = tx - sx
dy = ty - sy
```

**12.** Get a random value for the speed factor and then close the method.

```
speed = Rnd(500, 700)
Return True
End
```

**13.** Add the `Update` method.

```
Method Update:Int()
```

**14.** Calculate the current `x` and `y` positions.

```
cx += dx / time
cy += dy / time
```

**15.** Check for collisions with cities and explosions via a call to the `CheckCollisions` method, which we will implement later on.

```
CheckCollisions()
```

**16.** If the target `y` position is reached, remove the bomb from the bombs' list. Then, close the method.

```
If cy > ty Then bombs.Remove(Self)
Return True
End
```

**17.** Create a method called `Render`, to draw the bomb on the canvas.

```
Method Render:Int()
```

**18.** Draw the bomb's tail.

```
SetColor(255, 0, 0)
DrawLine(sx, sy, cx, cy)
```

**19.** Draw the bomb head and close the method.

```
SetColor(255, 55, 0)
DrawCircle(cx, cy, 2)
Return True
End
```

Now comes the interesting part. The collision check for the bomb. Without it, bombs won't be destroyed, and cities will live forever.

**20.** Add a new method called `CheckCollisions`.

```
Method CheckCollisions:Int()
```

**21.** Add a local variable called `dist`, which will store a distance factor.

```
Local dist:Float   'stores a distance
```

**22.** Loop through all explosions.

```
For Local explosion := Eachin explosions
```

**23.** Determine the distance between the bomb and the explosion.

```
dist =  GetDistance(cx, cy, explosion.x, explosion.y)
```

**24.** Check if the distance is smaller than the radius of the explosion.

```
If dist < explosion Then
```

**25.** Remove the bomb.

```
bombs.Remove(Self)
```

**26.** Add the explosion score value to the game score.

```
game.score += explosion.score
```

**27.** Increase the number of bombs that were destroyed, and increase the explosion score value by 100.

```
  game.totalBombsDestroyed += 1
  explosion.score += 100
Endif
Next
```

**28.** Loop through all cities. Repeat the same distance check with a city radius of 30.

```
For Local city := Eachin cities
  'Get distance to the bomb
  dist = GetDistance(cx, cy, city.x, city.y)
  'Check against city radius (30)
  If dist < 30 Then
    bombs.Remove(Self)
    cities.Remove(city)
  Endif
Next
```

**29.** Loop through all launchers and repeat the distance check with a radius of 15 pixels.

```
'Check if launcher got hit by the bomb
For Local launcher := Eachin launchers
 dist = GetDistance(cx, cy, launcher.x, launcher.y)
 If dist < 15 Then
  bombs.Remove(Self)
  launchers.Remove(launcher)
 Endif
Next
```

**30.** Close off the method and the class.

```
    Return True
  End
End
```

Voila! The last class is defined.

## What just happened?

We have built a class that reassembles our bombs. Inside this class, we have defined the usual wrapper functions and methods. What is special about this class is the `CheckCollisions` method, which does all the collision checks, for a bomb, against cities, launchers, and explosions.

## Implementing the bomb class into the game

Implement the `bomb` class into the game.

## Time for action – modifying the gameClasses file

To modify the `gameClasses` file, we will follow the ensuing steps:

**1.** Open the `gameClasses.monkey` file.

**2.** Add an `Import` statement for the `bombClass.monkey` file.

```
Import explosionClass
Import bombClass
```

**3.** Save the file and close it.

## What just happened?

You have added importing of the `bombClass.monkey` file so it can be used now.

## Updating bombs

Just like rockets, bombs will move down the screen, and so need to be updated each frame. For this, we need to call the function `UpdateBombs` within the `UpdateGame` method.

## Time for action – updating the bombs

Implement a call to the function UpdateBombs, inside the UpdateGame method.

```
Method UpdateGame()
  UpdateLaunchers()
  UpdateRockets()
  UpdateExplosions()
  UpdateBombs()
  Return True
```

## What just happened?

We havejust have added a call to UpdateBombs, inside the UpdateGame method.

## Rendering beautiful bombs

To render all existing bombs, we need to change the RenderGame method.

## Time for action – rendering the bombs

Add a call to the function RenderBombs, inside the RenderGame method.

```
    RenderLaunchers()
    RenderRockets()
    RenderExplosions
    RenderBombs
    Return True
```

## What just happened?

We have just implemented a call to our wrapper function RenderBombs. As you can see, implementing new objects into the game is easy.

If you let the game run, you will see some neat bombs falling from the sky, as shown in the following screenshot:

# Creating new bombs and checking for GameOver conditions, or new level conditions

Right now, we can update and render bombs. But how do they appear? For this, we need to modify the `UpdateGame` method of the `RocketCommander` class. Also, we want to check if the game is over or the next level has been reached.

## Time for action – modifying the UpdateGame method

To modify the `UpdateGame` method, we will follow the ensuing steps:

**1.** We need to modify the `UpdateGame` method in the `mainClass.monkey` file.

```
Method UpdateGame:Int()
```

**2.** Check if a random number is equal to `100` and the current active bombs are not more than the level number.

```
If Rnd(0,100) > 99 And (GetBombsCount() < levelNumber) Then
```

**3.** Create a new bomb.

```
    CreateBomb()
Endif
UpdateLaunchers()
UpdateBombs()
UpdateRockets()
UpdateExplosions()
```

**4.** If no city is left, remove all rockets, bombs, and explosions, and set the game mode to gmGameOver.

```
If GetCityCount() = 0 Then
  RemoveRockets()
  RemoveBombs()
  RemoveExplosions()
  gameMode = gmGameOver
Endif
```

**5.** Check if the next level is reached by comparing `levelNumber` times `10` with the total number of destroyed bombs.

```
If totalBombsDestroyed >= (levelNumber * 10) Then
```

**6.** Add 3000 points for each city left, and add 5 new rockets to each launcher. Also, raise the level number.

```
score += GetCityCount() * 3000
AddLauncherRockets(5)
levelNumber += 1
Endif
Return True
```

**7.** Now, save the mainClass.monkey file.

## What just happened?

You have now implemented code that will spawn new bombs, check if the game is over, and also ensure that the player will get new rockets.

# Displaying the game score

Of course, you want to display the score of the game. This can be done very easily.

## Time for action – displaying the game score

To display the game score, follow the ensuing steps:

**1.** Modify the RenderGame method again.

```
Method RenderGame:Int()
   'Render Ground
   SetColor(0, 0, 150)
   DrawRect(0, cHeight-40, cWidth, 40)
```

**2.** Draw text for the level number and the score, in the middle of the canvas.

```
SetColor(255, 255, 255)
DrawText("Level: "+levelNumber, cWidth/2, cHeight-34, 0.5, 0.0)
DrawText("Score: "+score, cWidth/2, cHeight - 20, 0.5, 0.0)

RenderCities()
RenderLaunchers()
```

## What just happened?

You have added some code to display the level number and the score of the game.

If you run the game, the score and level output will look like the following image:

# Summary

That was quite a chapter! And what did we learn? We created the game RocketCommander. During its development, we covered the following:

- Lists: Storing objects inside lists, iterating through them, and removing objects from a list.

- Lines and text: We learned how to draw lines, changed colors, and learnt how to draw text.

- Collision detection: We talked about simple collision detection that calculates the distance between two points. Once you put a radius into the calculation, you have a simple circle-collision check.

That's all for this chapter, but not all for this book. If you have completed this chapter as well as the previous one, *Chapter 2, Getting to Know your Monkey—a Trip to the Zoo*, you have now a good background on how you can work with the features of Monkey. In the next chapter, we will make use of third-party modules, so we can type less. Remember, modules are nothing more than extra classes and functions that give you specific extra functionalities.

# 4

# Game #3, CometCrusher

**Asteroids** *was a classic arcade game in the 80s. You could find it in every arcade hall. You had to control a little spaceship and blast asteroids which were flying around into pieces. Sometimes an enemy spaceship flew by and you had to avoid its deadly shots and try to shoot it down for additional points. If you don't know about this game, then have a look at the following:* `http://en.wikipedia.org/wiki/Asteroids_%28video_game%29`*.*

*In this chapter, we will create the game* **CometCrusher***, a game similar to Asteroids.*

*In the game, you are trapped inside a huge asteroid field, and you have to make sure that your little spaceship is not crushed by these huge rocks of heavy material. Three hits and your ship is gone! So blast your cannon at them and smash them into pieces. Once you are done, you can be sure that there is more work for you to do because space is full of rocks.*

During this chapter, we make heavy use of a game framework called **fantomEngine**. We will do the following:

- Create, load, and display images via the fantomEngine game framework
- Save and load a high score list via SaveState
- Load and play sound effects
- Learn where to store the game resources
- Install Flex, and a command-line compiler to create FLASH games

Since almost every game stores at least a high score list, you will learn how to create a high score list, save it, and also load it back into the game the next time the game loads.

Besides the actual game code, we will learn how to export to FLASH.

# Using a game framework—the fantomEngine

In *Chapter 3, Game #2, Rocket commander* we have created every single class and function required for our game. Sometimes we also created duplicate functionality. For example, every object had its render method. This bloats up the code of the game but it was also good to understand the concept of a whole game.

To avoid redundant coding and make your life easier, you can and will use the fantomEngine game framework for this game.

The source code file, `fantomEngine.monkey` is included with this book, but for the most recent version visit: `http://code.google.com/p/fantomengine/`.

The fantomEngine features some classes (objects) for different functionalities, which are described as follows:

- `ftEngine`: This is the main engine class
- `ftObject`: An object that can be an image, text, circle, or a box
- `ftSound`: This is to handle sound files
- `ftLayer`: A layer groups several objects together to update, render, and check collisions
- `ftFont`: This is a bitmap font object which can load EZGui compatible font files
- `ftTimer`: Using this, a timer will be called at will and you can automate processes with it

In this chapter, we won't go into every feature of the fantomEngine. For a detailed reference please visit its website.

# Game resources

Images, sounds, and other game data files are called **resource files**. For this game, we will need quite a few. With Monkey, all resource files have to be stored inside a subfolder of your project with a name such as `yourGameName.data`. For **CometCrusher**, we will need the following types of resource files:

- Player ship image
- Shield image

- ◆ Comet images
- ◆ Bullet image
- ◆ Explosion particle image
- ◆ Background star image
- ◆ Bitmap font image to draw game stats
- ◆ Explosion sound
- ◆ Shot sound

So, let's go over these different types of resources, and how you could create them.

# Images

Almost every game needs some graphics. In the initial chapters, we have used graphical primitives such as rectangles, circles, and lines. Monkey can draw these out of the box. For CometCrusher, we will now use images.

**Inkscape** is a very good freeware software. It's a vector drawing program in the style of Adobe Illustrator. The graphics for CometCrusher were created with it and then exported from it in the PNG file format. To get more information about it, visit its homepage at `http://inkscape.org/`.

Another good freeware program is **GIMP**. Instead of drawing in the vector style, you draw with pixels just like in Adobe Photoshop. GIMP is available at `http://www.gimp.org`.

# Sounds

CometCrusher is the first game we will create, that will support sound effects. To create these sounds, we can use a simple recording program, a microphone, and your voice. But you could also use a nice freeware program such as SFXR to create some nice arcade sound effects.

You can get the Windows version of SFXR at `http://www.drpetter.se/project_sfxr.html`.

The **OSX** version is called **CFXR**, and is available at `http://thirdcog.eu/apps/cfxr`.

Both programs export the sounds as WAV files. To convert them into the sound formats you need, you can use **Audacity**, which is available at `http://audacity.sourceforge.net/`.

To play games inside the web browser, the OGG file format is the best at the moment. For FLASH games, you should use the MP3 file format. With the `LAME` plugin, Audacity can export sound files to the MP3 format.

Of course, you can also use any other sound/music program to create the sound effects and music for your game. Just try!

# Bitmap fonts

To draw text well on the screen and with good performance, you should use bitmap fonts. There are several good programs on the Web to create them. A **bitmap font** is usually a combination of a font texture image, and a description file, which stores the position, size, and other information for each character inside the texture.

The fantomEngine initially supports bitmap fonts, which are stored in the **EZGui** font file format. One of the programs that can export to this file format is called **GlyphDesigner** and is available for OSX at `http://glyphdesigner.71squared.com/`.

The font file which is included in this chapter was also created and exported from GlyphDesigner. This app will create a single texture map with all the characters on it. Then it will also create another file, which describes where exactly each character is located on this texture map. It looks something similar to the following:

```
info face="Orbitron-Bold" size=18 bold=0 italic=0 charset="" unicode=0
stretchH=100 smooth=1 aa=1 padding=0,0,0,0 spacing=2,2
common lineHeight=18 base=14 scaleW=256 scaleH=128 pages=1 packed=0
page id=0 file="cc_font.png"
chars count=94
char id=106 x=2 y=2 width=8 height=19 xoffset=-3 yoffset=-1 xadvance=4
page=0 chnl=0 letter="j"
char id=36 x=12 y=2 width=14 height=18 xoffset=1 yoffset=-2
xadvance=14 page=0 chnl=0 letter="$"
char id=124 x=28 y=2 width=3 height=18 xoffset=1 yoffset=-2 xadvance=4
page=0 chnl=0 letter="|"
```

Don't worry about it, fantomEngine is able to interpret the file and load the font correctly.

# The game objects

Like it was stated earlier, CometCrusher will feature a few game objects. Most of them won't be stationary and all behave differently in the game.

Each object will be created via a call to the `CreateLayer`, `CreateImage`, `LoadSound`, or `LoadFont` methods of fantomEngine.

So let's talk about them one by one.

# Layers

The game will feature a few layers (groups). Each layer groups several objects. Thus, it makes sense to group objects that need to be handled together. The collision detection of fantomEngine will only work with objects that are in the same layer.

All layers are rendered in the order of their creation. The same goes for the corresponding objects in each layer, unless they are a child of an object.

For the game, we will have a few layers, as follows:

- Background
- Game
- ParticleFX
- UI
- Title
- High score list

Not every layer is visible at all times. For example, the high score list and the title are visible only when needed.

# Background stars

The background of the game is composed of a two-digit number of star images, which are scaled down and then spin around their own center. This spinning animation is automatically done by fantomEngine during the updating of events for the game. So basically, you set the start up in the OnCreate phase of the game and then forget about them.

To set up the spinning, we will use a call to the SetSpin method of each star object.

# Comets

In CometCrusher, you will find three sizes of comets. When a comet is created, it will have the biggest size. Once you shoot at it, it will be cracked (destroyed) into several medium-sized comets. And if these are cracked, they will spawn several small comets. The small comets will be destroyed without spawning new comets once they get hit by a shot.

New big comets will be created at random positions. Medium and small comets will be spawned from the center of the previously destroyed comet. Every comet will spin around its center at a random speed. The direction and speed of their movement is also randomly determined, and set with the call of the `SetSpeed` method. Once a comet reaches the border of the screen (canvas), it will be automatically wrapped to the opposite side of the screen by fantomEngine. We will need to set this behavior with a call to the `SetWrapScreen` method.

# The player ship

This is your vessel, your tool to get the job done. Controlling it is a little bit difficult and will be handled inside the `OnObjectUpdate` method. Hey, we are in space, so what do you expect? There is no grip of some tires here and if you turn your ship it isn't automatically flying into its new direction.

The following illustration will show you what that means:

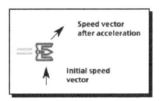

The vessel was flying upwards, and then turned to the right by 90 degrees. Then, its engine tried to push it into the new direction. The outcome was that the vessel was still heading at 90 degrees, but the ship was flying at a speed vector of 45 degrees. It was basically *sliding* through space.

So you have to push the ship with your engine. Directing the ship is a mix of turning the ship and adding speed to its new direction. As we don't want to go wild with the ship's speed, it will have a maximum speed. The `SetMaxSpeed` method will do that for us.

Even though we are in space, there is a little friction set for the ship. So if you don't speed up, it will stop after a while. The friction is set with the `SetFriction` method.

Turning your ship is done via a simple `SetAngle` method from fantomEngine. Increasing the speed and calculating its movement, via the `AddSpeed` method, is also supported by fantomEngine, so you don't need to worry about all the math that is done behind the scenes. Just like the comets, the player ship will wrap around the screen when it hits the edges of the screen canvas.

Be careful not to hit a comet with your ship without having your shield up. You will lose a life and when all your lives are gone, the game is over. Of course, the impact will crack that comet too.

# The shield

Just like every good spaceship, your vessel has a protection shield. It can be activated at will and will be active for a given amount of time. While being active, a collision with a comet will not harm your ship. Some players could use a "Shield up and hit" tactic.

The shield will be a child of the player ship. That means that fantomEngine will move it automatically with the player ship. Once set up correctly, you won't need to worry about its movement anymore. You only need to activate it and deactivate it after a certain amount of time. For setting up timer events, you can use the `CreateObjTimer` method. Once a timer fires, you can react to it in the `OnObjectTimer` method.

# Shots

Besides breaking the comets into pieces, your ship carries a deadly cannon that fires some nice fast bullets which can blast a comet with one hit.

Each bullet will travel at a given speed at the angle which the player ship was facing when the bullet was shot. Each bullet will also wrap around the screen once it hits the borders. fantomEngine will also check for collisions with comets, and let you know about them in the `OnObjectCollision` method, so you can act accordingly. That means remove the bullet, add points to the score, destroy the comet that was hit, and maybe spawn new smaller comets. When a shot is fired, a corresponding sound effect will be played via a call of the `Play` method of the sound object.

# Particles

When shots hit a comet or a player runs viciously into one of these huge rocks, an explosion will appear. This is just for visual kicks, so-called eye-candy. For an explosion, several particles will be spawned at the center of the explosion with a random speed and angle of movement. After a random time, they will be removed from the game. Also, an explosion sound effect will be played.

# Game info text

Inside the game, we will inform the player about different statistics such as the game score. Each text object will be created with the `CreateText` method and then later updated with the `SetText` method.

# The basic file structure

Now it is time to start the coding process. For CometCrusher, we will work with a single file structure again. In the end, how big a game is comes down to how easily you can manage its source code. We will have no more than 500 lines for this game and that should be manageable with just one file.

## Time for action – create the main source file and its folders

As this is the first time, we will work with the resources files and will need to set up the folder of our project in a slightly different manner:

1.  Create a new folder for the game, and give it the same name as your main source file.

2.  Then inside that folder, create another folder with the name of your main source file and the extension `.data`.

3. Copy all the resource files from the chapter's `cometcrusher.data` folder into your `.data` folder.

4. Copy the source file of fantomEngine from the chapter's folder into your project folder. Its name is `fantomEngine.monkey`.

5. Create a new, empty script file and save it under the name you have chosen.

   Inside the new script add the following lines; by now you will know them pretty well.

```
Strict
#rem
    Script:       cometcrusher.monkey
    Description:  Sample script from chapter #4 of the book
        "Monkey Game Development Beginners guide" by PacktPub
    Author:       Michael Hartlef
#end


Import fantomEngine
```

6. As you can see, we didn't import the **Mojo** framework; it is already imported by fantomEngine.

7. Next, create a global variable called `g`, which holds an instance of our main class called `game`.

```
Global g:game
```

   Then add the `game` class to our source file.

8. Create a new class called `game` with `OnCreate`, `OnUpdate`, and `OnRender` methods.

```
Class game Extends App
  Method OnCreate:Int()
    Return 0
  End
  Method OnUpdate:Int()
    Return 0
  End
  Method OnRender:Int()
    Return 0
  End
End
```

   The last thing that is needed for a valid Monkey app is the `Main` function.

**9.** Add the `Main` function header.

```
Function Main:Int()
```

**10.** Create an instance of the `game` class and store it inside the variable `g`. Then, close the function.

```
   g = New game
   Return 0
End
```

fantomEngine supports different object, layer, and timer-related event methods. To fill them with life, and of course use fantomEngine, we need to create an instance of the `ftEngine` class.

**11.** Create a new class called `engine`, as an instance of the `ftEngine` class. Inside it, create methods for its `OnObjectCollision`, `OnObjectTimer`, `OnObjectUpdate`, and `OnLayerUpdate` methods.

```
Class engine Extends ftEngine
   '----------------------------------------
   Method OnObjectCollision:Int(obj:ftObject, obj2:ftObject)
      Return 0
   End

   Method OnObjectTimer:Int(timerId:Int, obj:ftObject)
      Return 0
   End

   Method OnObjectUpdate:Int(obj:ftObject)
      Return 0
   End

   Method OnLayerUpdate:Int(layer:ftLayer)
      Return 0
   end
End
```

That's it. Save your file and if you like, let it build to see if any error shows up. Remember, save save save!

## What just happened?

We have seen some basic stuff that repeats itself in every Monkey app; plus interfacing with the fantomEngine. These methods are there, so we can act on different engine events.

# Open the storage please—the data structure of Comet-Crusher

The game class will hold several fields to store important game objects such as the player ship and also constants to represent game modes and other identifiers.

## Time for action – creating the data structure

Let's start modifying the game class.

**1.** Add a field to our `engine` class, the instance of the fantomEngine's `ftEngine` class.

```
Field eng:engine
```

**2.** Next, we have fields to store different `ftObject` instances, which need to be accessible at any time.

```
Field obj:ftObject          'A general object
Field player:ftObject       'Holds the player ship object
Field shield:ftObject       'the Shield of the player
```

**3.** To store different text information, we will need some objects for these as well.

```
Field txtScore:ftObject        'Stores the game store info text
Field txtLifes:ftObject        'The text info about the lifes left
Field txtLevel:ftObject        'Shows which level we are in
Field txtComets:ftObject       'Info about how many comets are left
Field txtHighScore:ftObject[10]    'Score list(array) with 10
entries
```

**4.** Add a field that will hold the instance for our bitmap font.

```
Field font1:ftFont
```

**5.** Now, we need several `ftLayer` class instances.

```
Field layerBackGround:ftLayer    'Groups all background stars
Field layerGame:ftLayer          'All game objects are stored
here
Field layerUI:ftLayer            'Holds the info text objects
Field layerFX:ftLayer            'ParticleFX objects
Field layerTitle:ftLayer         'the title screen
Field layerScore:ftLayer         'The high-score list
```

**6.** The last objects are the sound effects. Add one `ftSound` instance for the explosion, and one for a shot.

```
Field sndExplo:ftSound
Field sndShot:ftSound
```

**7.** For the sprite sheet, we will have one atlas as an image.

```
Field atlas:Image
```

**8.** Next, we have fields to store game logic related information.

```
Field cometCount:Int        'How many comets are active
Field levelNumber:Int       'The level number
Field score:Int             'Game score
Field lifes:Int             'Player lifes left
Field gameMode:Int = gmMenu 'Mode the game is in
```

The last fields we will add are related to the delta timing feature of our game.

**9.** To measure the delta time for each frame, we need a field to measure the difference in milliseconds from the last time measured, and a field for the last time measured.

```
Field lastTime:Int
Field deltaTime:Int
```

To finish off the data structure and to make the game logic easier to read, we will add some constants.

**10.** Add constants for the initial title menu, the game in play, and when it is over to show the high score list.

```
Const gmMenu:Int = 1
Const gmPlay:Int = 2
Const gmGameOver:Int = 3
Const gmScoreList:Int = 4
```

**11.** Next, we need three constants for the different sizes of the comets.

```
Const cmSmall:Int = 0
Const cmMiddle:Int = 1
Const cmLarge:Int = 2
```

**12.** During collision check, we need to have identifier objects for different collision groups.

```
Const grpShot:Int = 1
Const grpComet:Int = 2
Const grpPlayer:Int = 3
Const grpShield:Int = 6
```

**13.** The last constants will be IDs for the object timer events.

```
Const tmObjRemove:Int = 2
Const tmShieldTime:Int = 3
```

That's all for now. And later too!

Save your script, and build it to see if any error shows up.

## *What just happened?*

We have added different data fields to store information and objects of the game. Also, we have added different constants that make the script more readable.

# First changes to the OnCreate method

To build the base for every other method we will add to the game, we need to modify the OnCreate method of the game class.

## Time for action – modifying the OnCreate method

We need to set the update rate, create an instance of the ftEngine class from the fantomEngine, and load the texture (sprite sheet) that holds all the game graphics.

**1.** Modify the OnCreate method by setting the update rate.

```
Method OnCreate:Int()

    SetUpdateRate(60)
```

**2.** Set the eng variable with an instance of our engine class.

```
eng = New engine
```

**3.** Load the texture atlas.

```
    atlas = LoadImage("cctiles.png")

    Return 0
End
```

## *What just happened?*

By modifying the OnCreate method, we now have access to the fantomEngine. Also, we will set the update rate of the game to 60 frames per second.

# Detailing the Render process

The good thing is that we need only a few commands in the OnRender method of the game class to render every object in the game. Once we are done with that, we can forget about it.

## Time for action – detailing the OnRender method

We can detail the OnRender method as follows:

1. We start by adding the Cls statement to clear the screen before we render anything.

```
Method OnRender:Int()

    Cls
```

2. Next, call the Render method of the fantomEngine, which is stored inside the eng variable.

```
    eng.Render()

    Return 0
End
```

3. Save the script again and now actually try to run it. You should see a basic black canvas in the browser.

## What just happened?

With one simple call to the Render method of the fantomEngine, we have rendered every single object that was active and visible. By using this framework, you won't need to think about rendering your game objects anymore. Cool isn't it?

# This is a setup—creating the game objects

The next methods we will create will all deal with setting up the different objects in the game.

# Group yourself—layers

The concept of fantomEngine is built on layers and objects. Each layer is created via a call to the CreateLayer method of fantomEngine.

## Time for action – creating some layers

We can use the following steps to create some layers:

**1.** Add a new method called `CreateLayers` to the game class.

```
Method CreateLayers:Int()
```

**2.** Create the layers in the order they have to be rendered later on.

```
layerBackGround = eng.CreateLayer()
layerGame = eng.CreateLayer()
layerFX = eng.CreateLayer()
layerUI = eng.CreateLayer()
layerTitle = eng.CreateLayer()
layerScore = eng.CreateLayer()
```

**3.** Close the method.

```
    Return 0
End
```

## Let them shine—the background stars

The stars are objects of the `layerBackground` layer.

## Time for action – implementing some stars

We can use the following steps to implement some stars:

**1.** Create a method in the `game` class with the name `CreateStars`. It will have a parameter for the amount of starts to be created.

```
Method CreateStars:Int (scount:Int)
```

**2.** Start a FOR loop from `1` to the amount of stars to be created.

```
For Local i:Int = 1 To scount
```

Now, create a local `star` object, which will be a subimage from the texture atlas which we have loaded before. For this, we utilize the `CreateImage` method of the fantomEngine. At the same time we position it. We could use `DeviceWidth` and `DeviceHeight` of Mojo, but fantomEngine can work with virtual canvas sizes so we will use its own canvas size fields.

**3.** Create a local star object and position it randomly over the total canvas.

```
        Local star:ftObject = eng.CreateImage(atlas,
16,112,16,16, Rn(0,eng.canvasWidth),Rnd(0,eng.canvasHeight))
```

**4.** Set its scale factor, angle, and also spinning speed.

```
star.SetScale(Rnd(1,3)/10)
star.SetAngle(Rnd(0,359))
star.SetSpin(5)
```

**5.** Now, reset the layer of the star object to `layerBackGround`. Then close the method.

```
    star.SetLayer(layerBackGround)
Next
Return 0
End
```

## What just happened?

The last method you have implemented will create as many stars on the screen as you have set as its parameter.

## The Hero—creating the player ship

Our precious player ship is a little more complex to set up, since you will set up the shield object along with it, as it is a child of the ship.

## Time for action – setting up the player ship

**1.** Add a new method called `CreatePlayer` to the game class.

```
Method CreatePlayer:Int()
```

**2.** Set the player object by calling `CreateImage` with our texture atlas. The positioning doesn't matter because we will do this later on.

```
player = eng.CreateImage(atlas,0,0,32,32, 0,0)
```

**3.** Now, set the friction and the maximum speed of the ship.

```
player.SetFriction(0.2)
player.SetMaxSpeed(20.0)
```

**4.** To have the ship automatically wrap around the screen when it reaches its edges, set the wrapping to `True` via `SetWrapScreen`.

```
player.SetWrapScreen(True)
```

**5.** Reset the layer of the player object to `layerGame`.

```
player.SetLayer(layerGame)
```

**6.** The ship needs to be able to collide with comets, specifically. Set its collision group (`grpPlayer`) so that it can actually collide with comets set `grpComets`. The radius of the circle collision detection will be set to `12` pixels.

```
player.SetColGroup(grpPlayer)
player.SetColWith(grpComet, True)
player.SetRadius(12)
```

**7.** Now, set the player ship to be inactive so it doesn't show up at the start of the game automatically.

```
player.SetActive(False)
```

We now need to create the shield that protects the ship. The process of creation is similar to that of the player ship.

**8.** Create the shield object.

```
shield = eng.CreateImage(atlas,32,96,32,32,0,0)
```

**9.** Set its scale, spinning speed, and layer.

```
shield.SetScale(2.0)
shield.SetSpin(15)
shield.SetLayer(layerGame)
```

**10.** By setting the parent as the player object, the shield will automatically move and rotate with the player ship.

```
shield.SetParent(player)
```

**11.** Now, set its collision group so that it can collide with comets and set its collision radius to `13` pixels.

```
shield.SetColGroup(grpShield)
shield.SetColWith(grpComet, True)
shield.SetRadius(13)
```

***12.*** Also, set the shield to be inactive at the beginning of the game. Then, close the method.

```
shield.SetActive(False)
Return 0
End
```

## What just happened?

With the method `CreatePlayer`, you set up your ship in one go. It is always good to separate code in methods or functions, as it makes the code more readable.

# Did you hear that—loading sounds

Our little game will feature two sound effects. One for a shot and one for an explosion. The nice thing is that you can create the code for loading the sounds to be format independent. fantomEngine will automatically choose the correct format depending on the platform. For **HTML5**, the best format so far is **OGG**, and for a FLASH game, it is MP3. To load the sounds, we will create a new method called `LoadSounds`.

## Time for action – creating a method to load sounds

***1.*** Add the `LoadSounds` method to the `game` class.

```
Method LoadSounds:Int ()
```

***2.*** Set the sound objects via calls to the engine's `LoadSound` method. The parameter is the filename of the sound, but without a file extension.

```
sndExplo = eng.LoadSound("explosion")
sndShot = eng.LoadSound("shoot1")
```

***3.*** Close the method:

```
Return 0
End
```

## What just happened?

Even though we have only two sounds to load, with the `LoadSounds` method you have a code section that you can easily expand once you want to add more sounds to the game.

# Did you see that score—the game UI

In every game, you have a **user interface** (**UI**) that will let you control the game somehow and also inform the player about certain statistics of the game. For example, how high the score is, how many lives are remaining, and so on. In the following screenshot, for example, the red arrows point to the UI elements:

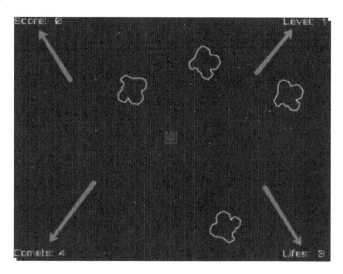

This can be done with graphics or text. In CometCrusher, you will print these values as text on the screen. fantomEngine supports you with a bitmap font object called ftFont, which is needed for a text object when you create it with the CreateText method.

## Time for action – creating some game info text objects

1. Add a new method in the game class called CreateInfoText.

   ```
   Method CreateInfoText:Int ()
   ```

2. Create the text objects txtScore. It is reset to the layer layerUI.

   ```
   txtScore  = eng.CreateText(font1,"Score:    "+score,0,0)
   txtScore.SetLayer(layerUI)
   ```

3. Now, create the text objects txtScore, txtComets, and txtLifes. Again, they are set to the layer called layerUI.

   ```
       txtLevel = eng.CreateText(font1,"Level:    "+levelNumber,eng.
   canvasWidth-5,0,2)
       txtLevel.SetLayer(layerUI)
       txtComets = eng.CreateText(font1,"Comets:
   "+cometCount,0,eng.canvasHeight-font1.lineHeight)
   ```

```
        txtComets.SetLayer(layerUI)
        txtLifes = eng.CreateText(font1,"Lifes:    "+lifes,eng.
canvasWidth-5,eng.canvasHeight-font1.lineHeight,2)
        txtLifes.SetLayer(layerUI)
```

**4.** Close this method.

```
    Return 0
End
```

## What just happened?

To create all info text objects at once, you have created a separate method to do this at one call. This method just creates the text object; it doesn't update them during the gameplay. For this, we will create another method later on.

## Headlines—adding a title screen

When the term screen is used, think about layers or groups. The good thing about layers is that you can activate them or make them visible when you need them to be. Our game needs a title screen too. It will be a simple one, with just the name of the game printed on the screen, and instructions on how to start the game.

## Time for action – adding a title screen

**1.** Inside the game class, add a new method called CreateTitleScreen.

```
    Method CreateTitleScreen:Int ()
```

**2.** Add a local text object for the game title. Its draw mode is set to CENTER (1), so fantomEngine will automatically draw the text centered around the given position parameters.

```
        Local txtTitle:ftObject = eng.CreateText(font1,"Comet
Crusher",eng.canvasWidth/2,eng.canvasHeight/2-40,1)
        txtTitle.SetLayer(layerTitle)
```

**3.** Now, add local text objects for instructions to start the game and show a high score list, which we will create later on.

```
        Local txtTitle2:ftObject = eng.CreateText(font1,"*** Press
'P' to play ***",eng.canvasWidth/2,eng.canvasHeight/2+10,1)
        txtTitle2.SetLayer(layerTitle)
        Local txtTitle3:ftObject = eng.CreateText(font1,"*** Press
'H' to see the high-score list ***",eng.canvasWidth/2,eng.
canvasHeight/2+40,1)
        txtTitle3.SetLayer(layerTitle)
```

**4.** Close the method.

```
    Return 0
End
```

## What just happened?

Again, this was another method that will set up a part of your game once you call it. This time it will create a simple title screen which is made of the logo, and two instructions for the player.

## How good are you—the high score list

A game is not complete without some kind of high score list. That is why we will implement a high score list into the game.

## Time for action – setting up the high score list

We can set up the high score as follows:

**1.** Inside the game class, create a new method called CreateHighScoreList.

```
Method CreateHighScoreList:Int ()
```

**2.** The list has a title; guess which one? Create a text object for it that is set to the layerScore layer.

```
    Local txtTitleHightScore:ftObject = eng.CreateText(font1,"H I G
H S C O R E S",eng.canvasWidth/2,70,1)
    txtTitleHightScore.SetLayer(layerScore)
```

**3.** Now, start a FOR loop for 10 entries.

```
For Local y:Int = 1 To 10
```

**4.** Each score entry will have a number on the left, indicating the rank inside the list.

```
        Local txtScoreNum:ftObject = eng.
CreateText(font1,"#"+y,eng.canvasWidth/4+50,80 + (eng.
canvasHeight/20)*y)
        txtScoreNum.SetLayer(layerScore)
```

**5.** Now, create a new text object for the score values. It is stored inside the txtHighScore array, which we have created earlier in the *Creating a data structure* section.

```
        txtHighScore[y-1] = eng.CreateText(font1,"0000000",(eng.
canvasWidth/4)*3-50,80 + (eng.canvasHeight/20)*y,2)
        txtHighScore[y-1].SetLayer(layerScore)
```

**6.** Close the FOR loop, set the layer to be inactive, and close the method.

```
Next
layerScore.SetActive(False)
Return 0
End
```

## What just happened?

This method is a good example where you use local objects which you will never access individually in the game and also the use of global objects. These global objects are required when you want to change them later on, and need direct access to them.

## Rocks rocks rocks—fill the space with some comets

The next two methods will be typical helper methods. The first one, `CreateComet`, is to create and set up a single comet at a given position. The second one, `SpawnComets`, will be used to spawn several large comets randomly over the total canvas space.

## Time for action – create a comet

**1.** To create a comet, we need a new method called `CreateComet`. The parameters are the kind of comet, its position, the travel speed, and angle.

```
Method CreateComet:ftObject(k:Int, xp:Float, yp:Float,
speed:Float, speedAngle:Float)
```

**2.** Define a local `ftObject` called `com`.

```
Local com:ftObject
```

**3.** Depending on the size of the comet, create the comet object from different locations of the sprite atlas. Also, set the radius depending on the size.

```
If k = cmSmall Then
  com = eng.CreateImage(atlas, 0,32,16,16, xp, yp)
  com.SetRadius(4)
Endif
If k = cmMiddle Then
  com = eng.CreateImage(atlas, 32,0,32,32, xp, yp)
  com.SetRadius(12)
Endif
If k = cmLarge Then
  com = eng.CreateImage(atlas, 64,0,64,64, xp, yp)
  com.SetRadius(24)
Endif
```

4. Now, set the speed and the angle that the comet will move at.

```
com.SetSpeed(speed, speedAngle)
```

5. Next, we set a random starting angle and spinning speed.

```
com.SetAngle(Rnd(0,359))
com.SetSpin(Rnd(-4,4))
```

6. Store the comet size constant into the `tag` field.

```
com.SetTag(k)
```

7. Tell the engine that the comet will wrap the screen once it hits the canvas edge.

```
com.SetWrapScreen(True)
```

8. Now, set its collision group to `grpComet` and the layer to `layerGame`.

```
com.SetColGroup(grpComet)
com.SetLayer(layerGame)
```

9. The last things you need to do before you close the method is to set the ID with the `grpComet` constant and raise `cometCount` by 1.

```
  com.SetID(grpComet)
  cometCount += 1
  Return com
End
```

## What just happened?

Using the `CreateComet` method, you can create a new comet in one call. With its various parameters, you can define the position, the type of comet, and where it will travel during its life time.

## Time for action – creating some comets

1. As always, inside the `game` class, create a new method called `CreateComets`. Its parameter will be the amount of comets that have to be created.

```
Method SpawnComets:Int (ccount:Int)
```

2. Add a FOR loop from 1 to the amount of comets you want to create.

```
For Local i:Int = 1 To ccount
```

3. Call up the method CreateComet with the size set to `large`, and random values for position, angle, and speed.

```
            obj = CreateComet(cmLarge,Rnd(64,eng.canvasWidth-
64),Rnd(64,eng.canvasHeight-64),Rnd(1,4)/2,Rnd(0,359))/
```

4. Close the FOR loop, and the method.

```
    Next
    Return 0
End
```

## What just happened?

To actually spawn comets, you have created a method that will do this randomly over the canvas area. You just tell how many comets you need and it will spawn them.

## Mission complete... finalizing the OnCreate process

We have now created all the methods to create the initial objects. It is time to finalize the OnCreate method of the game class.

## Time for action – finalizing the OnCreate method

1. Head over to our OnCreate method and add the call to CreateLayers.

```
Method OnCreate:Int()
  SetUpdateRate(60)
  eng = New engine
  atlas = LoadImage("cctiles.png")
  CreateLayers()
```

2. Now, insert a call to CreateStars for 50 stars.

```
CreateStars(50)
```

3. Create the player and load the sounds.

```
CreatePlayer()
LoadSounds()
```

4. Before you create text objects, you need to load a bitmap font.

```
font1 = eng.LoadFont("cc_font")
```

**5.** Now, create all the text related objects.

```
CreateInfoText()
CreateTitleScreen()
CreateHighScoreList()

Return 0
End
```

## What just happened?

That's all. We have created several methods that will create our game objects. The OnCreate method is also set and done. No further changes are required. If you save the script now and let it run, you should see something similar to the following screenshot:

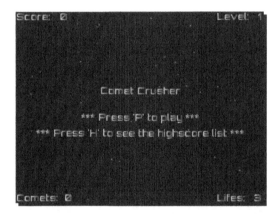

# We need help—more methods for the Update process

Right now you can't play the game. To finalize the OnUpdate method and the gameplay in general, we need more helper (support) methods. If you create smaller methods for more detailed tasks, it is easier to interface with them in other places and also easier to maintain.

## Loading and showing the high score list

To show the high score list, we first need a function that will load it from the app state. As the app state is just a string of characters, we will utilize the LoadFromString method of the engine's score list.

# Time for action – loading a high score list

1.  Create a new method called LoadHighScore.

    ```
    Method LoadHighScore:Int ()
    ```

2.  Call LoadState and store the result inside a local String variable called state.

    ```
    Local state:String = LoadState()
    ```

3.  Check if an app state was found and loaded.

    ```
    If state Then
    ```

4.  A call to LoadFromString from the engine's score list will load the high score list.

    ```
    eng.scoreList.LoadFromString(state)
    ```

5.  Close the IF check, and the method.

    ```
        Endif
        Return 0
    End
    ```

## What just happened?

To actually show the list, we need to update the text object array that holds the score values. For this, we will create a method in the next section.

# Time for action – showing the high score list

1.  Add a method called ShowScoreList.

    ```
    Method ShowScoreList:Int()
    ```

2.  Load the high score list.

    ```
    LoadHighScore()
    ```

3.  Loop through the score list entries, determine their values with GetValue, and fill the text object array via the SetText method.

    ```
    For Local y:Int = 1 To eng.scoreList.Count()
      txtHighScore[y-1].SetText(eng.scoreList.GetValue(y))
    Next
    ```

4. To show the high score list, set the `layerScore` layer to `active` and the `layerTitle` layer to `inactive`. Then, close the method.

```
layerScore.SetActive(True)
layerTitle.SetActive(False)
Return 0
End
```

## What just happened?

To load the high score data from storage and set up our list objects, we can now use the `ShowScoreList` method. Besides taking care of the loading and storing the values in the list, it will actually show the high score list on the screen.

## Activating the shield of the player ship

At some point in the game, we need to activate the shield of the player ship. One such time is at the start of a new game.

## Time for action – the ActivateShield method

1. The new method will be called `ActivateShield`.

```
Method ActivateShield:Int()
```

The shield object is already created, so we just want to make it active. As we want it to be deactivated after 5 seconds, we need to create a timer to do this.

2. Create a new object timer. The parameters are the shield object, the timer ID `tmShieldTime`, and when it should fire (in 5000 milliseconds).

```
eng.CreateObjTimer(g.shield, g.tmShieldTime, 5000)
```

3. While the shield is active, the player ship should not take any collisions.

```
g.player.SetColGroup(0)
```

4. Set the shield to active and close the method.

```
g.shield.SetActive(True)
Return 0
End
```

## *What just happened?*

The last method you have created will activate the shield of the player ship and create the timer that will deactivate the shield when it fires.

# Delta time related movement

If you want to have your objects move at the same speed no matter how fast the computer that the game is running on is, then you need to measure the time it will spend between each OnUpdate call.

## Time for action – determine the time delta

**1.** Add a new method call, UpdateGametime.

```
Method UpdateGameTime:Int()
```

**2.** Store the difference between the current Millisecs value and the global variable lastTime into deltaTime.

```
deltaTime = Millisecs() - lastTime
```

**3.** Add the delta to the time of the last call.

```
lastTime += deltaTime
```

**4.** Return the deltaTime and close the method.

```
    Return deltaTime
End
```

## *What just happened?*

This is a simple method which determines the time in milliseconds since its last call. The delta time can be used to factor speed values or other factors that are time dependent.

# Updating the game statistic info text objects

In each frame, we want to update the text objects that will display our most important game fields, such as score, lifes, levelNumber, and cometCount.

## Time for action – updating the info text

**1.** Insert a new method called `UpdateInfoText`.

```
Method UpdateInfoText:Int()
```

**2.** Set the text field of the text objects with their corresponding values.

```
txtScore.SetText("Score:    "+score)
txtComets.SetText("Comets:   "+cometCount)
 txtLevel.SetText("Level:    "+levelNumber)
txtLifes.SetText("Lifes:    "+lifes)
```

**3.** Close the method.

```
   Return 0
End
```

## What just happened?

Within the `UpdateInfoText` method, we update all of our UI text objects so they display the current values regarding score, the level number, how many lives are left, and also how many comets are left on the screen.

## Starting a new game

There are two points where you want to start a new game by resetting some variables: at the beginning of the game, and after one game is over and you want to start a new one.

## Time for action – creating a StartNewGame method

**1.** Add the `StartNewGame` method to the `game` class.

```
Method StartNewGame:Int()
```

**2.** Set the game relevant fields to their initial values.

```
cometCount = 0
lifes = 3
 score = 0
levelNumber = 1
```

**3.** Deactivate the layers `layerTitle` and `layerScore`.

```
layerTitle.SetActive(False)
layerScore.SetActive(False)
```

4. Position the player ship in the middle of the virtual canvas.

```
player.SetPos(eng.canvasWidth/2,eng.canvasHeight/2)
```

5. Set its angle and speed to 0.

```
player.SetAngle(0.0)
player.SetSpeed(0)
```

6. Activate the player ship and activate its shield.

```
player.SetActive(True)
ActivateShield()
```

7. Spawn 4 new large comets by calling SpawnComets.

```
SpawnComets(4)
```

8. Set the game mode to gmPlay and close the method.

```
    gameMode = gmPlay
    Return 0
End
```

## What just happened?

Every time the game starts again, you need to reset some values, create new objects, and so on. The last method you have created does just that.

## Let the engine glow

Every game also needs eye candy. In our case, the engine of our precious ship will leave a trail from the engine, which will fade away over time.

## Time for action – spawning some engine particle FX

1. Insert the SpawnPlayerEngine method into the game class.

```
Method SpawnPlayerEngine:Int()
```

2. Determine the position 20 pixels right behind the ship with the GetVector method.

```
Local d:Float[] = player.GetVector(20,180.0+player.angle)
```

3. Create a new object for the engine particle from the sprite atlas.

```
obj = eng.CreateImage(atlas, 16,96,16,16, d[0],d[1])
```

**4.** Set the angle to the ship angle, scale it down to a half, and set the layer to `layerFX`.

```
obj.SetAngle(player.angle)
obj.SetScale(0.5)
obj.SetLayer(layerFX)
```

**5.** To remove the trail after `100` milliseconds, call `CreateObjTimer`. After that, close that method.

```
eng.CreateObjTimer(obj, tmObjRemove, 100)
Return 0
End
```

## What just happened?

The method `SpawnPlayerEngine` creates a nice particle effect that reassembles the thrust of an engine. It also creates a timer for each particle so it will be removed after its lifetime.

## And it goes boom—creating an explosion

Another source of eye candy would be the explosions when an object gets hit.

## Time for action – creating some explosions

**1.** To spawn an explosion, create an method called `SpawnExplosion`. The parameters will be the particle amount, and the center position of the explosion.

```
Method SpawnExplosion:Int(c:Int, xp:Float, yp:Float)
```

**2.** Add a FOR loop from `1` to the amount of particles.

```
For Local i:Int = 1 To c
```

**3.** Create a local object of the particle from the sprite atlas.

```
Local explo:ftObject = eng.CreateImage(atlas,
0,112,16,16, xp, yp)
```

**4.** Scale and rotate it randomly.

```
explo.SetScale(Rnd(3,15)/10)
explo.SetAngle(Rnd(0,359))
```

**5.** Add a random spin and speed.

```
explo.SetSpin(Rnd(-4,4))
explo.SetSpeed(Rnd(1,2))
```

**6.** Reset the layer to `layerFX` and create an object timer with the ID `tmObjRemove` to remove the particle after a random time between `100` to `2000` milliseconds.

```
explo.SetLayer(layerFX)
eng.CreateObjTimer(explo, tmObjRemove, Rnd(100,2000))
```

**7.** Close the FOR loop and play the `sndExplo` sound.

```
Next
sndExplo.Play()
```

**8.** Close the method.

```
    Return 0
End
```

## What just happened?

Again, this method helps you to spawn some nice explosions. It also creates a timer that will ensure that each particle is removed after its lifetime.

## Give me that gun—spawning a shot

This game is about blasting some rocks into pieces. And what is the best tool for it? The deadly cannon of our lovely spaceship. So we need to shoot something.

## Time for action – spawning some shots

**1.** As always, create a new method. This time it is called `SpawnPlayerShot`.

```
Method SpawnPlayerShot:Int()
```

**2.** We need to get the position that is `20` pixels in front of the ship. For this, we can use the `GetVector` method. It needs the distances and the angle from it, which will be the same as the ship's angle.

```
Local ds:Float[] = player.GetVector(20, player.angle)
```

**3.** Create a local shot image from the sprite atlas.

```
        Local sht:ftObject = eng.CreateImage(atlas, 0,96,16,16,
ds[0],ds[1])
```

**4.** Set the angle of the shot to the same as the ship.

```
sht.SetAngle(player.angle)
```

**5.** Set the maximum speed to 25 and the actual speed to the player speed + 10.

```
sht.SetMaxSpeed(25.0)
sht.SetSpeed(player.speed+10.0)
```

**6.** Scale the object down to a half and let it wrap around the screen edges.

```
sht.SetScale(0.5)
sht.SetWrapScreen(True)
```

**7.** Reset the layer of the shot to layerGame.

```
sht.SetLayer(layerGame)
```

**8.** Add an object timer with the ID tmObjRemove to remove the shot after 2500 milliseconds.

```
eng.CreateObjTimer(sht, tmObjRemove, 2500)
```

**9.** Set the collision parameters.

```
sht.SetColGroup(grpShot)
sht.SetColWith(grpComet, True)
sht.SetRadius(2)
```

**10.** Play the sndShot sound and close the method.

```
sndShot.Play()
Return 0
End
```

## What just happened?

Besides spawning the shot from the player ship and letting it travel in the direction your ship was heading to, this method will also play the corresponding sound effect for the shot.

## Save some high scores, will ya!

To save the high score list to the app's state, we will create a new method.

## Time for action – saving the high score list

**1.** Create a new method called SaveHighScore.

```
Method SaveHighScore:Int ()
```

2. Use the `SaveToString` method of the engine's `scoreList` to save it to a string.

```
Local hs:String = g.eng.scoreList.SaveToString()
```

3. Save this string with a call to `SaveState`. Then close this method.

```
    SaveState(hs)
    Return 0
End
```

## What just happened?

By creating more specialized help methods, we can easily plug them into the game where we need them. Also, we have avoided creating redundant code, which means we don't have duplicate code sections in the game.

# Finalizing the OnUpdate method

Now, we can also set the `OnUpdate` method of our game class in stone. It will control the game depending on how the `gameMode` variable is set.

## Time for action – finalizing the OnUpdate method

1. Head over to the `OnUpdate` method and add a `Select` statement with the `gameMode` as a parameter.

```
Method OnUpdate:Int()

    Select gameMode
```

2. When the game mode is `gmPlay`, update the engine with the `deltaTime` divided by `60` as a speed parameter.

```
Case gmPlay
    eng.Update(Float(UpdateGameTime())/60.0)
```

3. Do a collision check only on the `layerGame` layer.

```
eng.CollisionCheck(layerGame)
```

4. Update the info text objects.

```
UpdateInfoText()
```

**5.** When the game mode is `gmMenu` or `gmGameOver`.

```
Case gmMenu, gmGameOver
```

If the *P* key was hit, then start a new game.

```
If KeyHit(KEY_P) Then
  StartNewGame()
Endif
```

If the *H* key was hit, then show the high score list.

```
If KeyHit(KEY_H) Then
  ShowScoreList()
Endif
```

**6.** When the game mode is `gmScoreList`.

```
Case gmScoreList
```

If the *P* key was hit, start a new game.

```
If KeyHit(KEY_P) Then
  StartNewGame()
Endif
```

**7.** End the `Select` statement.

```
    End

    Return 0
End
```

## *What just happened?*

Now, if you build the game without any errors and press the *P* key, then you should see some comets moving over the screen and the spaceship in the middle.

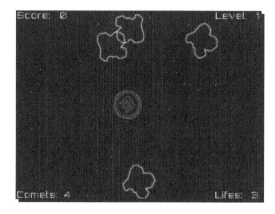

# Bring in the action—shaping the engine class

At the moment, you still can't move your ship or shoot anything. Also, the collision detection works in the background, but our game doesn't act on it. That is why we need to detail the `engine` class now. We need to act on collision, object updating, timer events, and also when a layer is updating.

## Crack these objects—object collision handling

We need to act on collision of comets with shots, the player ship, and an activated shield.

## Time for action – detailing the collision detection

The `OnObjectCollision` method has two parameters. The first object is the one that actually checks against a collision with the second object. To identify an object, we will compare against its collision group field, `collGroup`.

1. Add a local integer variable called `i` to the `OnObjectCollision` method.

   ```
   Method OnObjectCollision:Int(obj:ftObject, obj2:ftObject)

       Local i:Int
   ```

2. Now, check if the `collGroup` field of the second object is `g.grpComet`. As this is a constant from the `game` class, we need to add the prefix `g.` which stores it.

   ```
   If obj2.collGroup = g.grpComet Then
   ```

3. Compare the `tag` field with the constant comet size `g.cmLarge`.

   ```
   If obj2.tag = g.cmLarge Then
   ```

4. Spawn an explosion of `15` particles via `g.SpawnExplosion` at the position of the first object.

   ```
   g.SpawnExplosion(15,obj.xPos, obj.yPos)
   ```

5. Now, create two new comets of the size `g.cmMiddle`.

   ```
   For i = 1 To 2
      g.CreateComet(g.cmMiddle,obj2.xPos, obj2.yPos,
   Rnd(1,4)/2,Rnd(0,359))
   Next
   ```

6. Add `100` points to the game score. Then close the IF check.

   ```
   g.score = g.score + 100
   Endif
   ```

**7.** Repeat the same check, but check if `tag` is equal to `g.cmMiddle`. This time create only `10` particles, three small comets, and add `250` points to the game score.

```
If obj2.tag = g.cmMiddle Then
  g.SpawnExplosion(10,obj.xPos, obj.yPos)
  For i = 1 To 3
    g.CreateComet(g.cmSmall,obj2.xPos, obj2.yPos,
Rnd(1,4)/2,Rnd(0,359))
  Next
  g.score = g.score + 250
Endif
```

**8.** Repeat the same check but check if a `tag` field of the second object equals `g.cmSmall`. Create only `5` particles and add `500` points to the score. Don't create any new comets.

```
If obj2.tag = g.cmSmall Then
  g.SpawnExplosion(5,obj.xPos, obj.yPos)
  g.score = g.score + 500
Endif
```

**9.** Now subtract `1` from `g.cometCount` and remove the second object.

```
    g.cometCount -= 1
    obj2.Remove()
Endif
```

That's all for collision checks against comets. The next stop will be the player shots. Why? Because when they hit a comet they need to be removed too.

**10.** Check if the `collGroup` field of the first object equals `g.grpShot`. If yes, then remove it.

```
If obj.collGroup = g.grpShot Then
  obj.Remove()
Endif
```

**11.** Now, check if the player ship ran into a comet.

Check if the `collGroup` field of the first object equals `g.grpPlayer`. If yes, subtract `1` from `g.lifes`.

```
  If obj.collGroup = g.grpPlayer Then
    g.lifes -= 1
  Endif

  Return 0
End
```

## *What just happened?*

During a collision, a lot of things happen. Depending on which objects have collided with each other, you have removed them and updated the game score. If a large or medium-sized comet was destroyed, you have also created a set of smaller comets. This gives the illusion that the former comet was blasted into smaller pieces.

## It's about time—acting on timer events

An object timer was created for some objects, either to remove an object (particles, shots) when the timer fires or to deactivate (shield) it.

## Time for action – detailing the OnObjectTimer method

The method `OnObjectTimer` in the `engine` class has two parameters. The timer ID and the object it is related to.

**1.** Inside the `OnObjectTimer` method, check if the timer ID equals `g.tmObjRemove`.

```
Method OnObjectTimer:Int(timerId:Int, obj:ftObject)

    If timerId = g.tmObjRemove Then
```

**2.** Remove the object and close the IF check.

```
    obj.Remove()
Endif
```

**3.** Check if timer ID is equal to `g.tmShieldTime`.

```
If timerId = g.tmShieldTime Then
```

**4.** Deactivate the object.

```
obj.SetActive(False)
```

**5.** Set the collision group of the player ship to `g.grpPlayer` again. Then, close the IF check.

```
    g.player.SetColGroup(g.grpPlayer)
    Endif

    Return
End
```

## What just happened?

We have created timers during the game. When these fire, the preceding method will determine the corresponding object and act on it accordingly.

## Everything is under control—object update events

Every time an object gets updated, the `OnObjectUpdate` method is called automatically from the engine. So this is a great place to check for input by the user and control our ship with it.

## Time for action – detailing the OnObjectUpdate method

The `OnObjectUpdate` method has one parameter, the object that is updated.

1.  Check if the object is equal to `g.player`.

    ```
    Method OnObjectUpdate:Int(obj:ftObject)

        If obj = g.player Then
    ```

2.  If the up arrow key is pressed, add `1.5` times the engine `delta` field value to the object (player) with the `AddSpeed` method. Also, spawn a player engine particle with `g.SpawnPlayerEngine`.

    ```
    If KeyDown(KEY_UP)        'Speed up
        obj.AddSpeed(1.5*delta)
        g.SpawnPlayerEngine()
    Endif
    ```

3.  Check if the left arrow key is pressed. Then set the angle, `15*delta` degrees relative to its current angle with `SetAngle`.

    ```
    If KeyDown(KEY_LEFT)       'turn left
        obj.SetAngle(-15.0 * delta,True)
    Endif
    ```

4.  If the right arrow key is pressed, set the angle, `+15*delta` degrees relative to its current angle with `SetAngle`.

    ```
    If KeyDown(KEY_RIGHT)        'turn right
        obj.SetAngle(15.0 * delta,True)
    Endif
    ```

**5.** Check if the *S* key was pressed, then spawn a player shot with `g.SpawnPlayerShot`.

```
If KeyHit(KEY_S)              'Shoot your gun
   g.SpawnPlayerShot()
Endif
```

**6.** To fire up the shield, check if the *Space* key was hit. If the shield is not active, then activate it with `g.ActivateShield`.

```
   'Fire up shield
   If KeyHit(KEY_SPACE) And g.shield.isActive= False Then
      g.ActivateShield()
   Endif
Endif

Return 0
End
```

## What just happened?

Inside the `OnUpdateObject` method, you have added some logic to read the input from the player and control the movement of the player ship. Also, you can now activate the shield and fire a shot from your deadly cannon.

## Did I win—checking the losing conditions with OnLayerUpdate

Every game needs winning conditions. Or at least losing conditions. A perfect place is the `OnLayerUpdate` method which is called when the engine updates a layer. In our game, the relevant layer is `layerGame`.

## Time for action – detailing the OnLayerUpdate method

The `OnLayerUpdate` method has the layer as a parameter.

**1.** Check if the layer is equal to `g.layerGame`.

```
Method OnLayerUpdate:Int(layer:ftLayer)

   If layer = g.layerGame Then
```

**2.** Check if `g.lifes` are equal to or below `0`.

```
If g.lifes <= 0 Then            'GameOVER
```

**3.** Set `gameMode` to `g.gmGameOver`.

```
g.gameMode = g.gmGameOver
```

**4.** Activate the layer `g.layerTitle`.

```
g.layerTitle.SetActive(True)
```

**5.** Add `g.score` to the high score list of the engine.

```
g.eng.scoreList.AddScore(g.score,"---")
```

**6.** Deactivate the player object.

```
g.player.SetActive(False)
```

**7.** Remove all particle objects and all remaining comets using their ID values.

```
g.layerFX.RemoveAllObjects()
layer.RemoveAllObjectsByID(g.grpComet)
```

**8.** Save the high score list via `g.SaveHighScore`. Then `Return` from the method.

```
    g.SaveHighScore()
    Return 0
Endif
```

**9.** Check if all comets are destroyed and `g.gameMode` still equals `g.gmPlay`.

```
'All comets destroyed-> next level
If g.cometCount <= 0 And g.gameMode = g.gmPlay Then
```

**10.** Activate the player shield.

```
ActivateShield()
```

**11.** Raise the level number, and spawn new comets. Also, add a player life.

```
        g.levelNumber += 1
        g.SpawnComets(3 + g.levelNumber)
        g.lifes += 1
    Endif
  Endif

  Return 0
End
```

## What just happened?

In the preceding four methods, we basically set all the controls and condition checks for our gameplay.

Of course there are other ways to handle all this. Remember, this is just one way to do it. The whole game code is about 450-500 lines. That is not much. But fantomEngine took a lot of work from us. You could easily add another 800-1000 lines to the game if you had to create all this yourself.

## Have a go hero—adding an enemy ship

One thing that is missing from an Asteroids clone is the enemy ship that showed up randomly and shot at your ship. You could also try to destroy it, and if you hit it you get a good amount of points rewarded to you. It would be a good challenge for you to add an enemy ship. If you look at the sprite sheet, then you will find a green enemy ship right there. Try it, it is easy!

# One last thing—creating a FLASH game

Creating a FLASH game is as easy as creating an HTML5 game. You have just installed the **FLEX** compiler on your system. If you are on Windows, then you also need to install the **JAVA SE** development kit. For more detailed instructions about this, please refer to the *Getting started* section in the Monkey documentation.

After you have installed these software kits, then just restart Monk. When you build your game, you should now see a new FLASH entry in the list of build targets. After a successful build, you will find a FLASH folder inside your build folder, which contains all the files that you will need to copy to your web space if you want to publish your game there.

# Summary

In this chapter, we learned how to use the fantomEngine game framework.

Some of the things we have covered are as follows:

- ◆ How to load/create image objects
- ◆ How to load bitmap fonts and display text objects
- ◆ How to play sound effects
- ◆ How to act on collision detection
- ◆ How to create a FLASH game

We will also use the fantomEngine more intensively in *Chapter 5*, *Game #4, Chain Reaction*, where we will create a completely different game for the **Android** platform, called **Chain Reaction**. See you there!

# 5
# Game #4, Chain Reaction

*Here we are, over a third of the way through the book already, and now we finally hit our first mobile game. Well, this game is not the typical mobile or desktop game; this game, **Chain Reaction**, will be built for the Android platform. So, get your Android-powered phone/tablet and get cooking!*

*Have you ever worked inside a nuclear power plant? There, you have to avoid a chain reaction that could cause a nuclear meltdown. In Game #4, Chain Reaction, we want to create exactly that—a chain reaction. You will have a map of atoms in front of you and can trigger just one atom to start spinning. Will you be able to pick the right one and cause the biggest and longest chain reaction?*

In this chapter you will:

- Create your sprites/game objects mostly from sprite sheets to save memory and speed up the draw process
- Play back sprite animations
- Read the touch input of the device
- Act on the `OnResume` and `OnSuspend` events
- Create an Android application
- Learn how to scale the game content, depending on the size of the device display

In Chain Reaction, the player will see a grid of 8 x 11 atom elements in front of him/her. There are elements with 1, 2, or 3 connectors. The player now has to choose one by touching it. Now, this element will rotate clockwise by 90 degrees. After the rotation is done, the game will check if the neighboring elements connect to the previous element. If yes, a sound will be played, the score will be raised by 1, and these connected elements will start to rotate. The goal of the player is to touch the elements that will hopefully start the longest chain reaction.

Do you want to develop this game? Of course you do! So let's get on with it.

# Modifying the HTML5 canvas size

HTML5? We are creating an Android app, so why modify the HTML5 canvas size? Well, you will notice that compiling for the Android platform will take a while, much longer than for HTML5. In the game, we don't use Android-specific features. Hence, we can develop and test the game in the HTML browser. For this, we want to change the canvas size of the HTML5 build. By default, it has a size of 640 x 480 pixels. As we have a target canvas size of 480 x 800 pixels, we want to change that.

## Time for action – modifying canvas size

When you have your first playable results, you do the following:

1. Compile for HTML5.

2. Using Monk, open the `MonkeyGame.html` file, which is located inside the `build/HTML5` folder of your project.

3. Locate the line that looks like the following:
   ```
   <canvas id="GameCanvas" on click="javascript:this.focus();"
     width=640 height=480 tabindex=1></canvas><br>
   ```

4. Change the `width` value to `480` and the `height` value to `800`, and then save and close the file.

Now, when you build and run your project, the HTML5 canvas is similar to the targeted Android canvas size.

# Some development basics

Before we dive into the development of Chain Reaction, we should talk a little about some terms and techniques in game development. After all, you should learn some general things too and not only follow instructions on how to develop a certain type of game. Some of them are important when it comes to game development for mobile platforms.

# Frameworks/modules

In the previous chapter, we used a game framework called **fantomEngine**. As it provides a lot of game-related features that are perfect for the games in this book, we will use it further. But there are different third-party modules that you can use for your game development and enhance the feature set of Monkey, big-time. The following link will bring you to the Monkey module list:

```
http://www.monkeycoder.co.nz/Community/modules.php.
```

The newest version of the fantomEngine framework is available at:

```
http://code.google.com/p/fantomengine/.
```

Use these third-party modules/frameworks, or build one of your own. Practice makes perfect, but it makes no sense to recode everything over and over again.

# Sprite sheets

Using a sprite sheet, also known as a sprite atlas, is one way to preserve memory and also speed up the drawing process of a game. In every OpenGL-based engine, texture change takes some time. Imagine that, for each game object, you load a different image (texture). Now, when the engine wants to draw each image, it now has to tell OpenGL to provide a different texture. A lot of state changes are required and that simply takes time. A much faster way is to use sprite sheets. There, you find several (if not all) images placed onto one surface. When you want to draw a part of the big texture, you tell monkey to only draw a small part using the `DrawImageRect` command.

Otherwise, grab a subimage from a previous loaded image (atlas). Monkey supports this with the `GrabImage` command.

Here is an example of a small sprite sheet you know from the previous chapter:

You can create these sheets manually with software such as **Gimp**, **InkScape**, or **Photoshop**.

Otherwise, use specialized texture packer tools, such as **Texture Packer** or **Zwoptex**, which are available at `http://www.texturepacker.com/` and `http://zwoptexapp.com/` respectively.

# Content scaling

Especially with Android-based devices, you will find a lot of different screen resolutions. Some are 320 x 480 or 480 x 800 pixels and some are 480 x 855 pixels. Or, they could be something completely different. The more the devices that come onto the market, the more the variations that you will have to deal as a developer.

Thankfully, Monkey provides the canvas size at runtime via `DeviceWidth` and `DeviceHeight`. When you develop your game, you have to either place the game objects dynamically or scale everything so that it fits into the canvas with the `Scale` and `Translate` statements, before you start drawing.

A framework such as fantomEngine provides a virtual canvas size, which you can set with the `SetCanvasSize` method. After that, the `render`, `update`, and `touch` functions of fantomEngine will scale to the device's real canvas size, properly.

# Touch input

On a mobile device, such as an Android-powered mobile phone, you have two ways to control a game. One is by tilting the phone and retrieving corresponding values from the device's accelerometer and the other is by touching the screen with one or more fingers. We will use the one-touch solution in our game. Monkey provides methods to detect how many fingers touch the screen—`TouchDown` and `TouchHit`, and also their coordinates, via `TouchX` and `TouchY`. For Chain Reaction, we will utilize fantomEngine's `GetTouchX` and `GetTouchY` methods, so we don't have to deal manually with a possible content-scaling issue.

 Not all Android devices provide multi-touch information! Keep this in mind, if your code seems to not work on your test device.

# Suspend and Resume events

When you play these Android-based games, you can switch to the home screen via one touch of the home button. Your app will still be running in the background. A lot of times, you need to act on this. For example, the game should not update further when it isn't active for the player or you want to save the state of the game quickly; this is so that, if the running process gets killed, nothing gets lost. This is where Mojo's `OnSuspend` and `OnResume` methods come in handy. We will utilize these in the game too.

# Animation

There are different types of animations of a sprite/object. One deals with things such as the scale, angle, color, and alpha values of an object, and the other changes the sprite image that will be drawn on the canvas during a period of time. In Monkey, you can load these different images via a sprite sheet and an additional parameter of the `LoadImage` and `GrabImage` methods. The animation would have to be done manually through your code. fantomEngine will support you here too, with a new method called `CreateAnimImage`. During the update process, the engine will automatically switch the image that has to be drawn.

Here is an example of a sprite sheet that has game objects prepared for a typical sprite animation (look at the circles):

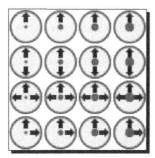

And here is what the game will look like, when it is done:

# Game resources

For the game, we will only have a few resource files this time:

- The title screen image
- The game background image
- The Atom tile sprite sheet
- Game bitmap font
- A sound to be played when a reaction starts

 The sound format for Monkey and the Android platform is the `.ogg` sound format. Use a tool such as Audacity to convert sounds if you need to.

# Game objects

Like every game, Chain Reaction is made out of several objects. Let's go through them one by one.

## Layers

In this game we will use only three layers (groups):

- Background
- Game
- Title screen

These layers help us to draw the game objects in the correct order, draw only the ones needed for a certain game mode, and also reduce the amount of objects to be checked during collision detection.

## Title screen

The title screen of our little game is an image with the title written on it and with a a button to start the game. As the button is already drawn on it, we will utilize a new feature of the fantomEngine, a **Zone** object. You can use a zone object to detect collisions on it and also check for touch events.

## Game background

The game background screen will cover the whole canvas of the device. In addition, there are two buttons drawn on it that let us exit the game and restart it. Beside the actual play field, there is also a header area where the game score and the current **FPS (frames per second)** value are displayed.

## Atom tiles

Finally, our main game object! The player has to touch one of the atom tiles; it then depends on its kind, rotation, and also the neighboring atoms as to whether a chain reaction is started. The atom tiles are drawn on one sprite sheet for the different types of atoms' elements. Each tile comes in four different variations that are used for the sprite animation.

## Game info text

While in game mode, the player will be provided with two fields of information in text form. One is the game score and the other will be the current FPS value. It will indicate how many times your device is able to draw the whole game screen in the last second. Anything less than 20 FPS becomes sloppy animation-wise. It is better to have it at around 30 FPS or higher.

# The basic app structure

Ok, we are done with the description part; let us create the game now. Just as our previous game, we will work with a single file structure again.

## Time for action – creating the main source file and its folders

At the time of writing this book, Monk didn't create the needed folder structure for you. So, you need to manually set up the folder for our project:

1. First, create a new folder for the game; name it `chainreaction`.

2. Inside this folder, create a data folder for all the resources with the name `chainreaction.data`.

3. Next, copy all the resource files from the chapter's `chainreaction.data` folder into your `.data` folder.

4. Now, also copy the source file of fantomEngine from the book's chapter folder into your project folder. As before, the name is `fantomEngine.monkey`.

5. All that is left is to create a new empty script file and save it under the name `chainreaction.monkey`.

**6.** An empty script doesn't do much; it won't even compile. Let's add a few lines.

```
Strict
#rem
  Script:     chainreaction.monkey
  Description:  Sample script from chapter #5 of the book
    „Monkey Game Development Beginners guide" by PacktPub
  Author:     Michael Hartlef
#end

Import fantomEngine
Global g:game
```

It looks familiar, right? If not, then please study *Chapter 4, Game# 3 Comet Crusher*, where we did the same. What's next? Adding the game class to our file.

**7.** Add a new class called game with the OnCreate, OnUpdate, and OnRender methods.

```
Class game Extends App
  Method OnCreate:Int()
    Return 0
  End
  Method OnUpdate:Int()
    Return 0
  End
  Method OnRender:Int()
    Return 0
  End
```

Remember, we want to utilize the OnSuspend and OnResume events.

**8.** Add new methods for OnSuspend and OnResume, and close the class.

```
  Method OnResume:Int()
    Return 0
  End
  Method OnSuspend:Int()
    Return 0
  End
End
```

And like with every Monkey app, we need to add the Main function.

**9.** Insert the `Main` function header.

```
Function Main:Int()
```

**10.** Create an instance of the `game` class, store it inside the variable `g`, and then close the function.

```
    g = New game
    Return 0
End
```

 Your `game` class is there to set up the game and handle, depending on the game mode, the general update, and render process.

To interface with fantomEngine, we will now create an instance of its `ftEngine` class.

**11.** Add a new class called `engine`, which is an instance of the `ftEngine` class. Next, insert methods for its `OnObjectTouch`, `OnObjectTransition`, `OnObjectCollision`, and `OnObjectTimer` methods.

```
Class engine Extends ftEngine
  Method OnObjectTouch:Int(obj:ftObject, touchId:Int)
    Return 0
  End

  Method OnObjectTransition:Int(transId:Int, obj:ftObject)
    Return 0
  End

  Method OnObjectCollision:Int(obj:ftObject, obj2:ftObject)
    Return 0
  End

  Method OnLayerTimer:Int(timerId:Int, obj:ftObject)
    Return 0
  end
End
```

This is the basic structure of our game. Save the file and build it to see if any errors appear.

# What just happened?

They say, just like history, Monkey game development repeats itself. We are once again interfacing with the fantomEngine; this is a huge timesaver.

> The data folder (which stores the images, sounds, and data files of your game) inside your source code folder has to be always named as follows:
>
> `yoursourcename.data`
>
> So, if your main source code file is named `furryballs.monkey`, then the data folder has to be named `furryballs.data`.

# The data storage

The `game` class holds, as usual, our definitions for various game objects and game-related fields. They help you in keeping track of the game score, the mode the game is in, and other stuff.

## Time for action – creating the data structure

The following modifications have to be made to the `game` class:

1. Insert the `eng` field, which will store the instance of the `engine` class.

   ```
   Field eng:engine
   ```

2. Now, add a general object called `obj`. We will use this field during game setup.

   ```
   Field obj:ftObject
   ```

3. To display some text in the game, we need one object for the game score and one to display the FPS value we have talked about previously.

   ```
   Field txtScore:ftObject
   Field txtFPS:ftObject
   ```

4. We will use a bitmap font in the game and store this font inside the `font1` object.

   ```
   Field font1:ftFont
   ```

5. Next, add the three layers for the background, the game itself, and the title screen.

   ```
   Field layerBackGround:ftLayer
   Field layerGame:ftLayer
   Field layerTitle:ftLayer
   ```

**6.** For the only sound effect in the game , we need a sound object called `sndBing`.

```
Field sndBing:ftSound
```

**7.** Now, add the `atlas` field to store the sprite sheet for the atom elements.

```
Field atlas:Image
```

**8.** Usually a game has a score and so does Chain Reaction.

```
Field score:Int = 0
```

**9.** To store the frames per second value, add a field called `fps`.

```
Field fps:Int=0
```

**10.** Now, add the `gameMode` field, which will be initialized with the `gmMenu` constant that we will add very soon.

```
Field gameMode:Int = gmMenu
```

**11.** Add various points inside the game; we will need to store a time value, and for this, we need two fields.

```
Field lastTime:Int
Field deltaTime:Int
```

**12.** To store the collision count, which will also be used as an object ID later on, we need the `collCount` field.

```
Field collCount:Int=0
```

**13.** When the game is suspended, we will set a field to `true` so that we can act on it later on.

```
Field isSuspended:Bool = False
```

These are all fields that the game Chain Reaction needs. Now, let's add some constants.

**14.** In the game, we need only two game mode constants—one for being inside the menu (title screen) and one for gameplay.

```
Const gmMenu:Int = 1
Const gmPlay:Int = 2
```

**15.** To do proper collision checks, we will need two object groups—one for the atom elements and one for circle collision objects.

```
Const grpAtom:Int = 3
Const grpCircle:Int = 4
```

In the game, we will use the timer feature of fantomEngine to change some values on an object. For this, we need a timer ID.

**16.** Add the `tmObjSwitch` timer ID.

```
Const tmObjSwitch:Int = 5
```

**17.** The last constants we add are for our three buttons in the game.

```
Const btnPlay:Int = 10
Const btnReset:Int = 11
Const btnExit:Int = 12
```

## What just happened?

Fields store game-relevant variable data that can change over time. Constants are values that don't change and make your game code more readable.

# First changes to the OnCreate event

Inside the `OnCreate` method of the `game` class, we will set up the game itself. So, let us make some modifications there.

## Time for action – first changes to the OnCreate method

Inside the `OnCreate` method of a monkey app, you basically set up the game. For example, loading some graphics can be done here:

**1.** First set the update rate of the game to `60` frames per second.

```
Method OnCreate:Int()
  SetUpdateRate(60)
```

**2.** Now, create an instance of the `engine` class.

```
eng = New engine
```

We want to work with a virtual resolution and let the fantomEngine take care of the scaling of our graphics and touch events.

**3.** Set the virtual canvas size to 480 x 800 with a call to the `SetCanvasSize` method.

```
eng.SetCanvasSize(480,800)
```

**4.** Load the texture atlas of the atom elements.

```
atlas = LoadImage („CR_Tiles.png")
```

**5.** Set the `font1` object with our bitmap font.

```
font1 = eng.LoadFont("cr_font")
Return 0
End
```

## What just happened?

We have set the update rate of the game, set its virtual canvas size, and loaded the texture atlas for the atom elements. Some basic definition is done, but we are far from being finished.

# Detailing the OnRender event

You will notice that the `OnRender` method is always very small. Nothing much happens here as the main work is done internally with the fantomEngine. However, we want to measure how many frames per second are displayed during gameplay. With the `SetUpdateRate` method, you will set exactly that—the update rate. The render rate can, and most likely will, be smaller. Monkey will skip render frames when the projected update rate is in danger.

## Time for action – detailing the OnRender method

To determine an FPS value in fantomEngine, a call to its `GetFPS` method will return the current FPS value, as follows:

**1.** Store the output of the `GetFPS` call in the `fps` field of the `game` class.

```
Method OnRender:Int()
    fps = eng.GetFPS()
```

**2.** Now tell the engine to render its objects.

```
eng.Render()
Return 0
End
```

## What just happened?

Inside the `OnRender` method, we determine the current frames per second value that indicates how many times the game is able to display the content. We will later create a method to update the corresponding text object called `txtFPS`. We also told the engine to render all objects in one batch.

# Setting up the game objects

Inside the `OnCreate` event of the game, most objects will be created and initialized. Some objects such as the atom elements will be created at the start of a game and when we reset the game field.

## Sound effects

Let's start with sounds. Creating your own method to load just one sound is kind of overkill, but if you want to extend the game later on, you know then in which method you should load new sounds.

## Time for action – loading the game sound effects

To load sounds into the game, we will create a method called `LoadSounds`.

1. Inside the `game` class, add a new method header called `LoadSounds`

   ```
   Method LoadSounds:Int ()
   ```

2. Load the `"bing"` sound into the `sndBing` object. Remember: don't add the file extension of your sound file to the filename. Now, close the method.

   ```
   sndBing = eng.LoadSound("bing")
   Return 0
   End
   ```

## What just happened?

With this separate method to load sounds, it will be easy for you to add other sounds as well. Just create another sound object in the data section, and then load the sound here.

## Game layers

Layers are like groups. They are rendered in their order of creation, unless you tell the engine to do it otherwise.

## Time for action – creating layers for the game

Just as in the previous chapter, we will add a method called `CreateLayers`:

1. Add a method called `CreateLayers` into the `game` class.

   ```
   Method CreateLayers:Int()
   ```

2. Create new layers for the background, the game, and the title screen.

```
layerBackGround = eng.CreateLayer()
layerGame = eng.CreateLayer()
layerTitle = eng.CreateLayer()
```

3. Close the method.

```
Return 0
End
```

## What just happened?

We want to group (layer) the game into three sections—one for the background, one for the actual game, and one for the title screen. Therefore, we have created the CreateLayers method.

# Game screen

The game screen is composed of the background image, the two info text objects for the game score and the FPS value. Also there are two buttons to reset or exit the game.

## Click here – Adding buttons

The buttons could be created from images, but they are drawn into the background image. To detect a touch event, you can use the **ZoneBox** object.

## Time for action – creating buttons

As we have several buttons in the game, we will add a method to the game class that will set up a button for us:

1. Insert the CreateButton method into the game class. Its parameters are the button width and height, its position, layer and an ID.

```
Method CreateButton:Int (width:Int, height:Int, xp:Int, yp:Int,
    id:Int, layer:ftLayer)
```

2. Create a new ZoneBox via the CreateZoneBox statement.

```
Local but:ftObject = eng.CreateZoneBox(width, height, xp, yp)
```

**3.** To identify the button, later in the `OnObjTouch` event of the engine, we will set the tag property of the object with the ID.

```
but.SetTag(id)
```

**4.** Now, set the touch mode (collision detection) to use the bounding box.

```
but.SetTouchMode(2)
```

**5.** Lastly, set the layer and then close the method

```
but.SetLayer(layer)
Return 0
End
```

## What just happened?

Since we need to create several buttons in the game, we have created a method that will set them up for us. Later on, we can use the `TouchCheck` method to determine if a button was hit.

## The info text objects

The game screen will have two text objects: One to display the game score and the other for the FPS value.

## Time for action – creating info text objects

The next method will set up the two text objects for us:

**1.** Inside the `game` class, add a new method called `CreateInfoText`.

```
Method CreateInfoText:Int ()
```

**2.** Create the `txtScore` text object from the `font1` font object. Set it to the background layer.

```
txtScore = eng.CreateText(font1,"Score:   „+score,40,46)
txtScore.SetLayer(layerBackGround)
```

**3.** Repeat this with the `txtFPS` text object.

```
txtFPS = eng.CreateText(font1,"FPS:  „+999,
  eng.canvasWidth-45,46,2)
txtFPS.SetLayer(layerBackGround)
```

**4.**   Close the method.

```
Return 0
End
```

## What just happened?

To display some info text values, we have created two text objects with the `CreateText` method of fantomEngine. Later in the game, we will update them with the `SetText` method of each object.

## The actual game screen

Now, let's create a method to compose the actual game screen.

## Time for action – composing the game screen

Remember that the game screen is composed of one background image, two text objects, and two button objects:

**1.**   To compose the screen, add a method called `CreateGameScreen` in the `game` class.

```
Method CreateGameScreen:Int()
```

**2.**   Load the background image into a local object, as we don't need to access it separately later on. Set its layer to `layerBackGround`.

```
Local ts:ftObject =
    eng.CreateImage("CR_GameScreen.png",eng.canvasWidth/2,
    eng.canvasHeight/2)
ts.SetLayer(layerBackGround)
```

**3.**   Now create the **RESET** button at a location where it is drawn on the background image.

```
CreateButton(180,60,130,eng.canvasHeight-50, btnReset,
    layerBackGround)
```

**4.**   Repeat this for the **EXIT** button and then close the method.

```
CreateButton(180,60,eng.canvasWidth-130,eng.canvasHeight-50,
    btnExit, layerBackGround)
CreateInfoText()
Return 0
End
```

## *What just happened?*

As you can easily see, splitting up tasks into smaller methods makes a code more readable, and you will appreciate this later when you want to make changes to your code. We have split up the game screen into three methods—one for creating buttons, one for the text objects, and one for the actual screen composing.

# Title screen

The title/menu screen is somewhat simpler than the background screen. We just have to load an image and create a **PLAY** button.

## Time for action – creating the title screen

For this we will create another method inside the game class.

1.  Insert a new method called CreateTitleScreen.

    ```
    Method CreateTitleScreen:Int ()
    ```

2.  Load the title screen image into a local object and set its layer to layerTitle.

    ```
    Local ts:ftObject =
        eng.CreateImage („CR_TitleScreen.png",eng.canvasWidth/2,
        eng.canvasHeight/2)
    ts.SetLayer(layerTitle)
    ```

3.  Create a **PLAY** button at the location the button is drawn onto the image.

    ```
    CreateButton(eng.canvasWidth-220,60,eng.canvasWidth/2,
        eng.canvasHeight-260, btnPlay, layerTitle)
    ```

4.  Close the method:

    ```
    Return 0
    End
    ```

## *What just happened?*

Continuing with our method to have several creator methods, we have one to assemble the title screen on its own layer. Since it is on its own layer, we can make it visible or hide it whenever we need it. As the layerTitle layer was created as the latest one, it will cover other layers, anyway.

# Finalizing the OnCreate event

We can set another method in stone, which means that, once we have made the changes you will read in the next *Time for action* section, this method will be complete and can be left as it is for the rest of the development.

## Time for action – finalizing the OnCreate method

The `OnCreate` method was previously created by you. But now you need to add the calls to the methods you have build over the last pages.

1. Inside the `OnCreate` method of the `game` class, add calls to our previously created methods `LoadSounds`, `CreateLayers`, `CreateGameScreen`, and `CreateTitleScreen`:

```
atlas = LoadImage („CR_Tiles.png")
font1 = eng.LoadFont („cr_font")
LoadSounds()
CreateLayers()
CreateGameScreen()
CreateTitleScreen()
Return 0
End
```

## What just happened?

Now, we have set up the game objects, but not all, because the atom elements are missing. These will be set up dynamically during the update process and so can't be done in the `OnCreate` event. This book comes with the complete source of the game. If you need to check against it, look in the `chainreaction.monkey` file.

# Helper functions for the update process

Just as in the creation process, where we have created several smaller *helper* methods to split up the process and make it more readable, we will have the same for the update process. Another reason besides readability is reusability. You don't want to code the same thing several times. That is why you use functions and methods.

## Creating the atom elements

Each atom object is also a composed object—the image object that you can see and, depending on how many connectors the atom has, several invisible circles, which we will use to detect a connection (collision) with a connector next to it.

## Collision circle objects

Every object can be invisible but still act on updates and collision detection.

## Time for action – creating collision circles

The next method, `CreateColCircle`, will create an object that is used for collision checks only and will not be visible.

1. To create the collision circles, insert a new method named `CreateColCircles` into the game class. The parameters are the parent object and the position of the circle.

   ```
   Method CreateColCircle:Int (parent:ftObject, xp:Float, yp:Float)
   ```

2. Now, add a local circle object via `CreateCircle`, with a radius of `1.5` pixels.

   ```
   Local colObj:ftObject = eng.CreateCircle(1.5,xp, yp)
   ```

3. Set the layer to `layerGame` and the parent to `parent`.

   ```
   colObj.SetLayer(layerGame)
   colObj.SetParent(parent)
   ```

4. Now, set the collision group and with whom to collide with to `grpCircle`.

   ```
   colObj.SetColGroup(grpCircle)
   colObj.SetColWith(grpCircle,True)
   ```

5. Since you don't want to see each circle, you set it to be invisible and then close the method.

   ```
   colObj.SetVisible(False)
   Return 0
   End
   ```

## What just happened?

By creating invisible collision objects, we can automize the collision detection later on. We don't have to check at which angle an atom will be, because the circles will spin with their parent atom element.

## Atom elements

To create the actual atom elements we will use another method.

# Time for action – creating the atom elements

At the start of a game, or when you want to reset the game field, you will call this method to set up a new tile set:

**1.** The new method inside the game class will be named `CreateAtomElements`.

```
Method CreateAtomElements:Int()
```

**2.** We want to randomize the grid setup. For this we will seed the random number generator with the value of a call to `Millisecs`.

```
Seed = Millisecs()
```

**3.** The distance from a collision circle to the center of an atom will be 23 pixels and stored inside a local variable.

```
Local cd:Int = 23
```

**4.** Now, we need a grid of 8 x 11 elements. Start two `For` loops for this purpose.

```
For Local y:Int = 1 To 11
For Local x:Int = 1 To 8
```

**5.** Next, we determine randomly in the range of 0 to 3 the kind of element which represents the different kinds of atom connectors.

```
Local ek:Int = (Rnd(0,3)+0.4)
```

**6.** As we do not want the game to go on forever, we modify the ek value to a different one. This depends on another random number call with a range from 0 to 100.

```
If ek = 2 And Rnd(0,100) > 20 Then ek = 3
If ek = 1 And Rnd(0,100) > 80 Then ek = 0
```

For a little bit of eye candy, we want to add some kind of sprite animation. Here, we will use the `CreateAnimImage` method of fantomEngine.

**7.** Create a local anim object. The Y location on the sprite sheet depends on the ek value. For each sprite, we have four different anim images.

```
Local tile:ftObject = eng.CreateAnimImage(atlas, 0 ,ek*32
   ,32,32, 4, x*48+24, y*48+88)
```

**8.** Set the tag field of the atom to `grpAtom`.

```
tile.SetTag(grpAtom)
```

9. As the actual images are a little bit small, scale them to 150 percent of their actual size. Then set the layer to `layerGame`.

```
tile.SetScale(1.5)
tile.SetLayer(layerGame)
```

10. Set their ID to 0. Later, we will store the current `collCount` value in it.

```
tile.SetID(0)
```

11. To touch the first element, we need to set its touch mode to bounding box touch hit check.

```
tile.SetTouchMode(2)
```

12. Now create, depending on the element type (`ek`), some collision cycles at the positions of the atom element connectors:

```
Select ek
  Case 0
    CreateColCircle(tile,x*48+24, y*48+88-cd)
  Case 1
    CreateColCircle(tile,x*48+24, y*48+88-cd)
    CreateColCircle(tile,x*48+24, y*48+88+cd)
  Case 2
    CreateColCircle(tile,x*48+24, y*48+88-cd)
    CreateColCircle(tile,x*48+24+cd, y*48+88)
    CreateColCircle(tile,x*48+24-cd, y*48+88)
  Case 3
    CreateColCircle(tile,x*48+24, y*48+88-cd)
    CreateColCircle(tile,x*48+24+cd, y*48+88)
End
```

13. Randomly determine the animation frame in a range from 0 to 3.

```
Local f:Int = (Rnd(0,3)+0.4)+1
```

14. Set the animation time for each frame to 5 units.

```
tile.SetAnimTime(5)
```

15. Set the animation frame to the previously determined frame value `f`.

```
tile.SetAnimFrame(f)
```

16. Again, calculate the random starting angle (0, 90, 180, and 270 degrees) and set it.

```
Local a:Int = (Rnd(0,3)+0.4)
tile.SetAngle(a*90.0)
```

**17.** Close both `For` loops and the method.

```
        Next
    Next
    Return 0
End
```

## What just happened?

We just created two methods that let us dynamically build a grid of atom elements and their corresponding child collision detectors.

## Starting a new game

At one or two points in the game, we may want to (re)start the game—when you hit the **PLAY** button on the title screen and when you hit the **RESET** button on the game screen.

## Time for action – creating a StartNewGame method

In this method, make use of the `CreateAtomElements` method that we have built before:

**1.** In the `game` class, add a new method called `StartNewGame`.
```
Method StartNewGame:Int()
```

**2.** First, set the game score to `0`.
```
    score = 0
```

**3.** Next, deactivate the title layer. Because of this, it won't be rendered and doesn't act on touch hits from the user.
```
    layerTitle.SetActive(False)
```

**4.** Now, remove all objects from the game layer (if there are any).
```
    layerGame.RemoveAllObjects()
```

**5.** Set the `collCount` field to `0`. This will be used as an increasing ID for collision checks.
```
    collCount = 0
```

**6.** Finally, call the method that will create the grids of atom elements.
```
    CreateAtomElements()
```

**7.** The last step is to set the game mode to `gmPlay` and close this method:

```
gameMode = gmPlay
Return 0
End
```

## What just happened?

We have created a method that let us (re)start the game at any time. It takes care of all fields that need to be set to zero and removes any existing atom elements from the game layer.

## Time-related movement

Imagine you are playing the game on two devices that are very different when it comes to computing power and render speed. One is very fast and one is crawling. The fast one will be able to compute/update more times in a second, than the slow one. The game would run much faster on one system. To avoid this, we will measure the time it took from the last frame to the current one. This value in milliseconds will be one part of the speed factor for the `Update` method of fantomEngine. This will ensure that the game updates at the same speed, no matter which device you play the game on.

## Time for action – implementing the GetDeltaTime method

This method will calculate the time it took from its last call in milliseconds:

**1.** Insert a new method called `GetDeltaTime`. It will return an `Int` value.

```
Method GetDeltaTime:Int()
```

**2.** Compute `deltaTime` as the result of a call to `Millisecs` minus `lastTime`.

```
deltaTime = Millisecs() - lastTime
```

**3.** Then, add the current `deltaTime` value to `lastTime`.

```
lastTime += deltaTime
```

**4.** Return `deltaTime` and close the method.

```
Return deltaTime
End
```

## *What just happened?*

To calculate how long it took between two update processes, we created a method that will do just that. Determine the current time in milliseconds, and calculate how long it took from the last time this method was called. The result will be used to determine a speed factor for the engine's update process.

# Updating the info text objects

We have two info text objects in the game layer—one displays the current game score and one indicates the FPS value.

## Time for action – creating a method to update the text information

To update these text objects, we will create the `UpdateInfoText` method. Each text object has a text field that stores the text string value. The content of this field will be drawn on the screen.

**1.** Add a new method called `UpdateInfoText` to the `game` class.

```
Method UpdateInfoText:Int()
```

**2.** Set the text fields of both objects corresponding to their purpose.

```
txtScore.SetText("Score:    "+score)
txtFPS.SetText("FPS:    "+fps)
```

**3.** Close the method.

```
    Return 0
End
```

## *What just happened?*

Since we created a separate method to update the info text objects, we can call it at any time we wish. Later on, we will do this in the `OnUpdate` event on the game class, but the `OnRender` event would be good, too.

# Detailing the OnUpdate event

The last of our main methods of the `game` class will now be finalized. Depending on the mode of the game, we will act differently and also do touch checks to different layers.

# Time for action – finalizing the OnUpdate method

The OnUpdate event is the place to update all game objects and control the flow of the game in general. You do everything in the method line-by-line and with hundreds of statements. However, we took the approach with building a lot of helper methods, which will now be called inside this method:

**1.** Inside the OnUpdate method, store the result of a call to the method GetDeltaTime in the local variable d.

```
Method OnUpdate:Int()
    Local d:Int = GetDeltaTime()
```

**2.** Check with an If statement, whether the field isSuspended is FALSE.

```
If isSuspended = False Then
```

**3.** Add a Select statement with the field gameMode. Then, insert the Case statement for the constant gmPlay.

```
Select gameMode
    Case gmPlay
```

**4.** Now, call the Update method of your engine instance. As a speed parameter, we use the local d variable divided by 60. The speed parameter is a FLOAT value so you need to cast d to FLOAT.

```
eng.Update(Float(d)/60.0)
```

**5.** Now, check whether a TouchHit for the first finger is reported. On HTML5, this also reports a click with the left mouse button.

```
If TouchHit(0) Then
```

**6.** Because when you touch an atom element you create a new chain reaction, you need to set the game score to 0.

```
score = 0
```

**7.** Now, do a TouchCheck for the game and background layers. This will test each touchable object in these layers, if the touch coordinates are within the borders of that object. If yes, it will call the engine's OnObjectTouch method.

```
        eng.TouchCheck(layerGame)
        eng.TouchCheck(layerBackGround)
    Endif
```

**8.** Now add a Case statement for the gmMenu constant.

```
Case gmMenu
```

**9.** Again check for a touch hit, and if yes, do a `TouchCheck` on the `layerTitle` layer. It will basically check if the **PLAY** button was hit.

```
If TouchHit(0) Then
   eng.TouchCheck(layerTitle)
Endif
```

**10.** End the `Select` statement and update the info text objects.

```
End
UpdateInfoText()
```

**11.** Now close the first `If` check.

```
Endif
Return 0
End
```

## What just happened?

That is it. We have the `OnUpdate` method set in stone. If the app is not suspended, we will do touch hit checks and update all the objects in the engine. If you are missing any collision checks, we will do this inside the engine class.

# Introducing the OnSuspend event

So far, we haven't had to act on an app being suspended earlier. With mobile devices, this can happen pretty often. For example, you will get a phone call when you are playing.

## Time for action – modifying the OnSuspend event

The `OnSuspend` method will be called from Monkey, when the app is not completely ended from the operation system and still runs in the background:

**1.** Inside the `OnSuspend` method, set `isSuspended` to `TRUE`.

```
Method OnSuspend:Int()
   isSuspended = True
```

**2.** Since we don't need to update the game so quickly now, set the update rate to `5`. This might conserve battery power.

```
SetUpdateRate(5)
Return 0
End
```

## What just happened?

Inside the `OnSuspend` event, we have set the `isSuspended` field to `False`, so we can act on it during the `OnUpdate` event. At the same time, we set the update rate to 5 FPS. This might conserve battery power, as the CPU doesn't need to update the game that often.

Another thing you might like to do is to save the state of the game.

# Introducing the OnResume event

Things that were suspended will be resumed at some point. And for this, Monkey has the `OnResume` event. This will be called when the user clicks on the apps icon again, after an Android app was suspended by a click to the home button.

## Time for action – updating the OnResume method

In the `OnResume` event, we will switch back to the settings we had specified inside the `OnSuspend` method, as follows:

*1.* Set `isSuspended` to `False`.

```
Method OnResume:Int()
    isSuspended = False
```

*2.* Then, set the update rate of the game back to 60.

```
    SetUpdateRate(60)
    Return 0
End
```

## What just happened?

In the `OnResume` event, we just changed the settings we had specified inside the `OnResume` event. The engine will now update the game normally. You could also load some settings in the event that you had saved before.

Save your script again. I haven't mentioned this much, but save, save, save! One simple power failure and you will lose hours of work.

So what is next? The game will run, but it won't do anything. By now, you will only see the game title screen.

Hitting the **PLAY** button does nothing. Why? Because, we haven't acted on it so far. All this will be done inside the `engine` class, which we will fill with life shortly.

Follow me closely!

# The heart of the game - the engine class

The `engine` class is the heart of the game. fantomEngine supports several callback methods which it calls automatically when certain things happen. For an example, a collision check was successful, a touch check to an object was positive, and so on.

## What are transitions?

In the `OnObjectTouch` method, you will use transitions. Hmm What are they, you might ask. A transition of an object is an automatic change of the position, angle, size, color, or alpha value, over a defined period of time.

For example, you tell the engine to move an object to a certain point within 2000 milliseconds and forget about it. The engine will do that automatically for you. If you had set a transition ID when you created one, the engine will call the `OnObjectTransition` method after the former transition is finished. Very convenient, isn't it?

## Touch me – acting on touch hits

Remember that we have set some objects to be touchable and did some touch checks on the title, game, and background layer. One type of object is button and the other is an atom element. To be able to identify them, we set the tag field of the objects with a corresponding constant value.

## Time for action – enhancing the OnObjectTouch method

Inside the `OnObjectTouch` method of the `engine` class, we want to start a new game when the **PLAY** or **RESET** button are hit. If the **EXIT** button was hit, we want to end the game. And if an atom element got hit, we want to start a chain reaction.

**1.** Insert a `Select` statement with a call to the object's `GetTag` method.

```
Class engine Extends ftEngine
  Method OnObjectTouch:Int(obj:ftObject, touchId:Int)
    Select obj.GetTag()
```

**2.** Add a `Case` statement with the game's `grpAtom` constant. This identifies an atom element.

```
Case g.grpAtom
```

**3.** Now, check if this object already has a transition going on.

```
If obj.GetTransitionCount() = 0 Then
```

**4.** Create a new rotation transition by relative `90` degrees to its current angle and with a transition ID of `1`. This ID needs to be set so that the `OnObjectTransition` method is called, once the transition is completed.

```
obj.CreateTransRot(90,200, True,1)
```

**5.** Now, raise the game's `collCount` field by `1` and set the objects ID with a negative `collCount` value. We do this because we check against the ID later on.

```
g.collCount += 1
obj.SetID(-g.collCount)
Endif
```

**6.** Now, add a `Case` statement with the game's `btnPlay` and `btnReset` constants.

```
Case g.btnPlay, g.btnReset
```

**7.** Call the game's `StartNewGame` method.

```
g.StartNewGame()
```

**8.** Insert a `Case` statement with the game's `btnExit` statement.

```
Case g.btnExit
```

**9.** End the game by a call to the `Error` statement with an empty error text. Weird, but it works! Then, close the `Select` statement:

```
    Error(„")
End
Return 0
End
```

Save your code now, and then build and run it. All buttons are functional; you can even tap on an element, and it will rotate by 90 degrees.

## What just happened?

The `OnObjectTouch` event is called when the user hits the object with a finger or on a desktop with the left mouse click. We acted on the buttons to change game modes and started the first transition of a new chain reaction.

# The eagle has landed—a transition is finished

Once a transition is done, and a transition ID was set during its creation, the engine will call `OnObjectTransition`.

## Time for action – detailing the OnObjectTransition method

We will use this method to fire a timer that will switch the ID of an object. The ID is important for our collision checks. As we don't want to check the collision right away, we use a timer for a little delay:

**1.** Inside the `OnObjectTransition` method, create an object timer with the game's `tmObjSwitch` constants. It should fire in `100` milliseconds:

```
Method OnObjectTransition:Int(transId:Int, obj:ftObject)
  g.eng.CreateObjTimer(obj, g.tmObjSwitch, 100)
  Return 0
End
```

## What just happened?

Since we don't want to check for collisions of the atom elements' connectors right away, we fire an object timer to do this with a little delay.

# It's about time—timer events

Whenever a timer event fires, you want to act on it. If you don't, then it makes no sense to fire it in the first place, or does it?

## Time for action – acting on timer events

To act on timer events, we need to detail the `OnObjectTimer` method inside the `engine` class. We will set the ID of an object to positive once again, and then check for collisions of its child collision circles:

**1.**  Check whether `timerID` is equal to `g.tmObjSwitch`.

```
Method OnObjectTimer:Int(timerId:Int, obj:ftObject)
    If timerId = g.tmObjSwitch Then
```

**2.**  Get the object's ID and store it locally in the `id` variable.

```
Local id:Int = obj.GetID()
```

**3.**  If `id` is negative, set it back to positive.

```
If id < 0 Then obj.SetID(obj.GetID()*-1)
```

**4.**  Start a `For` loop now, for every child collision circle of the object.

```
For Local i:Int = 1 To obj.GetChildCount()
```

**5.**  Do a collision check for each collision circle.

```
g.eng.CollisionCheck(obj.GetChild(i))
```

**6.**  Close the `For` loop and the `If` check.

```
            End
        Endif
        Return 0
    End
End
```

## What just happened?

Once a timer event got fired, we will do a collision check now for each child collision circle of an object. This reduces the number of collision checks big time. As we do this here and not in the update method, we also keep the frame rate up. Imagine checking every collision circle in each frame. This is total overkill and your game will slow down a lot.

## Captain! Collision ahead!—doing collision checks

Now take a deep breath. The last method that has to be modified is all about finding out if the chain reaction can go further. The method `OnObjectCollision` is called when a collision check is positive.

# Time for action – detailing the collision detection

The problem in this game is that sometimes it will report collisions of objects that are still in action, basically, when they pass by each other. For this, we check if the ID of the object's parent is bigger than the one of the second object's parent. If yes, the second object will start a transition.

1. Inside the method OnObjectCollision, check if the collision group is equal to g.grpCircle.

```
Method OnObjectCollision:Int(obj:ftObject, obj2:ftObject)
    If obj.collGroup = g.grpCircle Then
```

2. Now, check whether the ID of the first parent obj is bigger than the second one and also that the second parent ID is positive. Negative ones are still in transition.

```
If (obj.GetParent().GetID() > obj2.GetParent().GetID())
    And (obj2.GetParent().GetID() >= 0) Then
```

3. Raise the game score.

```
g.score += 1
```

4. Check whether the second parent object is in transition. If not, then start a rotation transition by relative 90 degrees to its current angle and a duration of 200 milliseconds. The transition ID is set to 1, so OnObjectTransition is called once the transition finishes.

```
If obj2.GetParent().GetTransitionCount() = 0 Then
    obj2.GetParent().CreateTransRot(90,200, True,1)
```

5. Raise g.collCount by 1 and set the ID of the parent object to negative g.collCount.

```
g.collCount += 1
obj2.GetParent().SetID(-g.collCount)
```

6. Play our famous *bing* sound.

```
g.sndBing.Play()
```

7. Close all open If checks.

```
    Endif
Endif
Return 0
End
```

## What just happened?

We checked if a collision is able to fire a new transition. We did this by comparing the ID values of the parent atom elements. If all checks were successful, we raised the game score and fired a new transition. And the chain reaction goes on! That's the goal.

The game is done. Save it again and run it. Hopefully, no errors appear and you can have a race to the highest score. Don't worry if you cause an endless chain reaction. It is all by design.

### Have a go hero – enhancing Chain Reaction

Now that the game is done, you can add a few things to it by yourself. How about a high-score list? How you could do this is described in *Chapter 4, Game# 3 Comet Crusher*. There, we used the internal high-score list functionality of fantomEngine.

Another thing you could try is an option screen to turn off sound effects or add different sounds that play in random order. I agree, the current sound becomes very annoying after a short time.

# Creating an Android app

Ok, so far and till this point, you could have tested everything as an HTML5 application. For the development process, this works, but with mobile devices you should also start testing on a device very early. They have much less computing power than a desktop PC. And if you run into a performance problem, well you can only detect this on the device.

Anyway, when you build and transfer your app onto a device, it will always have the name Monkey Game, by default, and a default icon. For sure, you want to change that.

## Changing icons

Google has a pretty good description of how icons have to be designed for certain usage. At the time of writing this book, the information is available at: `http://developer. android.com/guide/practices/ui_guidelines/icon_design.html`.

There, under *Providing Density-Specific Icon Sets*, is described which sizes they should have. Basically, you need three icons, 36 x 36, 48 x 48, and 72 x 72 pixels, in dimension. So, create these three icons as regular PNG files. Next, you have to build your Android project. Inside the `Build/Android` folder, you will find another `res` folder. There you find three drawable-... folders. In that folder you copy your icons depending on if it is for the lower (ldpi), medium (mdpi), or high (hdpi) resolution. The next time you build and transfer your project to the device, you will find that it now has the icons that you have copied into the folder structure.

# Do a name change

To change the name of the app, locate the file `yourProjectFolder/Build/android/ CONFIG.TXT`.

There, you have two fields that have to be set—`APP_LABEL` for the name and `APP_PACKAGE` to make it unique. Change both according to the description. The next time you build and transfer your project to the device, the app will have a new name.

# Signing an application for the market

We will talk about signing an application correctly for the Android market, in *Chapter 10*. However, this link will give you a little information on how to do it —`http://www.monkeycoder.co.nz/Community/post. php?topic=1014&post=8800`.

# Summary

This chapter was again a wealth of information, especially on where to use the fantomEngine framework. If we hadn't used that, we would need at least 40 pages more, that is for sure.

So what did we talk about?

- ◆ You learned about how to create buttons and check on touch hits.
- ◆ You have learned to use content scaling for different devices.
- ◆ Using different images for a sprite animation was also covered in this chapter.
- ◆ To automate things, you learned how to use transitions and how to act on them.
- ◆ Collision detection doesn't have to be done always and on all objects. On mobile devices, you have to be careful about your CPU resources.

Ok, that's all for now. See you in Chapter 6, *Game #5, Balls Out!* and with a new game called **Balls Out!**.

# 6
# Game #5, Balls Out!

*A lot of games use balls as their main objects. Pinball machines, marbles, break out, and of course sports games such as soccer, baseball, and many others. It is just natural to use them in computer games too. Everyone knows a ball and can predict how to use it or how it will behave. The game we will create together in this chapter is called* `Balls Out!` *It is heavily influenced by the classic game called BreakOut, which you will know if you are old enough. If you don't, then have a look at this link:* `http://en.wikipedia.org/wiki/Breakout_%28video_game%29`

Another version of this kind of game is called Arkanoid (`http://en.wikipedia.org/wiki/Arkanoid`).

`Balls Out!` doesn't have squared bricks for you to smash with your ball, but spheres, and that makes it rather tricky to control. Also, there won't be a paddle that controls your ball, but you will utilize the accelerometer of your iOS device and you will need to avoid some nasty fellows that run down the game field. If you collide with them, you are done!

As each game needs some eye candy, you will create some nice particle effects for your game and will learn how to display them. For this, you will create particle emitters, place them inside the game when needed, and control their behavior.

Together, we will go through the following topics:

- ◆ Create particles and display them with emitters
- ◆ Read the accelerometer data
- ◆ Create an iOS application
- ◆ Use Stacks, which are another form of list
- ◆ Move objects of predefined paths

# Which frameworks and modules are used?

Again, we will use the fantomEngine framework, which was created as an extra for this book and is available here at `http://code.google.com/p/fantomengine/`.

Make sure you use at least version 1.25 for this chapter. Under its hood, `fantomengine` will import `Mojo` so we don't need to import it ourselves.

# Game resources

For `Balls Out!`, we need the following resources:

- The ball image

- Enemy image

- The tile image

- A bitmap font description file and its corresponding bitmap

|$\Qj&W@%O
AVTGUCSX86
902dkbh/?{}Jf
J()[]!iMYNRH
ZDKBP4#EF3
L57flg;moens
c:wvqpuyaxzr
<>+^*=""'•^~--

◆ Sounds for an explosion, for when you select/touch a button, and for when the ball hits a tile

 The sound format for Monkey and the iOS platform is the M4A sound format. Use a tool such as Audacity to convert sounds, if you need to.

As you can see, not much is needed. The ball, enemy, and tile images will be located on one sprite sheet. Remember, using sprite sheets will speed up the rendering process.

# Our lovely game objects

Like every game, Balls Out! is made out of several objects that may or may not have their own life, of course, only if you code them to have a life. So which objects are part of the game?

## Layers

In this game we will use only three layers (groups):

◆ Background

◆ Game

◆ Title screen

The background layer will hold some info text and simple, colored rectangles. The title screen is just that with two extra buttons to start a game or to leave it completely. And the game layer will hold the main game objects, such as the balls, the enemies, and the tiles. Also, the particle effects will use the game layer. Just as a little reminder, with layers you can group sprites to handle them in one batch. Layers also control the order in which sprites are drawn.

## The title screen

In this game, we will keep it simple. No bitmap image graphic was harmed for Balls Out!, this time. No starving artist had to do unpaid overtime to create the title screen. We will use just a two-colored rectangle and then some text on the screen, for the title. For the buttons, we will use text objects and set them to be touchable. The fantomEngine framework makes it easy to use regular images as GUI objects.

# Game background

Again, for the game background, we will also make use of two colored rectangles drawn on top of each other. Also there is a button drawn on it, which lets the user go back to the title screen. And of course, in the header area, you will find two text objects for the game score, and the current **Frames Per Second** (**FPS**) value is displayed. The FPS is important to know you code for a mobile device. They are simply not as powerful as a desktop.

# The ball

The ball is the object that we want to control in the game. We have to make sure that we navigate it into the tiles and avoid the enemies that roam around the game field.

# Enemies

To separate the game a little from its classic ancestors, we will add enemies that roam around the game field on precalculated paths. Each time you have removed all the ball tiles, another enemy will appear and will make your life even harder.

# The ball tiles

These have to be hit by your ball. Once that happens, they will disappear and a nice sound will be played. Also, we will play some little particle effects for eye candy.

# The basic app structure

In the previous chapters, we have always built the basic structure of our script together. As we will utilize fantomEngine (which was created for this book) again, you can load in a file that holds this structure already. See, it's all about making your life as a rising game developer easier.

## Time for action – creating the basic file structure

So, let's set up our development folder. Follow the given steps:

1. Create a new project folder with a name you choose.

2. Load the `baseScript.monkey` file, which holds the basic structure for our game.

3. Change the information at the top of the script to your data, and save it under a name you choose and inside the new folder you created before.

4. Create a new `yourGameName.data` folder inside the project folder.

5. Copy the resources from the `ballsout.data` folder within your own data folder.

6. Now, build and run an HTML5 project.

That's all for now!

## What just happened?

We have set up the directory and file structure to start developing our game. The fact that we've already built an HTML5 project, will help us in the next step. At the moment, the screen looks like the following:

# Modifying the HTML5 canvas size for testing

Just like in *Chapter 5, Game #4, Chain Reaction*, we don't want to deploy the game to the device every time we want to test it. We are creating an iOS app, and iOS devices have specific screen dimensions. The older ones run by a resolution of 320 x 480. That will be a good size to test our game. For this, we will change the HTML5 build files that are created by Monkey.

## Time for action – modifying the HTML5 output

Again, when you have your first playable results, if you didn't do it already, do the following:

1. Compile for HTML5.

2. Next, open the `MonkeyGame.HTML` file, which is located inside the `build/HTML5` folder of your project. Use Monk for it; it can open HTML files.

3. Then, locate the line that looks like this:

```
<canvas id="GameCanvas" on click="javascript:this.focus();"
width=640 height=480 tabindex=1></canvas><br>
```

4. Change the width value to `320` and the height value to `480`. Then, save and close the file.

As you can see, the HTML5 canvas now has the same size as an iOS device.

# The data storage

Without a place to store the data for our game, there simply won't be a game at all, as simple as it may be.

## Time for action – creating the data structure

1. To store the relevant fields, we will create fields again in our main class, called `game`.

2. The `game` class already has fields for the instance of the `engine` class and a field that will store if the app is suspended or not.

```
Class game Extends App
  Field eng:engine
  Field isSuspended:Bool = False
```

3. Next, add fields to store text objects for storing the game score, *Game Over* text, and the FPS indicator.

```
Field txtScore:ftObject
Field txtGameOver:ftObject
Field txtFPS:ftObject
```

4. Our game ball will be a separate object and so are the fonts, which we will be using for our in-game text objects.

```
Field ball:ftObject
Field font1:ftFont
```

5. Later on, we will create two classes for particle emitters and the enemies that will hunt you down in the game. To store these, we will use lists.

6. Add fields for lists based on the `Enemy` class and the `ParticleEmitter` class.

```
Field enemyList:=New List<Enemy>
Field emitterList:=New List<ParticleEmitter>
```

**7.** Now, add the layers that we need—one for the background, one for the game, and one for the title screen.

```
Field layerBackGround:ftLayer
Field layerGame:ftLayer
Field layerTitle:ftLayer
```

**8.** The sound effects have to be stored. We need three of them.

```
Field sndHit:ftSound
Field sndSelect:ftSound
Field sndExplo:ftSound
```

**9.** Now, add fields to store the sprite sheet (atlas) and the game mode, which controls the flow of the update procedure.

```
Field atlas:Image
Field gameMode:Int = gmMenu
```

**10.** To make life more convenient through less typing, we will need fields to store the canvas width and height.

```
Field cw:Float
Field ch:Float
```

**11.** Some more fields are needed to store the current frames per second, the score, tile count, level number, and lives left in the game.

```
Field fps:Float
Field score:Int = 0
Field tileCount:Int = 0
Field levelNum:Int = 0
Field lifes:Int = 0
```

**12.** These are the data fields, but like always, we will add some constants to the game.

- First, add constants for the game mode.

```
Const gmMenu:Int = 1
Const gmPlay:Int = 2
Const gmGameOver:Int = 3
```

- To identify objects during the game, we need some group identifiers.

```
Const grpEnemy:Int = 1
Const grpBall:Int = 2
Const grpTile:Int = 3
```

- ❏ The three buttons in our game will need some IDs too.

```
Const btnPlay:Int = 10
Const btnExit:Int = 13
Const btnBack:Int = 14
```

- ❏ The last constants that we need to add are some transition IDs: one for particles and one for the *Game Over* text.

```
Const tidParticle:Int = 20
Const tidGameOver:Int = 21
'-------------------------
'Method OnCreate:Int()
```

Great, the data section is filled with everything that is needed.

## What just happened?

As soon you include media files in your project, you need a data folder. We created the folder structure that is needed. Then we added various constants and variables.

# First changes to the OnCreate event

We can start changing the `OnCreate` event right away, as some stuff has to be done now.

## Time for action – first changes to the OnCreate method

For example, let's look at loading the bitmap font and loading the sprite atlas:

1. Inside the `OnCreate` method of the game class, change the canvas size to the resolution of the iPhone 4. This way, we have more space for the game. It will be automatically scaled down on older devices.

```
Method OnCreate:Int()
  SetUpdateRate(60)
  eng = New engine
  eng.SetCanvasSize(640,960)
```

2. To make our life easier by typing less, we store the dimensions of the canvas inside cw and ch.

```
cw = eng.canvasWidth
ch = eng.canvasHeight
```

**3.** Now, load the sprite sheet and the bitmap font.

```
atlas = LoadImage("bo_tiles.png")
font1 = eng.LoadFont("bo_font")
Return 0
End
```

## What just happened?

We have loaded the media files required to go on with the game.

# Detailing the OnRender event

It is always great to have methods or other features of your code done, so that you can forget about them. Let's do that with the rendering process.

## Time for action – detailing the OnRender method

We won't change the OnRender method in the game class. We will only change the background color and set the text of the FPS indicator to see how fast our game renders everything:

**1.** Add the optional parameters to the CLS statement, which defines a nice orange color background.

```
Method OnRender:Int()
  Cls (255,155,0)
```

**2.** Then, set the text property of our txtFPS object with the current FPS value.

```
txtFPS.SetText("FPS: "+eng.GetFPS())
    eng.Render()
    Return 0
End
```

## What just happened?

The OnRender method is done. We determine the current FPS value inside it, as Monkey is skipping rendering frames if OnUpdate is taking to long. Only here will you get the true FPS value in its traditional meaning.

# Setting up the game objects

It is now time to prepare the objects for our game: sounds, images, buttons, and so on.

## Make some noise—sound effects

It is always good to create little helper functions to bundle a specific task, say for loading sounds. You can easily add more to them once you know where that part of code is located.

## Time for action – loading the game sound effects

To load sounds, we will create a method in the game class called `LoadSounds`.
There, we will load sounds for an explosion, a hit sound, and a select sound:

1. Create a new method called `LoadSounds`.

   ```
   Method LoadSounds:Int ()
   ```

2. Load the three sounds called `select`, `explosion`, and hit (remember, no file extension!).

   ```
   sndSelect = eng.LoadSound("select")
   sndExplo = eng.LoadSound("explosion")
   sndHit = eng.LoadSound("hit")
   ```

3. Close the method.

   ```
   Return 0
   End
   ```

## What just happened?

We have created a method to load sounds into the game. To load sounds, we used fantomengine's `LoadSound` method. You don't need to add the file extension to it, as fantomengine will load the one that is right for that platform. In the case of iOS, it is the MP4 file format.

## Lay your head on me—the game layers

Think about grouping game objects and then each group is updated and rendered after each other and on top of each other. These groups are called layers.

## Time for action – creating layers for the game

We will create these layers inside their own `CreateLayers` method. Follow these steps:

1. Insert a new method called `CreateLayers` inside the game class.

   ```
   Method CreateLayers:Int()
   ```

2. Now, create a new layer for the background, the game itself, and the title screen.

```
layerBackGround = eng.CreateLayer()
layerGame = eng.CreateLayer()
layerTitle = eng.CreateLayer()
```

3. Close the method.

```
Return 0
End
```

## What just happened?

We have added a method to create new layers. These layers help us with updating and rendering the game in an organized fashion.

## Our beloved play field—the background screen

This time, we will compose the background layer. It will be drawn as the background for the actual gameplay.

### Buttons—I need more text buttons!

To create text buttons, we will add our own method for it. It will automatically set up a text object that is able to be hit-tested against touches and/or mouse clicks.

## Time for action – creating text buttons

This new helper method will be added to the game class:

1. Insert a new class called CreateTextButton. Its parameters are a font object, the text, its position, button ID, and the layer that the button is added to.

```
Method CreateTextButton:ftObject (font:ftFont, txt:String,
xp:Int, yp:Int, id:Int, layer:ftLayer)
```

2. Create a new next object.

```
Local but:ftObject = eng.CreateText(font,txt,xp,yp,1)
```

3. It its tag with the ID and the touch mode to a rectangular hit test.

```
but.SetTag(id)
but.SetTouchMode(2)
```

**4.** Now, set the layer and close the method.

```
but.SetLayer(layer)
Return but
End
```

## What just happened?

With this method, we can easily add text buttons with one line of code. It is all about being more efficient when you develop games, because even your spare time is money!

## The background screen as usual

This is composed of different objects. We will have a nice single-colored background and a few text objects.

## Time for action – composing the game screen

We create the background screen in one batch and method. You will easily be able to add more stuff to it, if you need to:

**1.** Add the method `CreateBackgroundScreen` to the game class.

```
Method CreateBackgroundScreen:Int()
```

**2.** For the single-colored background, create a new box object, assign it to the background layer, and set its color to a dark blue.

```
Local box:ftObject = eng.CreateBox(cw-20,ch-20,cw/2,ch/2)
box.SetLayer(layerBackGround)
box.SetColor(0,0,100)
```

**3.** Next, add a **BACK** button at the top-center of the canvas.

```
CreateTextButton(font1, "Back",cw/2,46, btnBack,
layerBackGround)
```

**4.** To display the game score and the FPS value, create two text objects and assign them to the background layer.

```
txtScore = eng.CreateText(font1,"Score:    "+score,40,46)
txtScore.SetLayer(layerBackGround)
txtFPS = eng.CreateText(font1,"FPS: 999",cw-40,46,2)
txtFPS.SetLayer(layerBackGround)
```

**5.** Lastly, create a new text object to display the Game Over text message in the middle of the canvas.

```
txtGameOver = eng.CreateText(font1,"GAME OVER",cw/2, ch/2, 1)
```

**6.** Again, assign it to the background layer and also make it invisible. We only need to display it when the game is over.

```
txtGameOver.SetLayer(layerBackGround)
txtGameOver.SetVisible(False)
```

**7.** Close this method.

```
    Return 0
End
```

## What just happened?

We have just composed the game's background screen. The actual game objects (ball, tiles, and enemies) will be drawn on top of it, inside the game layer.

## Give it a name—the title screen

Most games have a title screen. Actually, you have to search hard to find a game without one. A title screen can also work as a menu screen—to start the game, go into its options, or exit the game.

## Time for action – creating the title screen

Our title screen will be composed of a nice single-colored background, the text Balls Out!, and two text buttons to Play and Exit the game:

**1.** Create the CreateTitleScreen method inside the game class.

```
Method CreateTitleScreen:Int ()
```

**2.** Create a new box object, assign it to the title layer, and set the color to a nice blue.

```
Local box:ftObject = eng.CreateBox(cw-20,ch-20,cw/2,ch/2)
box.SetLayer(layerTitle)
box.SetColor(0,0,255)
```

**3.** Now, create a text object that is also assigned to the title layer. Scale it to the factor 3.

```
    Local tx1:ftObject = eng.CreateText(font1,"Balls
Out!",cw/2,ch/5,1)
    tx1.SetLayer(layerTitle)
    tx1.SetScale(3.0)
```

**4.** To start and exit the game, we need two text buttons, both scaled to factor 1.5 and assigned to the title layer.

```
    Local b1:ftObject = CreateTextButton(font1, "Play",
cw/2,ch/5*3, btnPlay, layerTitle)
    b1.SetScale(1.5)
    Local b3:ftObject = CreateTextButton(font1, "Exit",
cw/2,ch/5*4, btnExit, layerTitle)
    b3.SetScale(1.5)
```

**5.** Close the method.

```
    Return 0
  End
```

## What just happened?

With this method, we will be able to create the title screen in one call. It's also a place that you can easily identify to add and change the screen in its total appearance.

# Finalizing the OnCreate event

Now that we have created all methods for our static objects, we can finish the changes to the OnCreate method of the game class.

## Time for action – finalizing the OnCreate method

We need to insert calls to all the methods we have created.

Insert calls to CreateLayers, CreateBackgroundScreen, CreateTitleScreen, and LoadSounds.

```
    atlas = LoadImage("bo_tiles.png")
    font1 = eng.LoadFont("bo_font")
    CreateLayers()
    CreateBackgroundScreen()
    CreateTitleScreen()
    LoadSounds()
```

```
    Return 0
End
```

## What just happened?

We just finalized the `OnCreate` method. The buttons are not functional at this moment, but the game will display the title screen when you run it.

It will probably look as follows, at the moment:

# Helper methods for the update process

At this stage, we have created all static objects, but there are no dynamic objects, and all objects that should interact don't do that right now. Let's start with more helper methods to create some dynamic objects.

## Creating the tiles

The tiles in `Balls Out!` are not blocks but balls or circles if you will. The sprite sheet we have loaded before includes a nice image to represent them.

## Time for action – creating the tiles

When we create the set of tiles, we want to place them inside a grid of three lines with five tiles in each. For this, we will create a new method:

1. Add the method `CreateTitles` to the `game` class.

   ```
   Method CreateTiles:Int()
   ```

**2.** To reset the tile count, which is needed to determine a new level, we set the variable TileCount to 0.

```
TileCount = 0
```

**3.** Now create two FOR loops, one for the y position factor from 1 to 3 and one for the x position factor from one to five.

```
For Local y:Int = 1 To 3
  For Local x:Int = 1 To 5
```

**4.** Create a local object through CreateImage. The position will be calculated as *one-sixth of the canvas width times the x factor, and 80 times the y factor, plus 100*. This will place the tiles equally over the top part of the screen.

```
Local tile:ftObject = eng.CreateImage(atlas,96,0,32,32,cw/
6*x,80*y+100)
```

**5.** Now, set the radius of the object to 16 pixels and its scale to factor 2.0.

```
tile.SetRadius(16)
tile.SetScale(2.0)
```

**6.** Assign it to the game layer.

```
tile.SetLayer(layerGame)
```

**7.** For collision detection, set its collision group to grpTile and that it will collide with the ball.

```
tile.SetColGroup(grpTile)
tile.SetColWith(grpBall, True)
```

**8.** Now, raise the tile count by one.

```
tileCount += 1
```

**9.** Close both FOR loops and the method itself.

```
      Next
    Next
    Return 0
  End
```

## What just happened?

To automatically create a new set of tiles, we have created a new method. It will be called later on, at the start of a new game, and also when all tiles are destroyed and the game proceeds to a new level.

# The main actor—creating the ball

Our main actor, the one we will have control of, is the ball. It won't be controlled by a paddle but by using the device's accelerometer feature. This means that, when you tilt the device in a particular direction, the ball rolls in that direction.

## Time for action – creating the ball

As it can be destroyed by the enemy, we will wrap up its creation inside its own method. That makes this process reusable.

1. Insert the method `CreateBall` into our `game` class.

   ```
   Method CreateBall:Int ()
   ```

2. The ball is a field set inside the game class, so assign an image object to it through the `CreateImage` method. It will be placed in the lower center of the canvas:

   ```
   ball = eng.CreateImage(atlas,64,0,32,32,cw/2,ch-50)
   ```

3. Set its radius and scale:

   ```
   ball.SetRadius(16)
   ball.SetScale(1.5)
   ```

4. Now, set the friction property. Once in movement, we don't want it to move forever, but slow down once you don't tilt the device:

   ```
   ball.SetFriction(0.8)
   ```

5. Assign it to the game layer:

   ```
   ball.SetLayer(layerGame)
   ```

6. To detect a collision, set its collision group to `grpBall`, so that it can collide with the enemies and the tiles:

   ```
   ball.SetColGroup(grpBall)
   ball.SetColWith(grpEnemy, True)
   ball.SetColWith(grpTile, True)
   ```

7. Finally, set its maximum speed to `20`, and close the method off:

   ```
   ball.SetMaxSpeed(20)
   Return 0
   End
   ```

## *What just happened?*

We have created a reusable method to create a ball whenever we need one. Fancy several player balls? Not at the moment, but it could be an enhancement that you could add on your own.

### Have a go hero – Add more player balls

You know what would be cool? Having the player control several balls at the same time. You could do this in different ways, either by modifying the preceding method to create several balls at different positions, or make this method flexible regarding its position and once you call it, give the position with the call.

# The bad guys—our beloved enemies

To demonstrate how you can add more objects with their own behaviors and have extra control over them, we will create a new class for the enemy objects. Each enemy will move along a pre-calculated path during its lifetime, and so it needs its own update procedure. All enemies will be stored inside the enemy list of the game class and their paths will be used inside a stack that is the property of each enemy.

So, let's play Dr. Frankenstein.

### Time for action – creating the enemy class

We will create this class in one batch, including data section, update, and constructor methods:

1.  Create a new class called Enemy. It won't be extended from anything.

    ```
    Class Enemy
    ```

2.  As we need a reference to the actual fantomEngine object, we will need a field to store it inside the class:

    ```
    Field enemyObj:ftObject = Null
    ```

3.  Now, add a stack for the path. The path is made of single 2D vectors, which are from a new object type of the fantomEngine called ftVec2D:

    ```
    Field pathStack:= New Stack<ftVec2D>
    ```

4.  Next, add a New constructor method, with the initial enemy position and the number of path nodes to be created as parameters:

    ```
    Method New(x:Float, y:Float, pathCount:Int)
    ```

**5.** Create an image object and assign it to the previous `enemyObj` field that we have added before:

```
enemyObj = g.eng.CreateImage(g.atlas,0,0,64,64, x , y)
```

**6.** Our enemies are bigger, so set the radius to `32`, and then assign it to the game layer:

```
enemyObj.SetRadius(32)
enemyObj.SetLayer(g.layerGame)
```

**7.** For collision detection, set its collision group to the game's `grpEnemy` constant:

enemyObj.SetColGroup(g.grpEnemy) **8.**    Add a local `FOR` loop with a variable `i` ranging from `1` to the `pathCount` parameter:

```
For Local i:Int = 1 To pathCount
```

**8.** Check whether `i` is equal to `1`. If it is, add a new path node at the top of the screen and a random x position:

```
If i = 1 Then
    pathStack.Push(New ftVec2D(Rnd(g.cw), 0.0))
```

This should make sure that the enemy moves back before it gets deleted after he has traveled along its path. We will read items from the stack, from the top. So, the first item will be the last one we will use.

**9.** Now, if `i` is not equal `0`, add a random position into the path stack. By subtracting `100` from the canvas height, we will give the player a little safety zone on the play field whenever an enemy appears:

```
Else
    pathStack.Push(New ftVec2D(Rnd(g.cw), Rnd(g.ch-100)))
Endif
```

**10.** Now, close the `FOR` loop and the method:

```
    Next
End
```

Later in the game, we need to remove enemies and their underlying fantom objects. Let's add a method to the `Enemy` class to do this:

**11.** Create a new method called `GetObj`, which returns the `ftObject`:

```
Method GetObj:ftObject()
  Return enemyObj
End
```

**12.** The last method we will add to the enemy class is the `Update` method:

**13.** Insert the `Update` method into the `Enemy` class. It will return a value from the type of `Bool`:

```
Method Update:Bool()
```

**14.** Check whether there are items left on the path stack:

```
If pathStack.Length() >= 1 Then
```

**15.** Now, check whether the object has any transitions attached to it. If not, it would mean it just started its life or finished a previous transition:

```
If enemyObj.GetTransitionCount()=0 Then
```

**16.** Retrieve a position vector form the path stack and store it inside the local `vec` variable from the type of `ftVec2D`:

```
Local vec:ftVec2D = pathStack.Pop()
```

**17.** Determine a local time factor, which takes the distance from the enemy to the destination path node into its calculation. This makes sure that shorter distances are traveled in a shorter period of time:

```
Local time:Float = 7500.0 / (1000.0/enemyObj.
GetVectorDist(vec.x, vec.y))
```

**18.** Now, create a new position transition with the path node's position values, the time we have calculated before. We don't set the transition ID, as we only need to check whether all nodes were traveled on; we don't need to check on a single transition:

```
        enemyObj.CreateTransPos(vec.x, vec.y, time , False, 0)
    Endif
Else
```

**19.** If no path stack entries are left and no transitions are assigned anymore, this means the enemy has reached its final destination. Return `FALSE`, then:

```
        If enemyObj.GetTransitionCount()=0 Then Return False
    Endif
```

**20.** Return `TRUE` for everything else. It means that this enemy is still alive. Then, close this method and the class:

```
    Return True
  End
End
```

## *What just happened?*

We have created a new class for our enemies. This class will create one at will, calculate its path, and also update it when one node of the path is reached.

# More helper functions

We are not done with our helper functions for updating processes and the `engine` class.

## Spawning an enemy

To spawn an enemy, we will create another method.

## Time for action – spawning an enemy

This new method called `SpawnEnemy` will create one enemy and initialize its position and the path to follow:

1. Create a new method called `SpawnEnemy`, inside the game class. It will have the x position as a parameter. The y position will be fixed and always on top.

   ```
   Method SpawnEnemy:Int (x:Float)
   ```

2. Add a new instance of the `Enemy` class to the `enemyList` field of the `game` class. The y position is always 0 and there are 25 path nodes to be created:

   ```
   enemyList.AddLast(New Enemy(x,0.0,25))
   Return 0
   End
   ```

## *What just happened?*

This method created an enemy with 25 path nodes and stored it inside the enemy list of the game class.

## Starting a new game

Things that should be done multiple times inside a game should be placed inside a function or a method. Starting a new game will be one of these things.

## Time for action – creating a StartNewGame method

To start a new game, we will create a new method in the game class. Follow the given steps:

**1.** Add a new method called StartNewGame.

```
Method StartNewGame:Int()
```

**2.** Seed the random number generator with the current millisecond value:

```
Seed = Millisecs()
```

**3.** Reset the Score value to 0, as shown in the following code:

```
Score = 0
```

**4.** Deactivate the title layer:

```
layerTitle.SetActive(False)
```

**5.** Remove all objects from the game layer:

```
layerGame.RemoveAllObjects()
```

**6.** Create a new ball:

```
CreateBall()
```

**7.** Create a new set of tiles:

```
CreateTiles()
```

**8.** Spawn a new enemy with a random x position. This position ranges from 20 to cw-20 (the canvas width minus 20):

```
SpawnEnemy(Rnd(20,cw-20))
```

**9.** Start with a level number of 1:

```
levelNum = 1
```

**10.** Set lifes to 3:

```
lifes = 3
```

**11.** Finally, set the game mode to gmPlay, and then close the method:

```
gameMode = gmPlay
Return 0
End
```

## *What just happened?*

This method reset all the game variables and started a new game. It brought up the game and background layer and created the ball, the tiles, and an enemy.

# Bring me up-to-date—detailing the OnUpdate event

We are done with setting up game objects. Now, it is time to detail the game's `OnUpdate` method.

## Time for action – detailing the OnUpdate method

The `OnUpdate` method will be called in the amount you have set the update rate to. The base script sets it to `60` times. Follow the given steps:

1. Start a `SELECT` statement with `gameMode` as a parameter.

   ```
   Method OnUpdate:Int()
     Local d:Float = Float(eng.CalcDeltaTime())/60.0
     If isSuspended = False Then
       Select gameMode
   ```

2. First, check if `gameMode` is equal to `gmPlay`:

   ```
         Case gmPlay
           eng.Update(d)
   ```

3. Start a collision check for the game layer:

   ```
           eng.CollisionCheck(layerGame)
   ```

4. Next, if there is a `TouchHit` method, do a touch check for the background layer:

   ```
           If TouchHit(0) Then
             eng.TouchCheck(layerBackGround)
           Endif
   ```

5. Set the text property of the `txtScore` object to the current score value:

   ```
           txtScore.SetText("Score: "+score)
   ```

6. Now, check whether the game mode is set to `gmMenu`:

   ```
           Case gmMenu
   ```

**7.** If there is a touch hit, perform a touch check for the title layer:

```
If TouchHit(0) Then
  eng.TouchCheck(layerTitle)
Endif
```

**8.** If the game mode is set to gmGameOver, update the background layer:

```
    Case gmGameOver
      eng.Update(layerBackGround, d)
  End
 Endif
 Return 0
End
```

## What just happened?

With detailing the OnUpdate method of the game class, we have the general control set of our game. When the game is not suspended, we check for touch hits, and then which touchable object of fantomEngine was hit. We also update objects depending on which mode the game is in.

At this stage, the game will look like the following screenshot:

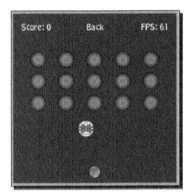

# Eye candy—particle effects

Of course, even in this little game, we want some eye candy; particles in games and little graphics that appear fast, move over a small or long distance, and then disappear. They usually don't collide with anything but give the impression that they are pieces of something that got destroyed or are made of gas, smoke, water, or whatever.

One method to create particles is to create them all at once and then let them move on automatically. When you want to create particles continuously over time, you need to have emitters to do the job for you. An **emitter** automatically creates particles and that is what we will create now.

# The particle emitter class

The `emitter` class to create particles will be taking care of creating new particles over a period of time. For this, we will use a constructor method and an update method.

## Time for action – creating the particle emitter class

Just like with the `Enemy` class, we will create the emitter class in one batch:

1.  Add a new class to our script, called `ParticleEmitter`. Again, this one isn't extended from anything.

    ```
    Class ParticleEmitter
    ```

2.  Add a field for the emitter position.

    ```
    Field xp:Float
    Field yp:Float
    ```

3.  Now, insert a field for the time that is left for the emitter to create particles.

    ```
    Field timeLeft:Float
    ```

4.  The last field in the data section is the `kind` field. Some particles will be colored, and so we need to tell the emitter to do that.

    ```
    Field kind:Int
    ```

5.  The `New` constructor method will have the `x` and `y` positions as parameters. Also it will take the `time` factor and the `kind` flag as values.

    ```
    Method New(x:Float, y:Float, time:Int, knd:Int)
    ```

6.  Set the calls fields with these values.

    ```
    timeLeft = time
    xp   = x
    yp   = y
    kind = knd
    ```

**7.** Close the method. Even in STRICT mode, our New method doesn't need a return value:

```
End
```

**8.** Insert the Update method. The parameter will be a delta value, which will later be subtracted from the time that is left:

```
Method Update:Bool(delta:Float)
```

**9.** Subtract the delta from timeLeft. Then, check whether timeLeft is still greater than 0, which means that the emitter has to create a particle:

```
timeLeft -= delta
If timeLeft > 0 Then
```

**10.** Next, create a local image object that will be taken from the sprite atlas. Its position is the one from the emitter class:

```
Local obj:ftObject = g.eng.CreateImage(g.
atlas,64,32,32,32,xp,yp)
```

**11.** Set the scale randomly and also its spin factor:

```
obj.SetScale(Rnd(10,100)/100)
obj.SetSpin(Rnd(-20,20))
```

**12.** Get a random vector with a random distance and angle:

```
Local vec:Float[] = obj.GetVector(Rnd(20,40),Rnd(360))
```

**13.** If the kind flag is not 0, set the color randomly:

```
If kind <> 0 Then obj.SetColor(Rnd(255),Rnd(255),Rnd(255))
```

**14.** Assign the object to the game layer:

```
obj.SetLayer(g.layerGame)
```

**15.** Now, create a position transition to the previously determined vector and a random running time. Here, the transition ID is set so we can remove the particle once it reaches its target position:

```
obj.CreateTransPos(vec[0], vec[1], Rnd(1000,3000),False,g.
tidParticle)
```

**16.** If no time is left, return FALSE so we can remove the particle emitter:

```
Else
  Return False
Endif
```

**17.** Return TRUE so we know the emitter is still active, and close the method and the class:

```
        Return True
    End
End
```

## What just happened?

We created a class that lets us create an emitter with its own constructor method; we also created an update method that creates new particles, as long the emitter is active.

## The last helper method

To spawn a particle emitter easily in the game, we will create a specialized method for it.

## Time for action – spawning a particle emitter

The only task of this class will be to create a new emitter and add it to the emitter list of our game class:

**1.** Add a new method called SpawnEmitter to the game class. Its parameters are the position, a time factor, and the kind flag.

```
    Method SpawnEmitter:Int (x:Float,y:Float,t:Float,k:Int=0)
```

**2.** Add a new instance of the ParticleEmitter class to the emitterList. Then, close this method:

```
        emitterList.AddLast(New ParticleEmitter(x,y,t,k))
        Return 0
    End
```

## What just happened?

Now, we are able to create emitters whenever and wherever we want. They will spit out particles for as long as we tell them to. Updating the emitters will be done inside the heart of our game, the engine class.

When you spawn particles later in the game, they will look like the following screenshot:

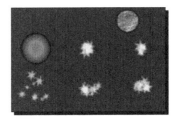

# The heart of the game—the engine class

All the objects can be created now—static objects such as text and also dynamic objects such as the tiles or particles. The could move now but there is no reaction to the input or collision checks, for example. That is where the engine class comes into play. To act on collisions and touch checks, and to update objects and layers, we will utilize the fantomEngine's callback methods.

## Touch me—acting on touch hits

Let's start with the touch events. The touchable objects in our game are the text buttons. They have a specific tag value and that is what we can check against. Remember, the OnObjectTouch method will be called when the mouse cursor or a touch is over the object during a call of the TouchCheck statement.

## Time for action – enhancing the OnObjectTouch method

The OnObjectTouch method has the object itself as a parameter, and the touch ID that was given optionally when the TouchCheck statement was called.

1. Inside the OnObjectTouch method, do a SELECT on the object's tag value.

   ```
   Method OnObjectTouch:Int(obj:ftObject, touchId:Int)
       Select obj.GetTag()
   ```

2. Check against the constant btnPlay, that is, the Play button:

   ```
           Case g.btnPlay
   ```

3. Play the Select sound and start a new game:

   ```
           g.sndSelect.Play()
           g.StartNewGame()
   ```

**4.** Check against the `btnBack` constant. This is the Back button:

```
Case g.btnBack
```

**5.** Play the Select sound, activate the title layer, and set the game mode to `gmMenu`:

```
g.sndSelect.Play()
g.layerTitle.SetActive(True)
g.gameMode = g.gmMenu
```

**6.** Check against the `btnExit` constant. This is the Exit button:

```
Case g.btnExit
```

**7.** End the game with a call to the `Error` method, with an empty string:

```
Error("")
```

**8.** Close the `SELECT` statement:

```
      End
      Return 0
End
```

## What just happened?

Our little game will react now to touch events. Every text button we will press is now functional. A new game will be started, but the objects still stay where they are. This will be changed in the update events of the `engine` class.

## Controlling the ball—acting on object update events

We will want to control the ball through the accelerometer in our device. The perfect place is the `OnObjectUpdate` method of the fantomEngine. It will be called every time an object is updated.

## Time for action – acting on object update events

**1.** Inside the method we will check if the ball reaches the edges of the game field and change its speed values according to the accelerometer values. The `OnObjectUpdate` method gives you the object as a parameter.

```
Method OnObjectUpdate:Int(obj:ftObject)
```

**2.** Perform a `SELECT` operation on the `obj` variable:

```
Select obj
```

**3.** If the object is equal to the object in `g.ball`, it is our ball:

```
Case g.ball
```

**4.** Now, check whether the ball reaches the top or bottom edge and whether its y speed value indicates that it is moving towards the corresponding edge:

```
        If (obj.yPos < obj.GetHeight()/2 And obj.GetSpeedY() < 0)
Or (obj.yPos > (g.ch - obj.GetHeight()/2) And obj.GetSpeedY() > 0)
Then
```

**5.** Reverse the Y speed factor so it will bounce off the edge. Also play the *Hit* sound effect:

```
        obj.SetSpeedY(-obj.GetSpeedY())
        g.sndHit.Play()
    Endif
```

**6.** Next, check whether the ball reaches the left or right edge and whether its speed x value indicates that it is moving towards that edge:

```
        If (obj.xPos < obj.GetWidth()/2 And obj.GetSpeedX() < 0)
Or (obj.xPos > (g.cw - obj.GetWidth()/2) And obj.GetSpeedX() > 0)
Then
```

**7.** Reverse the X speed factor, so it will bounce off the edge. Also play the *Hit* sound effect:

```
        obj.SetSpeedX(-obj.GetSpeedX())
        g.sndHit.Play()
    Endif
```

**8.** Now, read the accelerometer values. By using fantomEngine's `GetAccelXY` method, you can simulate these by using the up, down, left, and right keys. That is great for testing.

**9.** Store the engine's accelerometer values in the local `ac` array:

```
        Local ac:Float[] = g.eng.GetAccelXY()
```

**10.** Check whether either the x or the y value is different from 0:

```
        If ac[0]<> 0.0 Or ac[1]<> 0.0 Then
```

**11.** Add the current position values to the `ac` array:

```
            ac[0] += obj.GetPosX()
            ac[1] += obj.GetPosY()
```

**12.** Finally, add a speed value of `1` into the direction, which will be calculated from the object's position to the previous coordinates:

```
        obj.AddSpeed(1,obj.GetVectorAngle( ac[0], ac[1] ))
    Endif
End
Return 0
End
```

## *What just happened?*

In this method, we are now controlling the ball object. It will bounce off the edges of the screen and we will be able to control it on the device by tilting it, or by the arrow keys on the keyboard if we are on a desktop.

## What's the situation? Layer update events

fantomEngine also has `callback` methods when a layer is updated. It is a good place to check if the game is in a certain state and act on it.

## Time for action – acting on layer update events

In the `OnUpdateLayer` method, we want to update emitters and enemies. Also we want to check whether all tiles were removed and start the next level. If all lives of the player's ball are gone, we want to display the Game Over text. Follow the given steps:

**1.** Let's add a check to see if the layer parameter of the method is equal to `layerGame`.

```
Method OnLayerUpdate:Int(layer:ftLayer)
    If layer = g.layerGame Then
```

**2.** Now, do a FOR EACHIN loop of the emitter list of the `game` class:

```
For Local emitter := Eachin g.emitterList
```

**3.** Check whether a call to the emitter's `Update` method returns `FALSE`. We will use the engine's current delta time as a parameter for the emitter's `Update` call. If it is, then the emitter is done and we will remove it from the list:

```
        If emitter.Update(g.eng.GetDeltaTime()) = False Then
            g.emitterList.Remove(emitter)
        Endif
    Next
```

**4.** Next is a `For EachIn` loop through the enemy list of the `game` class:

```
For Local enemy := Eachin g.enemyList
```

**5.** Call the enemy's `Update` method and check whether it returns `FALSE`:

```
If enemy.Update() = False Then
```

**6.** Retrieve the corresponding fantomEngine object of the enemy instance:

```
Local eo:ftObject = enemy.GetObj()
```

**7.** Remove the first entry from the game's `enemyList`, and then the object from the engine:

```
g.enemyList.Remove(enemy)
eo.Remove()
```

**8.** Also spawn a new enemy at a random x position:

```
g.SpawnEnemy(Rnd(20,g.cw-20))
  Endif
Next
```

We handled particle emitters and enemy objects. Next will be the conditions to reach a new level, that is, when all tiles are destroyed.

**9.** Check whether all tiles are gone and the game mode is set to `gmPlay`:

```
If g.tileCount <= 0 And g.gameMode = g.gmPlay Then
```

**10.** Create a new tile set and add `1` to the level number:

```
g.CreateTiles()
g.levelNum += 1
```

**11.** Spawn an additional enemy to make the player's life just a little bit harder:

```
g.SpawnEnemy(Rnd(20,g.cw-20))
```

**12.** Remove the ball and recreate it at the starting position:

```
g.ball.Remove()
g.CreateBall()
  Endif
```

Now, we should act on the fact that all lives are gone and the game is over.

**13.** Check if no lives are left and the game mode is set to `gmPlay`:

```
If g.lifes <= 0 And g.gameMode = g.gmPlay Then
```

**14.** Make the *Game Over* text object visible:

```
g.txtGameOver.SetVisible(True)
```

**15.** Set the game mode to gmGameOver:

```
g.gameMode = g.gmGameOver
```

**16.** If the *Game Over* text object has no transition running, create a new scaling transition. It should scale to the factor 2.0 over 2000 milliseconds and with a transition ID of tidGameOver:

```
        If g.txtGameOver.GetTransitionCount()<= 0 Then
g.txtGameOver.CreateTransScale(2.0,2000,False,g.tidGameOver)
        Endif
      Endif
      Return 0
   End
End
```

## What just happened?

Now that we act on the layer update events, we control the particle emitters totally and also all enemies. Adding to that, we check whether a level is cleared and the game is over.

# We reached our parking position—a transition is done

Our particle effects will use transitions to reach their final destination. Once they are there, we want to delete these particles. That is why their transitions are fired with an ID.

## Time for action – detailing the OnObjectTransition method

The OnObjectTransition method is called whenever a transition finishes and this transition had an ID assigned to it. So we will need to act on it:

**1.** First, perform a SELECT operation on the transition ID.

```
Method OnObjectTransition:Int(transId:Int, obj:ftObject)
   Select transId
```

**2.** Check against the tidParticle constant. If it is, the particle needs to be removed. Call the object's Remove method to do this:

```
        Case g.tidParticle
          obj.Remove()
```

**3.** Check against the `tidGameOver` constant. If it is, activate the title layer:

```
Case g.tidGameOver
   g.layerTitle.SetActive(True)
```

**4.** Make the Game Over text invisible and scale it back to `1.0`:

```
g.txtGameOver.SetVisible(False)
g.txtGameOver.SetScale(1.0)
```

**5.** Set the game mode to `gmMenu` and end the SELECT statement:

```
      g.gameMode = g.gmMenu
   End
   Return 0
End
```

## What just happened?

The code in the `OnObjectMethod` made sure that we removed the particles once they reached their destination and also switched the game back to the title screen once the Game Over text was scaled to its final size.

So what is left? Not much. Collision checks should come to mind, as the goal is to destroy the tiles.

## Bump bump—checking for collisions

Every time you call the engine's `CollisionCheck` method, for each collision that has happened, the engines `OnObjectCollision` method is called with both objects as parameters.

## Time for action – detailing the collision detection

Inside the `OnObjectCollision` method, we will remove tiles, and the ball, and will spawn some particle effects:

**1.** Check whether the collision group of `obj2` is equal to `grpEnemy`. That means the ball collided with the enemy:

```
Method OnObjectCollision:Int(obj1:ftObject, obj2:ftObject)
   If obj2.GetColGroup() = g.grpEnemy Then
```

**2.** Remove `obj1`, the ball:

```
obj1.Remove()
```

**3.** Spawn a new particle emitter at the ball's position, with a time factor of $300$ milliseconds and a `kind` flag of $1$:

```
g.SpawnEmitter(obj1.GetPosX(), obj1.GetPosY(), 300,1)
```

**4.** Play the explosion sound effect:

```
g.sndExplo.Play()
```

**5.** Now, reduce the `lifes` variable of the `game` class:

```
g.lifes -= 1
```

**6.** And create a new ball:

```
g.CreateBall()
Endif
```

This was the check against enemy collisions. Now, we handle the tile set.

**7.** Check whether the collision group of `obj2` is equal to `grpTile`:

```
If obj2.GetColGroup() = g.grpTile Then
```

We will do a very simple collision resolution. This means we will determine the angle from the ball to the tile and then calculate a new angle by adding 180 degrees to it.

**8.** Add that angle to the current speed angle of the ball, stored in the local variable `ca`:

```
Local ca:Float = obj.GetSpeedAngle() + obj.
GetTargetAngle(obj2) + 180.0
```

**9.** Set the speed angle of the ball with the new value:

```
obj.SetSpeedAngle(ca)
```

**10.** Add a factor of 10 times the level number to the game score:

```
g.score += (10 * g.levelNum)
```

**11.** Remove the tile object:

```
obj2.Remove()
```

**12.** Spawn a new particle emitter at the tile's position and with a time factor of $200$ milliseconds:

```
g.SpawnEmitter(obj2.GetPosX(), obj2.GetPosY(), 200)
```

**13.** Add some extra speed to the ball to make it behave like a pinball a little bit:

```
obj.AddSpeed(5)
```

**14.** Reduce the tile count by one:

```
g.tileCount -= 1
```

**15.** Play the hit sound effect and close the first IF check:

```
    g.sndHit.Play()
  Endif
  Return 0
End
```

## What just happened?

By adding the handling of the collision events, we have finished the game in this chapter. When the ball hits the enemy, it will be destroyed and the lives left will be reduced. If the ball hits a tile, the tile will be destroyed and the game score will be rise. And both events, particle emitters will be spawned and a explosion sound will be played.

## Have a go hero – enhancing a chain reaction

Now that you have done your homework, it is time to become a hero. There is still a lot that you can do to make the game more exciting:

- ◆ How about adding different particle effects or power-ups that appear randomly and maybe give some kind of shield to the player for a short period of time?
- ◆ Another thing you could add is how the tiles are set up. You could do that differently or maybe add extra walls to the level.

You see, there is so much to add. Go ahead and become a hero!

# Creating an iOS app

Creating the actual iOS app is pretty easy once you know how. First, you have to build an iOS app in Monk. Monk will also start the simulator of XCODE, but that is not what we want. We want to test the app on the actual device. Anyway, Monk will create an iOS folder inside the build folder of your project directory. Load up the created XCODE project by double-clicking on its MonkeyGame.xcodeproj file.

To build the app for the device, you need to switch the target in XCODE to DEVICE. Then, depending on how you have created your provisional profiles in the developer support area of your account, you need to set it inside the projects code's `signing` section as the corresponding identity and also maybe change the bundle identifier in the `MonkeyGame-Info.plist` file according to it.

For clear instructions on how to do it, please study the wealthy information on the Apple developer pages. Any information included while writing this book could be outdated by the time of printing, so it has been left out on purpose.

# Summary

In this chapter, we again went through some interesting stuff, such as:

- Using stacks and storing and retrieving data from them
- Reading the accelerometer data
- Storing enemies inside their own classes to have them move on predefined paths
- Creating particle emitters which, once they are spawned, do the job automatically
- And finally, testing your game on an iOS device

Ok, that's all for now. See you in *Chapter 7*, *Game #6, At The Docks* with a new game called `At The Docks`.

# 7
# Game #6, At The Docks

*Got pushed around when you were younger? Well, now it's time for payback! Not exactly against the bullies from your school times, but in Game #6, you are now working in a storage area at the docks. Your goal is to push the crates to the correct locations in storage. Someone just dropped them where they are now and it is up to you to finish the job they started. Start the engine of your machine and push these gigantic crates to their target positions. But be careful, you can only push them, not drag them.*

*Game #6 will be **At The Docks**, a Sokoban clone. For anyone who doesn't know the Sokoban kind of games, here is a link that explains them:* `http://en.wikipedia.org/wiki/Sokoban`.

*The game maps will be made of small tiles. The design of a map will be stored in simple text files, which we will read into the game at runtime. As we are targeting the Xbox 360 platform here, we will control the player's machine with the control pad.*

In this chapter, you will do the following:

- ◆ Read joystick input
- ◆ Do collision detection via Box2Box collision checks
- ◆ Use LoadString to read game map data
- ◆ Create an XNA application

So, let's get on with it...

# Frameworks and modules used

For our game, we will use the **fantomEngine** framework (found at `http://code.google.com/p/fantomengine/`). Why? Well, it was made for this book and it will shorten our development time tremendously.

The minimum version for this chapter will be 1.30. fantomEngine imports the **Mojo** framework (that is the heart of Monkey) and provides all the major functionality. The fantomEngine framework makes it easy for you to organize your game objects, use layers, and provide a lot of automation.

# Game resources

The resources for At The Docks will not cover sound files, at this time. The goal of this book is to show you important elements of a game and how to implement them. If you want to have sounds within the game, you are always welcome to add them yourself, once you are done with the chapter.

What kinds of resources will we have?

◆ A sprite sheet that will be used to create the maps in the game. This sheet includes a wall, a floor, a target, a crate image, and the player machine in three animated frames

◆ A bitmap font to display information in the game

That's all for now. Remember, it isn't about quantity, it's about quality!

# The game objects

Our Sokoban clone doesn't have many objects, but we should still go through them one by one. Ladies and gentleman... the following are the objects in our game

## Layers

In this game, we will use only three layers (groups). In version 1.30 of fantomEngine, the default layer was introduced. We will use this as our background layer, so we need to create only two more. The layers are as follows:

◆ Default layer

◆ Game layer

◆ Title screen layer

# The default layer

The default layer will only hold an info text object that displays the number of crates for a level and how many are on their target position.

# The title screen

The title screen is composed of a colored rectangle and two info text objects that will let the player know how to start and exit the game. There won't be any text buttons, this time, as we will only be reacting to input via the game controller of the Xbox 360. Well, not totally; during testing, we will interface with the keyboard of your development machine.

# Game screen

The game layer will be composed of the complete level map objects and the player machine that you can control. All the collision detection in the game is done on the game layer.

# Wall tiles

As the game field is limited in space, we need walls to surround it and also block the player's path, once in a while. We want to make the game a little more difficult, so we need walls.

# Floor tiles

To let the player know where he can drive with his machine, we need to render floor tiles. They are a nice and shiny blue. Don't dirty them or you will have to clean the mess up!

# Target tiles

Do you know where a crate has to be placed? The black-and-yellow striped tiles will show you the way. Place a crate on one, and you will be one step closer to getting the job done!

# Crate tiles

One of the main objects is a crate. It is very heavy, so don't try to move it by hand. Use your powerful machine to push it towards the target. Do it fast, but think first before you act. You can only push them forward, not drag them backwards. Depending on the layout plan of your storage unit, this can become rather tricky.

# The player machine

The machine is an animated sprite, made from three images. When you study the sprite sheet more closely, you will notice that the tracks of the machine are animated. This is the raw power, your tool to get the job done. But remember, you break it, you fix it!

# The basic app structure

Just like in *Chapter 6, Game #5, Balls Out!*, you will utilize the `basescript.monkey` file. It sets up the basic code structure and saves you some time to develop the game. You still need to copy some resources from the book and create some folders but that's all.

## Time for action – creating the basic file structure

Ok, set up the development folder with the following steps:

1. Create a new project folder with a name you choose, such as `At the docks`, for example.

2. Load the `baseScript.monkey` file, which holds the basic code structure for our game.

3. Change the information at the top of the script to your data, and save it under a name you choose, inside the new folder you created before.

4. Create a new `yourGameName.data` folder inside the project folder.

5. Copy the resources from the `atthedocks.data` folder inside your own data folder.

6. Now, build and run an HTML5 project.

## *What just happened?*

You have set up the directory and file structure for the game. And you have built an **HTML5** project that will help you further on. But wait, we need to do something so we can test conveniently on your development machine.

# Modifying the HTML5 canvas size for testing

You don't want to transport the game to the **Xbox 360** every time you want to test it. You will create an **XNA** app this time. XNA devices have different screen sizes. The phones are in the usual sizes you also find on Android phones. The Xbox 360 is more like a PC. The optimal size for a game is recommended as `1280x720`. But we can use sizes larger than regular sizes too. For our game, we will target a size of `800x600`. That will be a good size to test our game. For this, we will change the HTML5 build files that are created by Monkey.

## Time for action – modifying the HTML5 output

To change the HTML5 output to your needed canvas size, follow the ensuing steps:

1. Compile for HTML5.

2. Open the `MonkeyGame.HTML` file, which is located inside the `build/HTML5` folder of your project. Use Monk to do this as it can open HTML files.

3. Locate the line that looks like the following:

```
<canvas id="GameCanvas" on click="javascript:this.focus();"
width=640 height=480 tabindex=1></canvas><br>
```

4. Now, change the width value to `800` and the height value to `600`. Save and close the file.

## *What just happened?*

We have changed the size of the HTML canvas. It is now the size we need it to be so we can test the game easily in the HTML5 browser of your choice.

# The storage for our data

Isn't it funny how things repeat themselves? In every game, you need to store information and states. At The Docks is no exception to this.

## Time for action – creating the data structure

As always, we will place our data storage in the game class. You could also create these fields as global variables, but it is a better practice to encapsulate them inside a class, if you are mainly using an object-oriented coding style.

***1.*** Let's add the field for our layers first. We don't need one for the background, as this is the default layer anyway.

```
Class game Extends App
  Field eng:engine
  Field isSuspended:Bool = False

  Field layerGame:ftLayer
  Field layerTitle:ftLayer
```

***2.*** Next, we will add an object that will store the info text about how many crates are left to be placed on targets.

```
Field txtCrates:ftObject
```

***3.*** To store the bitmap font, we need another field.

```
Field font1:ftFont
```

***4.*** The sprite sheet (atlas) will be stored inside its own field.

```
Field atlas:Image
```

***5.*** Now, we add two fields to store the number of total crates and how many are on a target.

```
Field onTarget:Int = 0
Field crateNum:Int=0
```

***6.*** During collision checks, we need to check if we are close to a wall and store that information. As we have two points in front of the machine to check, we have two Boolean fields.

```
Field hitWall:Bool=False
Field hitWall2:Bool=False
```

***7.*** The same goes with crates. We need to store two crate objects.

```
Field hitCrate:ftObject=Null
Field hitCrate2:ftObject=Null
```

***8.*** The player machine has to be stored inside an object too, of course.

```
Field player:ftObject
```

**9.** Now, add a field for the level number and one for the game mode.

```
Field levelNum:Int = 0
Field gameMode:Int = gmMenu
```

**10.** During the loading of a map, we need to store the initial player position. For this, we need a FLOAT array with two entries.

```
Field plStPos:Float[] = [0.0, 0.0]
```

These were the fields to store dynamic data. Now we need some constants.

**11.** First, add constants for the game modes: Menu, Play, and NextLevel.

```
Const gmMenu:Int = 1
Const gmPlay:Int = 2
Const gmNextLevel:Int = 3
```

**12.** We need a few constants for the collision groups as well as the object tags. The two player constants are needed because we will have two collision zones in front of the machine.

```
Const grpPlayer2:Int = 6
Const grpPlayer:Int = 5
Const grpCrate:Int = 2
Const grpWall:Int = 1
Const grpFloor:Int = 3
Const grpTarget:Int = 4
```

**13.** The last constant we will add is one for a transition ID. We need this when we want to switch to a new level.

```
Const tidNextLevel:Int=1
Method OnCreate:Int()
```

That's all!

## What just happened?

We have added various fields for the game objects and also constants to control the game itself. Constants make reading your source code much easier.

# Setting up the game objects

For this game, we can skip a few things. For example, the `OnRender` method is already set like we need it. Another thing is the background layer. We will use the default layer of Monkey. We will define it during the `OnCreate` event, as it will only contain one text object. But let's concentrate on what have to create now.

## Slice over slice—game layers

For this game, we only need two extra layers—one for the game itself, and one for the title screen, so we can switch it on or off with one statement.

## Time for action – creating layers for the game

To set up the layers for the game, we will use a method inside the `game` class, as follows:

1. At first, add a new method header called `CreateLayers`.

   ```
   Method CreateLayers:Int()
   ```

2. Create a new layer for the game objects and store it inside `layerGame`.

   ```
   layerGame = eng.CreateLayer()
   ```

3. The top row of the game will hold some text objects. As the play field would cover them a little bit, we will move the game layer a little bit downwards.

   ```
   layerGame.SetPos((eng.canvasWidth-11*64)/2+32,+100)
   ```

4. Now, create another layer for the title screen and store it inside `layerTitle`. After that, close this method.

   ```
   layerTitle = eng.CreateLayer()
   Return 0
   End
   ```

## What just happened?

This time, we only created layers for the game objects and the title screen. For the text info objects, we will use the default layer of fantomEngine.

## The second-most important part—a title screen

The title screen in **At The Blocks** will be a simple one. Of course, you can use images as a title screen and menu screen, but we are keeping it simple here.

# Time for action – creating the title screen

Our title screen is composed of a single colored red rectangle and three text objects. One is for the title itself, and two are instructions about which keys the player has to press to start a new game or exit it.

1. Insert a new method header called `CreateTitleScreen`, inside the game class.

   ```
   Method CreateTitleScreen:Int ()
   ```

   Before version 1.30 of fantomEngine, you needed to assign each new object to a layer. Now, you can set a default layer and every new object will be automatically assigned to it.

2. Set the default layer to the title layer.

   ```
   eng.SetDefaultLayer(layerTitle)
   ```

3. To cover the complete title screen, you need to create a rectangle (box) that is centered in the middle of the canvas; it should be the same size as the canvas.

   ```
   Local box:ftObject = eng.CreateBox(eng.canvasWidth,eng.
   canvasHeight,eng.canvasWidth/2,eng.canvasHeight/2)
   ```

4. Color the box in a nice, full red.

   ```
   box.SetColor(255,0,0)
   ```

5. The title `At The Docks` will be made from a text object. Scale it up to a factor of 2.0.

   ```
   Local tx1:ftObject = eng.CreateText(font1,"At the docks",eng.
   canvasWidth/2,eng.canvasHeight/4,1)
   tx1.SetScale(2.0)
   ```

6. To start the game, the player needs to press the *A* key. Create a text object to instruct him to do so.

   ```
   Local tx2:ftObject = eng.CreateText(font1,"Press 'A' to play",
   eng.canvasWidth/2,eng.canvasHeight/2+40,1)
   ```

7. To exit the game, the player needs to press the *Y* key. Again, create a text object to inform the player about this.

   ```
     Local tx3:ftObject = eng.CreateText(font1,"Press 'Y' to exit",
   eng.canvasWidth/2,eng.canvasHeight/2+150,1)
     Return 0
   End
   ```

## *What just happened?*

The title screen was created in a separate method, which will let you enhance it easily later on. You can exchange everything with images if you want.

# Detailing the OnCreate event

You now have all the methods required for the OnCreate method in the game class.

## Time for action – finalizing the OnCreate method

Inside the OnCreate method, we will set the virtual canvas size and set up the layers and the title screen. Also, we will create the objects that will use the default layers for the game background.

**1.** Set the virtual canvas size to 800x600. By setting it, you will make sure that the game canvas will be the same size, no matter what resolution the Xbox 360 runs on.

```
Method OnCreate:Int()
  SetUpdateRate(60)
  eng = New engine

  eng.SetCanvasSize(800,600)
```

**2.** Now, load the tile set and store it inside the atlas field.

```
atlas = LoadImage("atd_tiles.png")
```

**3.** The same goes for the bitmap font. Load it, and store the reference.

```
font1 = eng.LoadFont("atd_font")
```

**4.** Now, make a call to the method that will create all the needed layers.

```
CreateLayers()
```

Remember, we only created new layers. The default layer is still the active one, so every object that is created now will be assigned to the default layer.

**5.** Add a text object that will display the number of crates on targets in the top-left corner of the canvas.

```
txtCrates = eng.CreateText(font1,"Crates on target:
"+onTarget+"/"+crateNum,20,10)
```

**6.** Insert another text object in the top-right corner to inform the player how to switch back to the title screen.

```
Local tx:ftObject = eng.CreateText(font1,"'X'=Back",eng.
canvasWidth-20,10,2)
```

**7.** Make a call to the method that will create the title screen.

```
    CreateTitleScreen()

    Return 0
End
```

## What just happened?

The method `OnCreate` is now finalized. If you want, you can build and run the game. By now, you should see something like the following:

Of course, there is no functionality when pressing any key at the moment. But you will get there, don't worry.

# Some flexible methods for the update process

During the update process, the game will be in a certain mode. At one point, for example, it will create a new game. During this part, it has to load a level map and create the player's powerful machine. Without it, there is no way to push the huge crates around inside the storage area.

It is always a good practice to organize these tasks in their own functions or methods. Maybe you are wondering why I mainly use methods inside classes for this. Well, it is more of a personal preference, as well as a feature, that a method can interface a field of a class to make it easier or shorter, if desired.

# Lads and gents... the main actor

The player of this game will control a huge pushing machine. With its 880 horsepower and its hard rubber tracks, you can easily navigate it through the tight corners of the storage space. The wide pusher at the front will grab onto a crate tightly when you want to push it.

## Time for action – creating the player

To create the player machine, you will add a new method to the game class:

1. Now, add a new method called CreatePlayer.

   ```
   Method CreatePlayer:Int ()
   ```

   The player is an animated image made up from three frames. If you study the images closely, you will see that the tracks are animated.

2. Load the animated image into the player field.

   ```
   player = eng.CreateAnimImage(atlas,0,128,64,64,3,
   plStPos[0],plStPos[1])
   ```

3. Set the animation speed for each frame to 1.

   ```
   player.SetAnimTime(1)
   ```

   To check if the player machine runs into crates or walls, we will need two collision zone boxes.

4. Create a new collision zone box, that is, place 64 pixels in front of the player machine.

   ```
   Local obj:=eng.CreateZoneBox(10,10,plStPos[0],plStPos[1]-64.0)
   ```

5. Set the parent of the box to the player. Also set the collision group to grpPlayer.

   ```
   obj.SetParent(player)
   obj.SetColGroup(grpPlayer)
   ```

   You will need another collision zone so you can still check if there is a wall when the machine pushes a crate.

6. Now, create another collision zone box, but this time 128 pixels in front of the player, and set its collision group to grpPlayer2.

   ```
   Local obj2:=eng.CreateZoneBox(10,10,plStPos[0],plStPos[1]-128.0)
   obj2.SetParent(player)
   obj2.SetColGroup(grpPlayer2)
   ```

**7.** Close the method.

```
    Return 0
End
```

## What just happened?

This method we have just created will load the animated image frames for the player's machine and create the collision zone boxes. By default, these have the bounding box flag set to them, so fantomEngine will use a bounding box to mark collision check to determine whether a collision has happened.

# The level maps—loading the tiles

The maps for At The Docks are made of single tiles with a size of $64x64$ pixels. To store the layout of these maps inside a text file, we will use a simple system of rows and columns of IDs, which will reassemble the map layout. These IDs have the following meanings:

| | |
|---|---|
| 1 | Wall |
| 2 | Crate |
| 3 | Floor |
| 4 | Target platform |
| 5 | Initial start position of the player |

The IDs 2 and 5 will not only create a crate or set the player's start position, but also create a floor tile. The following, is what the first level looks like in the text file:

```
1;1;1;1;1;1;1;1;1;1;1
1;3;3;3;3;3;3;3;3;3;1
1;3;3;3;3;3;2;3;3;3;1
1;4;1;3;3;1;1;3;3;3;1
1;3;1;2;3;3;4;3;5;3;1
1;3;3;3;3;3;3;3;3;3;1
1;3;3;3;3;3;3;3;3;3;1
1;1;1;1;1;1;1;1;1;1
```

Here is what it will look like in the game:

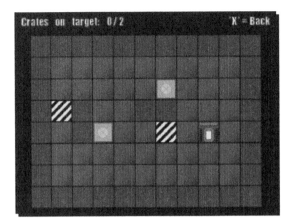

Please note that the levels of the game will be composed of 11 columns in 8 rows.

## Time for action – loading the level tiles

To load a level, you will create a new method for it. Depending on how the field `levelNum` is set, it will load a corresponding text file into a string variable. This will then be split up so we can determine the ID of each tile.

1. Create a new method inside the `game` class, called `LoadLevel`.

   ```
   Method LoadLevel:Int()
   ```

2. Set the default layer for new objects, from now on, to `layerGame`.

   ```
   eng.SetDefaultLayer(layerGame)
   ```

3. Remove all objects from the game layer, and reset the number of crates and the number that are on target.

   ```
   layerGame.RemoveAllObjects()
   crateNum = 0
   onTarget = 0
   ```

4. Next, load the text file and store the result in the local `String` variable `levelText`.

   ```
   Local levelText:String = LoadString("level"+levelNum+".txt")
   ```

5. Split each line of the string into a string array. For this, use the NewLine ASCII character code (`10`).

   ```
   Local lines:= levelText.Split(String.FromChar(10))
   ```

**6.** Determine how many lines (rows) a level has.

```
Local ly:Int = lines.Length()
```

**7.** Create an array with a maximum of `256` entries to store each tile of the map.

```
Local level:Int[]
level = level.Resize(255)
```

**8.** Reset the tile-ID marker.

```
Local levelTile:Int=0
```

**9.** Create a local variable that will store the number of columns.

```
Local lx:Int
```

**10.** Now start a FOR loop that goes through the `lines` array.

```
For Local line:= Eachin lines
```

**11.** Trim each line.

```
line=line.Trim()
```

**12.** If the line doesn't contain anything (if it is empty), continue with the FOR statement right away.

```
If line = "" Then Continue
```

**13.** Split the line into the `leveldata` array by each semicolon character.

```
Local leveldata:= line.Split(";")
```

**14.** Store the length of each line (number of rows) into the `lx` variable.

```
x = leveldata.Length()
```

**15.** Start a FOR loop that goes through each `leveldata` array entry.

```
For Local tile:= Eachin leveldata
```

**16.** Increase the number of level tiles.

```
LevelTile += 1
```

**17.** Store the ID of each tile and an INT value.

```
level[levelTile] = Int(tile.Trim())
```

**18.** Close both FOR loops.

```
    Next
Next
```

At this point, we have read the level file into a string and created an array that holds a sequence of level tile IDs. Now, we use this array to create and place each individual image object that will assemble the level map.

**19.** Reset the `levelTile` variable and create a temporary tile ID variable.

```
levelTile = 0
Local tempTile:Int
```

**20.** Start two new FOR loops for the number of rows and columns stored inside the `ly` and `lx` variables.

```
For Local y:Int = 0 To ly-1
  For Local x:Int = 0 To lx-1
```

**21.** Increase the `levelTile` variable.

```
LevelTile += 1
```

**22.** Start a `Select` statement depending on the current `levelTile` ID.

```
Select level[levelTile]
```

**23.** If the ID is FLOOR, CRATE, or PLAYER, set `tempTile` with `grpFloor`.

```
Case 5,2,3
  tempTile = grpFloor
```

**24.** If the ID is WALL, set `tempTile` to `grpWall`.

```
Case 1
  tempTile = grpWall
```

**25.** And if the ID is TARGET, set `tempTile` to `grpTarget`. Then, close the `Select` statement.

```
  Case 4
    tempTile = grpTarget
End
```

**26.** Now, create the image `obj` by grabbing a frame from the sprite `atlas`. The value in `tempTile` will control the actual X position on the sprite sheet. The position of the object on the canvas is controlled by the current `x` and `y` values.

```
Local obj:= eng.CreateImage(atlas,64*(tempTile-
1),0,64,64,x*64,y*64)
```

**27.** Set the collision group, if the tile is not a floor tile.

```
If tempTile<>grpFloor Then obj.SetColGroup(tempTile)
```

**28.** Start a new `Select` statement, depending on the value of `tempTile`.

```
Select tempTile
```

**29.** If it is equal to `grpWall`, then enable it to collide with `grpPlayer` and `grpPlayer2`.

```
Case grpWall
    obj.SetColWith(grpPlayer,True)
    obj.SetColWith(grpPlayer2,True)
```

**30.** If it is equal to `grpTarget`, the enable it to collide with `grpCrate`. Next, close the `Select` statement.

```
Case grpTarget
    obj.SetColWith(grpCrate,True)
End
```

**31.** Also, set the collision radius to `16` pixels and the collision type to bounding box, if the tile is not a floor tile.

```
If tempTile<>grpFloor obj.SetRadius(16)
If tempTile<>grpFloor obj.SetColType(eng.ctBound)
```

**32.** Close both FOR statements.

```
    Next
Next
```

We have now loaded all of the wall, floor, and target tiles. For every crate and the player, we also loaded a floor tile. Now, we loop over all tiles again, create the actual crates, and determine the player's start position.

**33.** Reset the `LevelTile` variable to `0`. It holds the index for the level map array.

```
LevelTile = 0
```

**34.** Start two FOR loops for the number of rows and columns stored inside the `ly` and `lx` variables.

```
For Local y:Int = 0 To ly-1
    For Local x:Int = 0 To lx-1
```

**35.** Increase the `LevelTile` index variable.

```
LevelTile += 1
```

**36.** If the current level tile is equal to PLAYER, then set the starting position.

```
If level[levelTile] = 5 Then
  plStPos[0] = x*64.0
  plStPos[1] = y*64.0
```

**37.** If the level tile is equal to CRATE, then create a new object by grabbing the corresponding frame from the sprite atlas. The position in the atlas is controlled by the levelTile ID and the position on the canvas by the x and y values.

```
Elseif level[levelTile] = 2 Then
  Local obj4:= eng.CreateImage(atlas,64*(level[levelTile]-
1),0,64,64,x*64,y*64)
```

**38.** Now, set the collision group to grpCrate and enable it to collide with the two collision zones of the player.

```
obj4.SetColGroup(grpCrate)
obj4.SetColWith(grpPlayer,True)
obj4.SetColWith(grpPlayer2,True)
```

**39.** The collision type of the crate needs to be set to Box collision. Also, scale it down a bit.

```
obj4.SetColType(eng.ctBox)
obj4.SetScale(0.9)
```

**40.** Raise the number of crates in this level.

```
    crateNum += 1
Endif
```

**41.** Close both FOR loops.

```
    Next
Next
```

**42.** Create the player and then close off the method.

```
    CreatePlayer()
    Return 0
End
```

## *What just happened?*

Phew, that was a rather huge method! At least for this book. But this method now loads the definition of the current level into an array and will create all the objects that reassemble the level map, including crates and the player.

# On your marks—starting a new game

The last helper method we need is the one to start a new game.

## Time for action – creating a StartNewGame method

This method will deactivate the title layer, set the level number to `1`, and load the level. To implement it, follow the ensuing steps:

1. Insert the new method called `StartNewGame` into the `game` class.

   ```
   Method StartNewGame:Int()
   ```

2. Deactivate the title layer.

   ```
   layerTitle.SetActive(False)
   ```

3. Set the level number to `1`  and load the level.

   ```
   levelNum = 1
   LoadLevel()
   ```

4. The field `gameMode` needs to be set to `gmPlay`. Close this method.

   ```
   gameMode = gmPlay
   Return 0
   End
   ```

## *What just happened?*

Our last helper method starts a new game. It set all corresponding fields and will load the first level map.

# Bring me up-to-date—detailing the OnUpdate event

To finalize the `game` class, we need to detail the `OnUpdate` method.

# Time for action – detailing the OnUpdate method

The update process will determine the current delta time, reset the collision markers, and do the collision checks. It also will check the buttons of the game pad.

***1.*** The first change is to add a `Select` statement inside the `If` statement that depends on the field `gameMode`.

```
Method OnUpdate:Int()
    Local d:Float = Float(eng.CalcDeltaTime())/60.0
    If isSuspended = False then

        Select gameMode
```

***2.*** Check whether the game mode is equal to `gmPlay`.

```
Case gmPlay
```

***3.*** Reset the number of crates that are on a target.

```
OnTarget = 0
```

***4.*** Also, reset whether the player's collision zones hit a wall or a crate.

```
hitWall = False
hitWall2 = False
hitCrate = Null
hitCrate2 = Null
```

***5.*** Perform a collision check on the game layer.

```
eng.CollisionCheck(layerGame)

eng.Update(Float(d))
```

While playing a level, we want the player to be able to switch back to the title screen.

***6.*** Check whether the *X* key was hit on either the keyboard or the Xbox controller.

```
If KeyHit(KEY_X) Or JoyHit(JOY_X) Then
```

***7.*** Activate the title layer and set `gameMode` to `gmMenu`.

```
g.layerTitle.SetActive(True)
g.gameMode = g.gmMenu
Endif
```

In a former chapter we check for the winning conditions inside the `engines` callback methods. This time, we implement it inside the update process of the game class. It is all a matter of preference. There is no strict rule for anything.

8. Check whether the total number of crates is equal to the number of crates on a target and that the game is in PLAY mode.

```
If crateNum = onTarget And gameMode = gmPlay Then
```

9. Set the game mode to gmNextLevel.

```
gameMode = gmNextLevel
```

10. Create a layer transition that will fade out the game layer within 2000 milliseconds. It will also have a transition ID attached to it so we can react to it when the transition is done.

```
layerGame.CreateTransAlpha(0.01,2000,False,tidNextLevel)
Endif
```

11. Check whether gameMode is equal to gmMenu.

```
Case gmMenu
```

12. If the player hits the *A* key on the keyboard or the controller, start a new game.

```
If KeyHit(KEY_A) Or JoyHit(JOY_A) Or TouchHit(0) Then
  StartNewGame()
Endif
```

13. If the player hits the *Y* key on the keyboard or the controller, end the game.

```
If KeyHit(KEY_Y) Or JoyHit(JOY_Y) Then
  Error("")
Endif
```

14. Check that gameMode is equal to gmNextLevel.

```
Case gmNextLevel
```

15. Update the engine with a speed one-sixtieth the delta time; this is determined at the beginning of the OnUpdate method.

```
eng.Update(Float(d)/60)
```

16. Close the Select statement.

```
End
```

**17.** As we only have one dynamic info text object, we will update it here with the number of crates on the targets. This is the last change we make to the `OnUpdate` method.

```
    txtCrates.SetText("Crates on target: "+onTarget+"/"+crateNum)
  Endif
  Return 0
End
```

## What just happened?

Congratulate yourself. We just finalized the `OnUpdate` method of the game class. It will control the game flow by checking against the gameMode variable and also check whether certain keys are hit. We still can't control the player's machine, and collision detection is not implemented so far. But we will get there soon.

Save the script and run it. If you hit the *A* key, you should see the level as shown in the image at the beginning of the section *The level maps—loading the tiles*, in this chapter.

# And action!—the engine class

The callback methods of the engine class are the ones that will finally control the player machine and check for collisions. They will also be responsible for what happens when a level has finished its fading out transition. We could also have checked for the winning conditions here, but have chosen to do it inside the `OnUpdate` method of the game class. You see that there is no strict rule to it. And that is a good thing!

## Move it... object updates

To control the player's machine, we will detail the `OnObjectUpdate` callback method of the fantomEngine framework. Every time an object gets updated, fantomEngine will make a call to this method with the object as a parameter.

## Time for action – updating each object

Inside the `OnObjectUpdate` method, we will control the player machine. For this, we will check if the collision markers are set and act accordingly.

**1.** First, check whether the object is our player object.

```
Method OnObjectUpdate:Int(obj:ftObject)
  If obj = g.player Then
```

**2.** Next, check that the object is not in some kind of transition. All movements will be made with transitions, so if there aren't any, it stands still.

```
If obj.GetTransitionCount() = 0   Then
```

**3.** Set the object to be unanimated for now.

```
obj.SetAnimated(False)
```

**4.** Check whether the *UP* arrow key on the keyboard, or the "UP" direction of the joypad on your controller, was pressed. Also check that the player doesn't run into a wall or whether a crate that the player pushes could run into another crate.

```
If (KeyDown(KEY_UP) Or JoyDown(JOY_UP)) And g.hitWall = False And
((g.hitCrate<>Null And g.hitWall2 = False And g.hitCrate2=Null) Or
g.hitCrate=Null) Then
```

**5.** Determine the vector position that is 64 pixels in front of the player.

```
Local vec:Float[] = obj.GetVector(64,0,True)
```

**6.** Transition the player to this vector within 500 milliseconds.

```
obj.CreateTransPos(vec[0],vec[1], 500,False,0)
```

**7.** Check whether the player runs into a crate and that there is no wall next to the crate.

```
If g.hitCrate <> Null  And g.hitWall2 = False Then
```

**8.** Determine the vector position 128 pixels in front of the player. That will be the target position for the crate's transition.

```
Local vecC:Float[] = obj.GetVector(128,0,True)
```

**9.** Transition the crate to the vector we determined before.

```
    g.hitCrate.CreateTransPos(vecC[0],vecC[1], 500,False,0)
  Endif
Endif
```

**10.** Next, check whether the *LEFT* arrow key was hit on the keyboard or the joypad. Then crate a rotation transition by -90 degrees within 500 milliseconds.

```
If (KeyDown(KEY_LEFT) Or JoyDown(JOY_LEFT)) Then
  obj.CreateTransRot(-90, 500,True,0)
Endif
```

**11.** Do the same for the *RIGHT* arrow key and turn the player's machine to the right.

```
If (KeyDown(KEY_RIGHT) Or JoyDown(JOY_RIGHT)) Then
  obj.CreateTransRot( 90, 500,True,0)
Endif
```

**12.** If the object is still in transition, set it to be animated. That will give the illusion that the tracks of the player's machine are running.

```
    Else
       obj.SetAnimated(True)
    Endif
  Endif

  Return 0
End
```

## What just happened?

By detailing the `OnObjectUpdate` method, we can control the player's machine now, and when collision detection is implemented, it won't move through the walls and will also be able to push the crates.

## Push push—checking for collisions

To be able to push the crates to their target positions, we need to act on collision detection.

## Time for action – detailing collision detection

During the `collision` callback method, we will set the collision markers and objects, so that we can act on them during the `OnObjectUpdate` method.

**1.** Start with a `Select` statement on the first object's collision group.

```
Method OnObjectCollision:Int(obj:ftObject, obj2:ftObject)
  Select obj.GetColGroup()
```

**2.** Check whether it is a wall.

```
Case g.grpWall
```

**3.** If the second object is in the player's second collision zone (`128` pixels away), then set `g.hitWall2` to `True`. We do this by checking the collision group of the second object.

```
If obj2.GetColGroup()=g.grpPlayer2 Then g.hitWall2=True
```

**4.** Now, check whether the second object is the first collision zone of the player (64 pixels away), and if yes, set `g.hitWall` to `True`.

```
If obj2.GetColGroup()=g.grpPlayer Then g.hitWall=True
```

**5.** Check whether the first object is a crate.

```
Case g.grpCrate
```

**6.** If the second object is the first collision zone of the player, then set `g.hitCrate` with the first object.

```
If obj2.GetColGroup()=g.grpPlayer Then g.hitCrate=obj
```

**7.** Again, if the second object is the second collision zone of the player, then set `g.hitCrate2` with the first object.

```
If obj2.GetColGroup()=g.grpPlayer2 Then g.hitCrate2=obj
```

**8.** Finally, check whether the first object is a target.

```
Case g.grpTarget
```

**9.** If yes, then check whether the second object is a crate and it isn't moving anymore. If yes, that means that a crate is on a target and we need to increase the `g.onTarget` field.

```
If obj2.GetColGroup()=g.grpCrate And obj2.GetTransitionCount()=0
Then g.onTarget += 1
```

**10.** Close the `Select` statement.

```
    End

    Return 0
End
```

## What just happened?

During the `collision` callback method, we first checked what kind of first object we have. And depending on that, we have set various collision markers and objects that help to act on them when we want to update the movement of crates and the player machine.

## I can't see it anymore—the transition is finished!

The absolutely last thing that we will add together is the action that occurs when the level is complete and it has finished its fading-out transition.

# Time for action – detailing the OnLayerTransition method

For this, we need to detail the `OnLayerTransition` method of the `engine` class, as follows:

1. First, we check if the transition ID is equal to `g.tidNextLevel`.

   ```
   Method OnLayerTransition:Int(transId:Int, obj:ftLayer)
      If transId = g.tidNextLevel Then
   ```

2. Then, reset the alpha value of the layer back to `1.0`. That means it would be fully visible.

   ```
   g.layerGame.SetAlpha(1.0)
   ```

3. Next, check whether the current level number is smaller than `4` (we have only four levels).

   ```
   If g.levelNum < 4 Then
   ```

4. Raise the current level number and load a new level.

   ```
   g.levelNum+=1
   g.LoadLevel()
   ```

5. Switch the game mode back to `g.gmPlay`.

   ```
   g.gameMode = g.gmPlay
   ```

6. If the last level is already reached, activate the title layer.

   ```
   Else
      g.layerTitle.SetActive(True)
   ```

7. Set the game mode to `g.gmMenu` and close off the two `If` checks.

   ```
         g.gameMode = g.gmMenu
      Endif
   Endif

   Return 0
   End
   ```

## What just happened?

We have detailed the `OnLayerTransition` method of the engine class. We can now switch to a new level or jump back to the title layer when the last level has been finished.

That is all for now. We have a running game with most elements present. We can switch to new levels and control the player and the winning conditions.

There are a few things left for you to do, and the next part will tell you what they are.

## Have a go hero – enhancing At The Docks

Some parts in this game were left out on purpose for you to implement on your own. For example, sounds. While the machine is moving, you can play back some nice heavy machinery sounds. You could also add sounds for when a crate hits a target or you bump into a wall.

Another thing to add is some kind of high-score mechanism. Give points based on how fast the player finishes a level. For this, you need to measure time. Another neat gimmick would be that if you bump the machine too many times into a wall, it breaks and the player loses.

You see, there is still enough room for you to enhance the game.

# Creating a XNA app

To create an actual XNA application, you have to choose the XNA target inside the build dialog on Monk. It will only show up if you have installed Microsoft Visual C# Express according to the documentation in Monkey's *Getting Started* guide. Please make sure you have followed these instructions and the ones that Microsoft supplies regarding development for Xbox 360 or Windows Mobile Phone 7.

# Summary

During the development of At The Docks, we covered the following things:

- Loading of level maps with the LoadString command
- Reading and acting on input from an XBOX 360 controller
- Using the Box2Box and Box2Bound collision types of fantomEngine
- Creating an XNA application

In the next chapter of this book we will cover the second-last game that we create together. Hopefully, you had a lot of fun so far, and if so, we will meet again in *Chapter 8, Game #7, Air Dogs 1942*!

# 8

# Game #7, Air Dogs 1942

*"Of course, with the increasing number of aeroplanes one gains increased opportunities for shooting down one's enemies, but at the same time, the possibility of being shot down one's self increases."—Baron Manfred von Richthofen*

*Everyone would like to be a hero. That is the cool thing about games; you can be one inside a game. So, let's create a game about heroes. How about the heroic pilots of the Second World War who risked their lives fighting major duels in their powerful planes high in the skies? In Game #7, called **Air Dogs 1942**, you can be one of them. Take your plane and shoot the enemy down. Be quicker than your opponent. Don't get hit, or you will be taken down from the sky.*

*You will see the planes from the top view and can control yours with the keyboard. Floating clouds will cover some space. The places will be wrapped around the screen just like CometCrusher. You will see that the player can use this as a tactic against the computer-controlled plane.*

*As this game will be a single-player game, the computer-controlled plane needs some kind of a brain (**AI** or **Artificial Intelligence**). It needs to try to follow your plane and also try to shoot you down. You will learn how to create AI that makes its own decisions and will try to be a hard opponent to beat.*

*Some particle effects, such as smoke and explosions, plus adding sound effects, will round up the whole gaming experience.*

In this chapter, we will learn how to do the following:

- Create computer AI so you have something to fight against in a single-player game
- Export the game as a desktop app via GLFW

# Frameworks and modules used

As with most of the games in this book, we will utilize the fantomEngine game framework. You can get the newest version at `http://code.google.com/p/fantomEngine`.

For this game, use at least Version 1.30.

# No silver, no gold, but... our game resources!

In Air Dogs 1942, we need the following resources:

- A sprite sheet, which includes the plane images, various cloud images, and some colored circles for our smoke and explosion effects
- The bitmap font description file and its corresponding bitmap
- A background image for the ground the planes will fly over
- Sounds for an explosion, for when you shoot, and for when a bullet hits a plane; also, an engine sound

**Hint**: The sound format for Monkey and the GLFW platform is WAV. Use a tool such as **Audacity** to convert sounds, if you need to.

That is all for Air Dogs 1942. All these files are located inside the corresponding `airdogs1942.data` folder in the code that is bundled with this chapter.

# The game objects

The game will be composed of several objects. fantomEngine provides numerous objects that are suitable for our needs.

## Layers

Separating the game in different layers helps organizing the drawing order of active sprites and also to blend them in when needed. The game will have the following layers:

- The background layer
- Game layer
- Cloud layer
- An info text layer
- The title screen layer

The background layer will hold just the background image. We place it inside the background layer, because we will only do collision checks with objects inside the game layer. We will see the action happen in the game layer. It will hold the player, enemy plane, and also the bullets that are shot from the planes. The cloud layer will hold all the clouds that will float around. Information will be displayed inside the info text layer. It will hold several text objects that will display certain information, such as the player score. The title screen layer will be the starting point for the game. It will display a composed logo and a message that informs the player about how to start the game.

# The title screen

The title screen of the game will be composed of a white rectangle, the plane images, the title text, and two info text messages that inform the player about how to start the game and how to exit it.

# Game background

The game background screen will just be a photorealistic image of some fields of this planet. You could also show the player going over some simple blue sky.

# The player plane

The plane controlled by the player is a British war plane. It will be controlled by the arrow keys on the keyboard, and the *S* key will shoot bullets.

# The enemy plane

The computer-controlled enemy plane is a German one. It will try to follow the player automatically, and once within a certain angle, will start shooting deadly bullets towards the player machine.

# Bullets

To shoot the opponent down, each plane is loaded with unlimited deadly bullets.

# Clouds

While floating around the game canvas, the clouds give a little cover to each of the fighters. They come in different sizes and float at random angles and speeds.

# Info text

The player will be informed about the score with two info text objects. One will show the player's successful shoot-downs, and the other, the computer controlled planes'. To win a game, you need to shoot down the enemy five times. The text will be displayed in the bitmap font.

# Smoke particles

Once a plane is hit, it will leave smoke along its traveling path.

# Explosions

Once a plane gets hit five times, it will explode. The explosion itself will be composed of different colored circles that grow in size and fade out over time.

# The basic app structure

To keep this chapter short, you need to load a basic script file that is provided with fantomEngine and also copy the resources from the book.

## Time for action – setting up the basic file structure

To set up the basic file structure, follow the ensuing steps:

1. From the chapter's code folder, load the `baseMonkey.script` file.

2. Save it under the name `airdogs1942.monkey`, inside a folder you have created before.

3. Copy the `airdogs1942.data` folder and its included resources into your game folder.

### What just happened?

You have created the basic file and folder structure for this project and also copied the resources that we need for the game. You can now start with the development of the game.

# Storing data

The game will have several objects and we need to store them. Also, we need several constants that will help controlling the flow of the game within our finite-state-machine approach.

## Time for action – creating the data structure

To store the data, we will enhance the `game` class with some fields and constants, as follows:

1. First, add two text objects that will display the scores of the player and the computer.

   ```
   Class game Extends App
     Field eng:engine
     Field isSuspended:Bool = False

     Field txtScore:ftObject
     Field txtScoreC:ftObject
   ```

2. Next, add two text objects that will display if the player wins or loses.

   ```
   Field txtYouWin:ftObject
   Field txtYouLoose:ftObject
   ```

3. The player plane and the enemy plane will be stored in separate objects.

   ```
   Field player:ftObject
   Field enemy:ftObject
   ```

**4.** The game font also has to be stored.

```
Field font1:ftFont
```

**5.** Now, add five layers for the background, the game and clouds, and also the information and the title screen.

```
Field layerBackground:ftLayer
Field layerGame:ftLayer
Field layerClouds:ftLayer
Field layerInfo:ftLayer
Field layerTitle:ftLayer
```

**6.** To hold all the sound effects, we need a sound object for each sound.

```
Field sndHit:ftSound
Field sndExplo:ftSound
Field sndShoot:ftSound
Field sndEngine:ftSound
```

**7.** Add an image object called `atlas`, which will hold the reference to the sprite sheet.

```
Field atlas:Image
```

**8.** To control the flow of the game, we need one field called `gameMode` It will be initialized with the constant `gmMenu`, which we will add shortly.

```
Field gameMode:Int = gmMenu
```

**9.** Next, add fields to store the score for the player and the computer.

```
Field score:Int = 0
Field scoreC:Int = 0
```

**10.** Also, add two fields that store the number of times one plane got hit.

```
Field hits:Int = 0
Field hitsC:Int = 0
```

**11.** Because coders are lazy typists, we need to enter fields that will store the width and height of the canvas.

```
Field cw:Float = 0.0
Field ch:Float = 0.0
```

**12.** To determine if the enemy plane can shoot, add a Boolean field.

```
Field canShoot:Bool=True
```

You are done adding fields. Now, add some constants. Constants make your code more readable, and they are easier to remember, as compared to numbers.

**13.** Add three constants for the three game modes that we will need—one for the title screen/menu, one for the game in play, and one for when a game is over.

```
Const gmMenu:Int = 1
Const gmPlay:Int = 2
Const gmGameOver:Int = 3
```

**14.** For collision check purposes, we need three collision groups—`Player`, `Enemy`, and a group for the bullet shots.

```
Const grpPlayer:Int = 1
Const grpEnemy:Int = 2
Const grpShot:Int = 3
```

**15.** Some objects have to be deleted after a transition, so add a transition ID for this.

```
Const triDelete:Int = 6
```

**16.** And lastly, some objects need to be acted on after a timer finishes. We need one constant for deleting objects, and one for enabling the enemy plane to shoot again.

```
Const tmDelete:Int = 15
Const tmCanShoot:Int = 16

Method OnCreate:Int()
  SetUpdateRate(60)
```

## What just happened?

You have added some fields to hold dynamic data and some constants to make your code more readable. Good job! But, you are far from being done with the project.

# First changes to the OnCreate event

Before we start to create some game objects, we need to add our first modifications to the `OnCreate` method of the class `game`.

# Time for action – first changes to the OnCreate method

Inside the `OnCreate` method, we want to determine the canvas size and load the sprite sheet and the game font. This is done as follows:

1. Set the virtual canvas size to `800` by `600` pixels, as the background image is of the exact same size.

```
Method OnCreate:Int()
  SetUpdateRate(60)
  eng = New engine

  eng.SetCanvasSize(800,600)
```

2. Determine the canvas size and store the values in the fields we just created in the preceding section. You code set them with hard values, but this approach makes them more modular.

```
ch = eng.canvasHeight
cw = eng.canvasWidth
```

3. Now, load the sprite sheet and store the reference in the `atlas` field.

```
atlas = LoadImage("ad_Tiles.png")
```

4. And lastly, load the bitmap font.

```
font1 = eng.LoadFont("ad_font")

Return 0
End
```

## What just happened?

The first modifications that we have just made in the `OnCreate` event will prepare the project as far as the canvas size, loading the graphics, and font we will use are concerned.

# Setting up the game objects

To finalize the `OnCreate` event, we will build more methods that will create more objects for the game.

# Making some noise... sound effects!

Air Dogs 1942 will have sound effects for shots, hits, explosions, and the plane engine.

## Time for action – loading the game sound effects

**1.** To load the sounds, add the `LoadSound` method to the `game` class.

```
Method LoadSounds:Int()
```

**2.** Load the non-looping sound effects.

```
sndHit = eng.LoadSound("hit")
sndExplo = eng.LoadSound("explosion")
sndShoot = eng.LoadSound("shoot")
```

**3.** The plane engine sound needs to be looped continuously. Add a TRUE parameter to the `LoadSound` call.

```
sndEngine = eng.LoadSound("engine",True)
```

**4.** Close this method.

```
   Return 0
End
```

## What just happened?

You have created a method that will load all sounds we need for the game. A file extension was not given to the `LoadSound` statement, as it will be added from fantomEngine, according to the platform on which you will build it. For the GLFW platform, you need WAV files.

## Lay your head on me... the game layers

Layers are like sheets of paper you draw on, that are laid on top of each other.

## Time for action – creating layers for the game

To control the order of drawing the game objects, do collision checks, and also to hide or show certain objects, we need several layers.

**1.** Insert a new method called `CreateLayers` into the `game` class.

```
Method CreateLayers:Int()
```

**2.** Set the background layer with the default layer.

```
layerBackground = eng.GetDefaultLayer()
```

3. Now, add layers for the game, the clouds, the info text objects, and the title screen.

```
layerGame = eng.CreateLayer()
layerClouds = eng.CreateLayer()
layerInfo = eng.CreateLayer()
layerTitle = eng.CreateLayer()
```

4. Close this method.

```
   Return 0
End
```

## What just happened?

With this method, all the required layers are created and can then be used to assign objects. Boxing these into one method will let you change them easily and in an organized fashion.

## Over high ground—the background screen

A background for a game can be very complex or very simple. We are using a complex one from the graphics point of view, but with no functionality. It is only there to give the illusion of flying high over some fields.

## Time for action – composing the background screen

The game background will be just one image of some fields. It needs to be assigned to the background layer. That is all.

1. Add the method `CreateBackgroundScreen` to the `game` class.

```
Method CreateBackgroundScreen:Int()
```

2. Set the default layer to `layerBackground`.

```
eng.SetDefaultLayer(layerBackground)
```

3. Create a local object that calls `CreateImage`. It will be displayed in the center of the canvas. After that, close the method.

```
   Local obj:= eng.CreateImage("background.png",cw/2,ch/2)
   Return 0
End
```

## What just happened?

With this new method, you have loaded the background image. For other platforms, you could also create some buttons to switch back to the title screen, but we will handle this differently.

## Hope it won't rain—creating the clouds

To have more animated objects on the screen besides the planes, we will let some clouds float around the canvas.

## Time for action – creating the clouds

The clouds will come in different sizes and shapes. The shapes are chosen randomly from the sprite sheet by the method of creation, as follows:

**1.** Insert the method `CreateClouds` into the `game` class.

```
Method CreateClouds:Int()
```

**2.** As we will be creating several clouds, create a local object variable.

```
Local obj:ftObject
```

**3.** To calculate the shape, add a local `shape` variable of the type FLOAT.

```
Local shape:Float
```

**4.** Set the cloud layer as the default layer; all new objects, from now on, will be assigned to it.

```
eng.SetDefaultLayer(layerClouds)
```

**5.** We want ten clouds. Start a FOR loop ranging from `1` to `10`.

```
For Local i:Int = 1 To 10
```

**6.** To determine the cloud shape, we need a random number ranging from `0` to `100`.

```
shape = Rnd(100.0)
```

**7.** Check if `shape` is less or equal to `20`. If yes, then load one cloud shape from the sprite atlas. Place it randomly on the canvas.

```
If shape <= 20.0 Then
  obj = eng.CreateImage(atlas,128,0,64,64,Rnd(10,cw-
10),Rnd(10,ch-10))
```

**8.** If `shape` is greater than `20` and less than or equal to `70`, then load the second cloud shape.

```
Elseif shape > 20.0 And shape <= 70.0 Then
  obj = eng.CreateImage(atlas,192,0,64,64,Rnd(10,cw-
10),Rnd(10,ch-10))
```

**9.** And, if `shape` is greater than `70`, load the last cloud sprite shape.

```
Else
  obj = eng.CreateImage(atlas,0,64,128,128,Rnd(10,cw-
10),Rnd(10,ch-10))
Endif
```

**10.** Set the speed and direction of the cloud randomly, and also its angle.

```
obj.SetSpeed(Rnd(0.2,2),Rnd(360))
obj.SetAngle(Rnd(360))
```

**11.** Let the cloud object wrap around the screen edges when it moves outside the canvas borders.

```
obj.SetWrapScreen(True)
```

**12.** Close the FOR loop and this method.

```
    Next
    Return 0
End
```

## What just happened?

The `CreateClouds` method will add `10` clouds on the canvas in a random fashion. It will determine the shape to use randomly.

To make this method more general, you could add a parameter to the method head, which determines the amount of clouds to be created. But for now, we will go by this fixed amount we have chosen.

## What is going on?—creating info text objects

Air Dogs 1942 will have support from four text objects which will inform the player about the current state and score of the game.

## Time for action – creating info text objects

Two of the four text objects are dynamic and will display the current score of the player and the computer. Dynamic means they will be updated during the game with the current score. They are predefined, but are made invisible later on. They will display the **WIN** or **LOSE** message.

**1.** Insert a new method into the `game` class, called `CreateInfoText`.

```
Method CreateInfoText:Int ()
```

**2.** Set the info layer as the default layer.

```
eng.SetDefaultLayer(layerInfo)
```

**3.** Create two text objects, one for the player score and one for the computer score. Place them at each corner of the top edge of the screen.

```
txtScore = eng.CreateText(font1,"Player: "+score,10,0)
txtScoreC = eng.CreateText(font1,"Computer: "+scoreC,cw-10,0,2)
```

**4.** Next, create two text objects for the **YOU WIN** and **YOU LOSE** messages. They are to be placed in the middle of the canvas.

```
txtYouWin = eng.CreateText(font1,"YOU WIN :=)",cw/2,ch/2,1)
txtYouLoose = eng.CreateText(font1,"YOU LOOSE :-(",cw/2,ch/2,1)
```

**5.** Close this method.

```
    Return 0
End
```

## What just happened?

You have created a method that will initialize and create text objects that will be used to inform the player about the current state of the game. The fields to store the references of these text objects were added in the data storage section.

# What are we playing here?—The title/menu screen

Most games have a title/menu screen. So does Air Dogs 1942.

# Time for action – creating the title screen

This screen will show some graphics of our planes, the game title, and two instructional messages on how to start the game or exit it.

**_1._** To create the title screen, add a method called `CreateTitleScreen` to the `game` class.

```
Method CreateTitleScreen:Int ()
```

**_2._** Set the default layer to `layerTitle`.

```
eng.SetDefaultLayer(layerTitle)
```

**_3._** Next, create a box object covering the whole canvas. We want it to be white and that is its default color.

```
Local box:ftObject = eng.CreateBox(cw,ch,cw/2,ch/2)
```

**_4._** Now, create a local text object for the game title. Place it in the center of the canvas and at one-fourth of the canvas height.

```
Local tx1:ftObject = eng.CreateText(font1,"Air Dogs
1942",cw/2,ch/4,1)
```

**_5._** Scale the text object up by a factor of `2.0`.

```
tx1.SetScale(2.0)
```

**_6._** To inform the player about how to start the game, add a text object at the middle of the canvas.

```
Local tx2:ftObject = eng.CreateText(font1,"Press 'P' to
play",cw/2,ch/2+20, 1)
```

**_7._** To exit the game, we need to add another text object.

```
Local tx3:ftObject = eng.CreateText(font1,"Press 'ESC' to end the
game", cw/2,ch/2+120,1)
```

**_8._** We want to display both planes over the game title. Load a local image object with the player plane image.

```
Local p1:ftObject = eng.CreateImage(atlas,0,0,64,64,cw/2-
ch/8,ch/6)
```

**_9._** Rotate it to an angle of `45` degrees.

```
p1.SetAngle(45)
```

**10.** Now, load the enemy plane and rotate it to 315 degrees.

```
    Local p2:ftObject = eng.CreateImage(atlas,64,0,64,64,cw/2+ch/8
,ch/6)
    p2.SetAngle(315)
```

**11.** Close the method.

```
  Return 0
End
```

## What just happened?

We have created a method that will assemble the title/menu screen. Besides including some text objects, this time we also have some graphics for our title screen.

# Finalizing the OnCreate event

By adding just a few more statements inside the OnCreate method of the game class, we can consider this method done.

## Time for action – finalizing the OnCreate method

You will now add the calls to all these new methods we have created.

**1.** First, add a call to LoadSounds and create the layers through a call of the CreateLayers method.

```
font1 = eng.LoadFont("ad_font")

LoadSounds()
CreateLayers()
```

**2.** Create the background screen and the clouds that will float around the screen.

```
CreateBackgroundScreen()
CreateClouds()
```

**3.** Last, but not least, add the info text objects and set up the title screen.

```
  CreateInfoText()
  CreateTitleScreen()

  Return 0
End
```

## *What just happened?*

You have finalized the `OnCreate` method of the game class. If you build and run this game now, you will see something like the following screenshot, on the title/menu screen:

# Methods for the update process

The game is now at a state where it will just display the title screen and nothing more. There is no interaction and all other game objects are not involved so far. The `OnUpdate` method of the game class controls the flow of the game. For this, we need some helper methods that can be called when updating the game.

## The hero—spawning the player plane

The player plane will appear and also disappear from the screen at certain situations.

## Time for action – spawning the player plane

We need a method that will make the player plane appear. The plane should appear on the left side of the screen, facing upwards. Like the clouds, the plane will wrap around the screen once it moves over the screen edges.

1. Add a new method called `SpawnPlayer` to the class `game`.

   ```
   Method SpawnPlayer:Int ()
   ```

2. Store the reference to the player plane object inside its corresponding field.

   ```
   player = eng.CreateImage(atlas,0,0,64,64,cw/4,ch/2)
   ```

**3.** Scale it down to a factor of `0.7` and set the speed of the plane to `8`.

```
player.SetScale(0.7)
player.SetSpeed(8)
```

**4.** The player should wrap around the screen.

```
player.SetWrapScreen(True)
```

**5.** For collision detection, set the collision group to `grpPlayer` and the radius to `24` pixels. As the plane is already scaled down, the actual radius will be stored as `24` times `0.7`.

```
player.SetColGroup(grpPlayer)
player.SetRadius(24)
```

**6.** Reset the `hit` points to `0`. Then, close the method.

```
hits=0
Return 0
End
```

## What just happened?

Using the `SpawnPlayer` method, you can always create a new player machine with a single call. Of course, only call it when the plane was previously destroyed, or you will end up with more than one plane, of which you can only control the newer one.

## Spawning an enemy

As the hero needs an enemy to fight against, we need to spawn at least one enemy plane.

## Time for action – spawning an enemy plane

Besides using a different image, which is placed and rotated differently, spawning the enemy plane works in a similar way to spawning the player plane.

**1.** Add a new method called `SpawnEnemy` to the `game` class.

```
Method SpawnEnemy:Int ()
```

**2.** Assign the image of the plane to the corresponding `enemy` field.

```
enemy = eng.CreateImage(atlas,64,0,64,64,cw/4*3,ch/2)
```

**3.** Scale it down to a factor of `0.7`.

```
enemy.SetScale(0.7)
```

**4.** Set its angle to `180` degrees and give it a speed of `8`.

```
enemy.SetAngle(180)
enemy.SetSpeed(8)
```

**5.** Let the enemy plane wrap around the screen edges.

```
enemy.SetWrapScreen(True)
```

**6.** For collision detection, set the collision group to `grpEnemy` and give it a radius of `24`.

```
enemy.SetColGroup(grpEnemy)
enemy.SetRadius(24)
```

**7.** Reset its hit points to `0` and close the method.

```
hitsC=0
canShoot=True
Return 0
End
```

## What just happened?

Now, you have added a method to spawn an enemy plane that will appear on the right side of the canvas, facing downwards. Call it with care! Just kidding!

## Starting a new game

Before we detail the update process of the game, we need one more helper method to start a new game.

## Time for action – creating a StartNewGame method

This method will reset all score fields, deactivate the title layer, spawn the planes, and deactivate possibly visible status messages. It also starts the playback of the engine sound.

**1.** Add a method called `StartNewGame` to the `game` class.

```
Method StartNewGame:Int()
```

**2.** Seed the random number generator with the current value of a call to `Millisecs()`.

```
Seed = Millisecs()
```

**3.** Reset both score fields.

```
score = 0
scoreC = 0
```

**4.** Deactivate the title layer.

```
layerTitle.SetActive(False)
```

**5.** Remove all existing objects on the game layer.

```
layerGame.RemoveAllObjects()
```

**6.** Set the default layer to be `layerGame`.

```
eng.SetDefaultLayer(layerGame)
```

**7.** Spawn the player and the enemy plane.

```
SpawnPlayer()
SpawnEnemy()
```

**8.** Set the game mode to `gmPlay`.

```
gameMode = gmPlay
```

**9.** Deactivate the text objects that display whether or not you have won.

```
txtYouWin.SetActive(False)
txtYouLoose.SetActive(False)
```

**10.** Start playing the engine sound, and then close this method.

```
sndEngine.Play()
Return 0
End
```

## What just happened?

We will set up a new game with this method. It resets some data fields and spawns both planes. It also switches the game into the play mode. We can now modify the update process of the game.

# Detailing the OnUpdate event

The update process of the `game` class will take of the flow of the game, depending on which mode the game is in.

# Time for action – detailing the OnUpdate method

During the `OnUpdate` method, we will do different things depending on the `gameMode` field. If the mode is `gmPlay`, we will update all objects and do collision checks. In other modes, we mostly check for certain keys that are hit on the keyboard to switch the game into a different mode.

1. Add a `Select` statement with the `gameMode` field as a parameter.

```
Method OnUpdate:Int()
  Local d:Float = Float(eng.CalcDeltaTime())/60.0
  If isSuspended = False Then

    Select gameMode
```

2. Check against the `gmPlay` constant.

```
    Case gmPlay

      eng.Update(Float(d))
```

The call to the `Update` method of the engine is now part of the `gmPlay` segment.

3. Now, check for any collisions happening on the game layer. The response for this will be detailed inside the `engine` class.

```
eng.CollisionCheck(layerGame)
```

4. Check if the *Esc* key was hit.

```
If KeyHit(KEY_ESCAPE) Then
```

5. If yes, activate the title screen and stop the plane engine sound.

```
layerTitle.SetActive(True)
sndEngine.Stop()
```

6. Also, set the game mode to `gmMenu`.

```
    gameMode = gmMenu
Endif
```

7. Update the `score` info text objects with the current score values.

```
txtScore.SetText("Player: "+score)
txtScoreC.SetText("Computer: "+scoreC)
```

8. Check whether `gameMode` is equal to `gmMenu`.

```
Case gmMenu
```

**9.** And then, check whether the *P* key was hit. If yes, start a new game.

```
If KeyHit(KEY_P) Then
    StartNewGame()
Endif
```

**10.** Now, check whether the *Esc* key was hit. If yes, stop the game via an `Error` call.

```
If KeyHit(KEY_ESCAPE) Then
    Error ("")
Endif
```

**11.** Lastly, check whether `gameMode` is equal to `gmGameOver`.

```
Case gmGameOver
```

**12.** During this mode, check whether the *Esc* key was hit.

```
If KeyHit(KEY_ESCAPE) Then
```

**13.** If yes, set `gameMode` to `gmMenu` and activate the title layer.

```
gameMode = gmMenu
layerTitle.SetActive(True)
```

**14.** Close the last IF check and the `Select` statement.

```
        Endif
    End

  Endif
  Return 0
End
```

## What just happened?

By detailing the `OnUpdate` method of the class `game`, we can now start a new game and also switch back to the title screen. The player can't control the plane for now, but we will implement this, later in this chapter.

If you build and run the game at this moment, and start a new game, the console should look like the following screenshot:

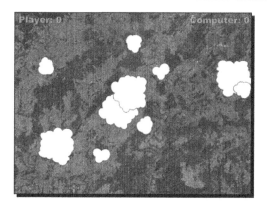

# Making it look nicer—some particle effects

In a game, eye candy is always good. For this, we will add some particle effects that will resemble smoke and explosions. The first will be emitted once a plane takes a hit, and the latter when it explodes into pieces.

The following methods will be added to the class `game`, but will be called during the callback methods of the `engine` class.

## Emitting smoke

We need to create a method to emit some smoke (not real smoke), that will do so whether the plane is the enemy's or the player's.

## Time for action – emitting the smoke

The method we have created to spawn smoke will be called once a plane gets hit. The more hits it takes, the higher the chance of emitting a smoke particle.

1. Create a new method called `SpawnSmoke` inside the `game` class. The parameters are the plane object and the number of hits.

   ```
   Method SpawnSmoke:Int(plane:ftObject, hits:Int)
   ```

2. Check whether a random number ranging from `0` to `100` will be greater than `100-hits` times `10`.

   ```
   If Rnd(0,100)>(100-hits*10)  Then
   ```

3. If yes, set the default layer to `layerGame`.

   ```
   eng.SetDefaultLayer(layerGame)
   ```

**4.** Determine a vector that is located in the back of the plane. The distance is `20` pixels and the angle is calculated randomly taking the hits into account.

```
Local vec:Float[] = plane.GetVector(20,180+Rnd(-
10*hits,10*hits),True)
```

**5.** Randomly determine an x offset for the next `CreateImage` call from the sprite atlas. This is used to choose the smoke images randomly.

```
Local xoff:Float = Int(Rnd(0,3))
```

**6.** Create a local image object that reassembles the smoke particle.

```
Local obj := eng.CreateImage(atlas,144+xoff*16.0,64,16,16,
vec[0],vec[1])
```

The smoke particles won't move, but the change in their alpha value over time means they will fade out.

**7.** Now, create an alpha transition to an alpha value of `0.1`, at a random time between `1000` and `3000` milliseconds. The transition ID will be `triDelete`.

```
Local trans:ftTrans = obj.CreateTransAlpha(0.1, Rnd(1000,
3000), False, triDelete)
```

**8.** Set the particle scale randomly from a factor of `0.1` to `0.5`.

```
obj.SetScale(Rnd(0.1,0.5))
```

**9.** Add a scale transition for a random scale of `1.0` to `4.0`.

```
obj.AddTransScale(trans, Rnd(1.0,4.0), False)
```

**10.** Close this method.

```
    Return 0
End
```

## What just happened?

You created a method that will let you emit smoke particles behind a plane, depending on how many hits that plane took.

## Boom!—Emitting explosions

What comes after smoke? Sometimes, it's a big explosion. If a plane takes too many hits, it will explode.

# Time for action – creating the explosion

The method to emit explosion particles works in a similar way to the one that emits smoke.

**1.** Insert a method called SpawnExplosion in the game class. The parameters are the x and y positions, and the amount of particles to create.

```
Method SpawnExplosion:Int(x:Float, y:Float, amount:Int)
```

**2.** Set the default layer to the game layer.

```
eng.SetDefaultLayer(layerGame)
```

**3.** Start a FOR loop for the local i variable ranging from 1 to the amount parameter of the method.

```
For Local i:Int = 1 To amount
```

**4.** Determine a random x offset that is used when an image object for the explosion particle is created.

```
Local xoff:Float = Int(Rnd(0,3))
```

**5.** Create a local object for the particle image. It will be placed at the coordinates given to the method.

```
Local obj:=eng.CreateImage(atlas,144+xoff*16.0,80,16,16, x,y)
```

**6.** Now, determine a random vector that will be 10 to 40 pixels and at a random angle around the given coordinates of the method.

```
Local vec:Float[] = obj.GetVector(Rnd(10,40),Rnd(360))
```

**7.** Create a position transition for the particle with the determined vector and a random duration of 1000 to 3000 milliseconds. The transition ID will be set to triDelete.

```
        Local trans:ftTrans = obj.CreateTransPos(vec[0], vec[1],
Rnd(1000,3000), False, triDelete)
```

**8.** Set the particle scale to a random factor of 0.1 to 1.0.

```
obj.SetScale(Rnd(0.1,1.0))
```

**9.** Add a scale transition with a random target scale ranging from 2.0 to 4.0.

```
obj.AddTransScale(trans, Rnd(2.0,4.0), False)
```

**10.** Lastly, add an alpha transition so it will fade out. The target alpha value is `0.5`.

```
obj.AddTransAlpha(trans, 0.5, False)
```

**11.** Close the FOR loop and the method.

```
Next
Return 0
End
```

## What just happened?

You just created a method that can generate any explosion, no matter how big you want it to be. If you want more particle effects, then it might be a good idea to create a new layer and place these particles in it, so that they won't loop over during the collision detection phase.

## Pow!—spawning a shot

We have smoke, we have explosions. But unless we add collision detection for the planes themselves, we will have nothing to hit the planes. We need bullets to be fired at your opponent.

## Time for action – spawning a shot

The following method will spawn a bullet that will be harmful for any plane that crosses its path.

**1.** Add the method `SpawnShot` to the `game` class. The parameter will be a `plane` object.

```
Method SpawnShot:Int (plane:ftObject)
```

**2.** Check whether the plane is the player's or the enemy's. If it is the enemy's, then also check whether it can shoot. This is to make sure that it cannot shoot each frame.

```
If (plane = enemy And canShoot = True) Or plane=player Then
```

**3.** Determine a vector that is located `40` pixels in front of the plane. That is the starting point for the bullet.

```
Local vec:Float[] = plane.GetVector(40,0,True)
```

**4.** Create a local object that will be a bullet.

```
        Local s:ftObject = eng.CreateImage(atlas,128,64,12,16,
vec[0],vec[1])
```

**5.** Set its angle to the plane's angle.

```
s.SetAngle(plane.GetAngle())
```

**6.** Set its speed to `15` and ensure that it will wrap around the screen edges.

```
s.SetSpeed(15)
s.SetWrapScreen(True)
```

**7.** Next, set the collision group to `grpShot`.

```
s.SetColGroup(grpShot)
```

**8.** Enable it to collide with both the player and the enemy plane.

```
s.SetColWith(grpPlayer, True)
s.SetColWith(grpEnemy, True)
```

**9.** The radius will be set to `6` pixels. By default, circle-to-circle collision detection is used.

```
s.SetRadius(6)
```

**10.** The bullet is allowed to fly for `2000` milliseconds. Create an object timer with a timer ID of `tmDelete`, which will fire in `2000` milliseconds.

```
eng.CreateObjTimer(s,tmDelete,2000)
```

**11.** Check whether `plane` is equal to `enemy`.

```
If plane = enemy Then
```

**12.** If yes, set `canShoot` to `False` and create an object timer with the ID `tmCanShoot` and a time of `300` milliseconds.

```
canShoot = False
eng.CreateObjTimer(plane,tmCanShoot,300)
Endif
```

Inside the `engine` class, we will detail the corresponding callback method and set the `canShoot` field back to `True`.

**13.** Now, play the shooting sound effect.

```
sndShoot.Play()
```

**14.** Close the first IF check and the method.

```
Endif
Return 0
End
```

## *What just happened?*

Woohoo! We can shoot bullets now, with the method we just created. Not totally, because we have no trigger to actually shoot, but the method is there.

# The brain—Computer AI (Artificial Intelligence)

Creating computer-controlled objects can be a very interesting part of game development. It can be sometimes also very difficult. For example, there are numerous variations and methods when it comes to path finding.

## Follow him!—creating a brain for the enemy pilot

Before we come to the heart of the game, the `engine` class, we need a method that will let our enemy planes act at least a little bit intelligent.

## Time for action – following the player

The brain of the computer-controlled plane will be a simple one. It will determine the angle difference towards the player plane. Then, it will turn towards that direction. If the player plane is in front of the computer controlled one, it will fire a shot.

*1.* Create a new method called `FollowPlayer` in the `game` class. The parameter is an object (usually the enemy plane).

```
Method FollowPlayer:Int(obj:ftObject)
```

*2.* Determine the relative angle from the object towards the player's plane.

```
Local angle:Float = obj.GetTargetAngle(player,True)
```

*3.* If the angle is less than zero (left side of the object) turn the object counterclockwise. The factor is determined by the delta time divided by `16`.

```
If angle < 0 Then
obj.SetAngle(-eng.GetDeltaTime()/16.0,True)
```

*4.* If the player plane is on the right side, turn the object clockwise.

```
Else
   obj.SetAngle(eng.GetDeltaTime()/16.0,True)
Endif
```

*5.* Now, if the absolute angle is less than `10` degrees, spawn a shot.

```
If Abs(angle) < 10.0 Then SpawnShot(obj)
```

**6.** Reset the speed angle of the object plane (the enemy) to the current angle of the object.

```
obj.SetSpeedAngle(obj.GetAngle())
```

**7.** Close this method.

```
   Return 0
End
```

## What just happened?

The `FollowPlayer` method will let a plane follow the player plane and, if possible, shoot at it. It is a simple example of artificial intelligence. The enemy plane doesn't follow the player at the moment, as we haven't implemented a call to this new method yet.

# The heart of the game—the engine class

Again, we still have no collision detection response, no control of the player plane, and no check for the winning conditions. All this will be handled in the callback methods of the `engine` class.

## Time management—acting on object timer events

We have objects that need to be deleted after a certain amount of time has passed, and also certain variables that need to be set.

## Time for action – enhancing the OnObjectTimer method

The `OnObjectTimer` method of the `engine` class needs to be detailed. For the bullets, the `canShoot` field of the `game` class needs to be set to `TRUE` and they also need to be deleted.

**1.** Check whether the timer ID is equal to `g.tmDelete`. If yes, call the `Remove` method of the object.

```
Method OnObjectTimer:Int(timerId:Int, obj:ftObject)

    If timerId = g.tmDelete Then obj.Remove()
```

**2.** Check whether the timer ID is equal to `g.canShoot`. If yes, set `g.canShoot` to True.

```
    If timerId = g.tmCanShoot Then g.canShoot = True

   Return 0
End
```

## What just happened?

Enhancing the OnObjectTimer method will let you delete objects and set the canShoot field of the game class to True, so the enemy plane can spawn bullets again.

# It is gone!—a transition is done

All particles are controlled by transitions. That is why you need to detail the OnObjectTransition method of the engine class.

## Time for action – detailing the OnObjectTransition method

Inside this method, we will only check for the transition ID, and if positive, we will delete the object.

Check whether the transition ID is equal to g.triDelete. If yes, then call the Remove method of the object.

```
Method OnObjectTransition:Int(transId:Int, obj:ftObject)

  If transId = g.triDelete Then obj.Remove()

  Return 0
End
```

## What just happened?

With this method, you can now use a single line, to automatically delete an object once its transition is done. We use it when a particle has faded out or reached its maximum scale factor.

# Controlling the player plane—acting on object update events

To control the player plane, you need to detail the OnObjectUpdate callback method of the engine class.

## Time for action – acting on object update events

In this method, we will check whether certain keys are hit on the keyboard. This is to turn the plane or change its speed. Also, we make sure that the player can shoot bullets himself and spawn some smoke if the planes are hit. And finally, we make the enemy plane follow the player.

**1.** Inside the `OnObjectUpdate` method, check whether the object is equal to `g.player`.

```
Method OnObjectUpdate:Int(obj:ftObject)

   If obj = g.player Then
```

**2.** If yes, set its basic speed to `8.0`.

```
obj.SetSpeed(8.0)
```

**3.** Check whether the *LEFT* arrow key is held down on the keyboard. If yes, turn the player plane to the left.

```
     If KeyDown(KEY_LEFT) Then obj.SetAngle(-g.eng.
GetDeltaTime()/16.0,True)
```

**4.** Check whether the *RIGHT* arrow key is held down. If yes, then turn the player plane to the right.

```
     If KeyDown(KEY_RIGHT) Then obj.SetAngle(g.eng.
GetDeltaTime()/16.0,True)
```

**5.** If the *UP* arrow key is held down, set the object's speed to `10`.

```
If KeyDown(KEY_UP) Then obj.SetSpeed(10.0)
```

**6.** Check whether the *DOWN* arrow key is held down. If yes, set the speed to `6.0`.

```
If KeyDown(KEY_DOWN) Then obj.SetSpeed(6.0)
```

**7.** If the *S* key is held down, then spawn a shot.

```
If KeyHit(KEY_S) Then g.SpawnShot(obj)
```

**8.** Now, check whether the number of hits on the player plane is greater than zero. If yes, spawn some smoke. Then close the IF check.

```
   If g.hits > 0 Then g.SpawnSmoke(obj, g.hits)
Endif
```

**9.** Next, check whether the object is equal to `g.enemy`.

```
If obj = g.enemy Then
```

**10.** Let the object (the enemy) follow the player plane.

```
FollowPlayer(obj)
```

**11.** Check whether the number of hits on the enemy plane is greater than zero. If yes, then spawn some smoke. Close the IF check.

```
    If g.hitsC > 0 Then g.SpawnSmoke(obj, g.hitsC)
  Endif

  Return 0
End
```

## What just happened?

Yes, we can finally control the player plane and the enemy plane will now follow the player plane and try to shoot at it. Build and run the game, and see for yourself.

## Hit it!—handling collision response

The initial collision check begins during the OnUpdate method of the game class. But, if a collision check is positive, the OnObjectCollision callback method is called. Here, you can handle the collision response.

## Time for action – detailing the collision response

During this method, we will add hit points, let the planes explode, and add scores.

**1.** Check whether the collision group of the first object is equal to g.grpShot.

```
Method OnObjectCollision:Int(obj:ftObject, obj2:ftObject)

If obj.GetColGroup()=g.grpShot Then
```

**2.** Play the sound effect of a plane being hit.

```
g.sndHit.Play()
```

**3.** Check if the second object is the player plane.

```
If obj2 = g.player Then
```

**4.** Add 1 to the player's hits field.

```
g.hits += 1
```

**5.** Check if it took five or more hits.

```
If g.hits >= 5 Then
```

**6.** Add 1 to the computer `score` field.

```
g.scoreC += 1
```

**7.** Play the explosion sound effect.

```
g.sndExplo.Play()
```

**8.** Spawn an explosion of 15 particles at the object's position.

```
g.SpawnExplosion(obj.GetPosX(), obj.GetPosY(),15)
```

**9.** Remove the second object (the player) and re-spawn the player. After that, close the last two IF checks.

```
    obj2.Remove()
      g.CreatePlayer()
    Endif
Endif
```

**10.** Now, check if the second object is equal to `g.enemy`.

```
If obj2 = g.enemy Then
```

**11.** Add 1 to the computers `hits` field.

```
g.hitsC += 1
```

**12.** Check if the enemy took five or more hits.

```
If g.hitsC >= 5 Then
```

**13.** If yes, raise the player score by 1 and play the explosion sound effect.

```
g.score += 1
g.sndExplo.Play()
```

**14.** Spawn an explosion of 15 particles at the object's position.

```
g.SpawnExplosion(obj.GetPosX(), obj.GetPosY(),15)
```

**15.** Remove the second object (the enemy) and re-spawn the enemy plane. After that, close the last two IF checks.

```
    obj2.Remove()
      g.CreateEnemy()
  Endif
Endif
```

**16.** Remove the bullet and close the initial IF check.

```
      obj.Remove()
   Endif

   Return 0
End
```

## What just happened?

Now that you have detailed the collision response, you can see that the bullets actually do something. Also you will see smoke appear if a plane gets hit, and after five hits, it will explode into pieces.

## Did I win?—layer update events

The last things you need to add are the winning conditions. After all, it is a game so it needs a goal.

## Time for action – acting of layer update events

A good place is the `OnLayerUpdate` callback method of the `engine` class. Check if one of the scores is 5 or bigger, and then set the game mode and also display a message.

**1.** Check if the `score` field of the game class is 5 or greater.

```
Method OnLayerUpdate:Int(layer:ftLayer)

   If g.score >= 5 Then
```

**2.** If yes, the player won. Activate the `g.txtYouWin` text object.

```
      g.txtYouWin.SetActive(True)
```

**3.** Set the game mode to `g.gmGameOver` and stop the engine sound effect.

```
      g.gameMode = g.gmGameOver
      g.sndEngine.Stop()
```

**4.** If the player score is lower than 5, check if the computer score is greater or equal to 5.

```
   Elseif g.scoreC >= 5 Then
```

**5.** If yes, the computer won. Display the **You Lose** message by activating the `g.txtYouLoose` object.

```
   g.txtYouLoose.SetActive(True)
```

6. Set the game mode to `g.gmGameOver`.

```
g.gameMode = g.gmGameOver
```

7. Stop the engine sound effect. Then close the initial IF check.

```
    g.sndEngine.Stop()
  Endif

  Return 0
End
```

## What just happened?

That is it. Using this method, we have set the winning conditions and when you build the game, you will have a playable full game. Have fun!

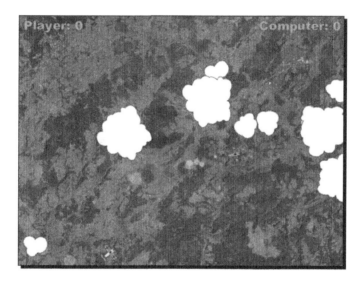

## Have a go hero—enhancing the game

Of course, this game can be enhanced. There is enough room for you to expand on. How about more than one enemy plane to fight with? How about different planes to choose from? How about enhancing the artificial intelligence of the enemy planes? Maybe the player plane can hide inside the clouds, and if he is covered by the clouds, the enemy plane will not turn towards the player. Or making the turn more random? Maybe you can let the enemy sometimes turn in the other direction instead of towards the player.

You see, there is enough room for expansion. Have fun and experiment with it. That is the most important thing in game development.

# Creating a GLFW app

Creating a GLFW app for Windows or OSX is pretty simple. Depending on the platform you develop on, you need to either install Visual C++ or XCode. Please follow the instructions in the *Getting started* section of the Monkey documentation. If everything was installed properly, you will see the GLFW target inside the **Build** dialog. Just pick that and Monk will create a GLFW application during the compiling process.

# Summary

In this chapter we have covered the following:

- How to give a computer-controlled object some kind of a brain. We have used a simple heading logic to let the enemy plane turn in the closest direction where the player plane is.

- Use of particles to simulate smoke that is emitted from a plane that was previously hit by a bullet. Also, showing an explosion when a plane was destroyed.

- Letting clouds float over the screen and wrap them at the edges of the visible area to the opposite site.

- How to create a GLFW app.

In the next chapter, we will create our last game together, **Treasure Chest**. Hopefully, you have enjoyed this chapter and will keep on reading till the end of the book.

# 9
# Game #8, Treasure Chest

*Wow! You've almost made it through this book. This is the last game we will develop together, and after we are done, you can proudly say that you have at least created eight games. That makes you definitely a game developer!*

*After all these action-packed games, it is time for another brain teaser. For this, we will create Game #8,* **Treasure Chest***. It is a game in the likeness of the famous* **Bejewled** *(http://en.wikipedia.org/wiki/Bejewled).*

*In Treasure Chest, you have to line up at least three gems with the same color in a row by switching pieces that lie next to each other. To do this, you click on the first gem with your mouse and then on a neighboring gem. The position of these two gems is exchanged. If their new position results in valid line ups, the game will allow the exchange and you will be rewarded with some points. Also, the gems will vanish and the empty space will be filled by the gems from above. Empty spaces on the top will be filled randomly with new gems.*

*In this chapter, you won't learn many new things. You will learn what a tile map is, but we will mostly include techniques we have learned in previous chapters. Take it as your final exam. If you manage to develop this game, you are ready to go and make lots of money! Or at least some great games! And that is what it is all about, right?*

Anyway, in this chapter we will cover the following:

- ◆ How to store a tile map
- ◆ Iterating through the tile map to find matching gems
- ◆ Dealing with 2D arrays
- ◆ Connecting the tile map to objects on the canvas

We will create an HTML5 game again, but you can definitely create one for GLFW, XNA, or the supported mobile platforms, too.

OK, it is time to get started. Let's go... one more time!

# Frameworks and modules used

Again, we will utilize the fantomEngine framework/module. It helps to shorten the code tremendously. Believe it or not, the code for this game would easily have spanned two chapters if we had not used a framework like this.

We need to use at least Version 1.40 of fantomEngine, and you can get the newest version at its website, `http://code.google.com/p/fantomengine`.

Please get familiar with its API, as this book does not explain the API in detail. It just shows you how to use it in Monkey.

# Reusing code

During this chapter, we will reuse some code from former chapters in one way or another. We have already written the code before, and there is no need to reinvent the wheel over and over again. For instance, you will also find an example in *Chapter 4*, *Game #3*, *CometCrusher*, on how to load and display the high score list.

# The parts of the game... resources

The game Treasure Chest will be made from the following resources:

- The sprite sheet that includes the images or the different gems, various particle images, a cell image for the map grid, and the gem selector graphic
- The bitmap font description file and its corresponding bitmap
- Sounds for an explosion, one for when you miss a matching line and one for when you select a button

> Hint: The sound format for Monkey and the HTML5 platform is the OGG sound format. The problem is that some of the popular browsers have problems playing back some sound formats. IE doesn't play WAV and OGG files. Firefox doesn't play MP3 and M4A. So, by using OGG you are covering most browsers today. Use a tool such as Audacity to convert sounds if you need to.

All these files are located inside the corresponding `treasurechest.data` folder in `chapter #9`.

# And here they are... the game objects!

The game will have the following objects:

- Layers
- A title screen
- A menu screen
- A game background
- Gems
- The gem selector
- Particle effects

## Layers

Just like before, layers will help us to organize other objects and just work on the ones we need at a certain state of the game. These layers will be used in the listed order:

- Background layer
- Game layer
- GFX layer
- Game over layer
- Menu layer
- Score layer
- Title layer

The background layer will hold some info text and the play field grid. The game layer will contain the various gems and the gem selector. The GFX layer holds the particle effects. To display the "Game Over" message, we will utilize the game over layer. To display the game menu, the menu layer will contain all the buttons to press. As we want to know which the highest score is, we need a score layer. And finally, the title layer will serve the purpose of displaying the game title.

# Our precious title screen

The title screen will be made of some text objects. One is prominently for the game title, and two are for the game's author and the version number of the game. We will let the title screen fade into the menu screen when you start the app.

# A menu screen

In previous games, we had made the title screen and the menu screen into one. Now that we have separated them, we have one text object for the title, and then three text buttons—one to start a new game, one for showing the high-score list, and one to exit the app.

# The "high-score" screen

Just like in *Game #4*, *Comet Crusher*, this game will feature the ability to store, save, load, and display a list of the ten highest scores reached in the game. It will be made up of several text objects and a text button to go back to the menu.

## A game background

The game background screen, which you will see when you actually play the game, displays multiple cell images that together display the map grid. Also, four text objects will be used to display the current score of the game and how much time is left.

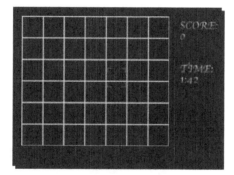

## The worthy gems

As this game is about a treasure chest, we are dealing with gems—lots of them, and different ones. Each type has a different color, so they are easier to identify.

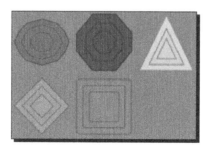

## The gem selector

To show that we have selected a tile, we have a selector image. It is basically a red frame that is displayed on top of the first selected gem of a pair.

## Particle effects

The sprite sheet contains several star-like images that we can use to display some particle effects when a matching line of tiles is removed from the map. It is eye candy, which every game should have.

# Preparation... the basic app and project structure

To prepare the project folder we will again utilize the base script from fantomEngine.

## Time for action – creating the basic file structure

To create the project folder for Treasure Chest, we have to do some things first:

1.  Create a folder called `treasurechest`, in a location you like.

2.  Next, open the `baseMonkey.script` file, from the resource files of the book for this chapter, and save it under the name `treasurechest.monkey` in the folder you created before.

3.  Copy the `treasurechest.data` folder from the chapter's data folder to your project folder.

## What just happened?

You have set up the project folder for the game. The file we will now work on is `treasurechest.monkey`.

# Creating 2D arrays

In this game, we want to store the tile map information inside a two-dimensional array. If you don't know what a 2D array is, imagine a table. The first dimension is represented by the rows and the second dimension by the columns. A 1D array is comparable with a table with just one column and several rows.

Here are two illustrations that show the difference:

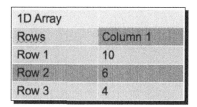

In the preceding image, you see an array with one dimension. It has just one column and the data is stored in a sequence, row after row. The following image shows an array with two dimensions. The difference here is that the second dimension is achieved by another column. You have two slots per row to store data. Actually, you will have as many slots per row as you define.

| 2D Array | | |
|---|---|---|
| Rows | Column 1 | Column 2 |
| Row 1 | 1 | 5 |
| Row 2 | 0 | 0 |
| Row 3 | 4 | 3 |

To access an array, here are small examples:

```
Print (my1Darray[2])    'With the array above, this will print 4
Print (my2Darray[0][1])   'With the array above, this will print 5
```

> Hint: Arrays in Monkey are zero-based. This means that the first index of a dimension is 0. A dimension defined with 10 elements has indices ranging from 0 to 9.

## Time for action – creating 2D arrays

Creating arrays with more than one dimension in Monkey is a little tricky. We can create a function that lets us set up a 2D array, using the following steps:

1. Add the function `Create2DArray` to the `treasurechest.monkey` file. Its parameters are the number of cells required for both the dimensions. The return type is a 2D array of the type INT.

   ```
   Function Create2DArray:Int[][]( columns:Int, rows:Int)
   ```

2. Define a local two-dimensional array of the type INT, initialized in the first dimension.

   ```
   Local a:Int[][] = New Int[columns][]
   ```

3. Start a FOR loop ranging from 0 to `columns`.

   ```
   For Local c:Int = 0 Until columns
   ```

4. Define a new array of rows in each column.

   ```
   a[c] = New Int[rows]
   ```

5. Close the FOR loop, return the array, and close the function.

   ```
      Next
      Return a
   End
   ```

## What just happened?

You have just created a function that will let you set up a 2D array in Monkey. It is reusable for other games that you will create in the future.

# Storing information... the data storage

In every game, you most definitely need to store data, be it the state of the game, the score, the number of enemies, and much more.

# Time for action – creating the data structure

To store data in Treasure chest, we will add some fields to the `game` class.

**1.** First, start with two FLOAT variables, which will hold the size of the canvas.

```
Class game Extends App
  Field eng:engine
  Field isSuspended:Bool = False

  Field cw:Float
  Field ch:Float
```

**2.** Next, add a field to store the mode of the game. Initialize it with a constant, which we will define shortly.

```
Field gameMode:Int = gmTitle
```

**3.** During the game, we need to measure how much time is left. For this, we need a field for minutes and one for seconds.

```
Field minutes:Int
Field seconds:Int
```

**4.** When a game begins, we need to store the time in milliseconds, to check when it will end.

```
Field endTime:Int
```

**5.** Add a field for the game score.

```
Field score:Int = 0
```

**6.** The time for one round will be stored as well. It is initialized to `2000` milliseconds. This makes it easy for testing.

```
Field gameTime:Int = (1000*60*2)
```

**7.** Next, add two fields to define the size of our game grid.

```
Field rows:Int = 6
Field columns:Int = 7
```

**8.** To store the grid, we need a two-dimensional array. It will be initialized later.

```
Field tileMap:Int[][]
```

**9.** We need to store the first and second selected gem during gameplay.

```
Field firstTile:ftObject=Null
Field secondTile:ftObject=Null
```

**10.** The gem selector graphic will be another object.

```
Field selector:ftObject=Null
```

**11.** For the first frame of a new game, when the grid has just been filled with gems, we need to have a starting Boolean field.

```
Field justStarted:Bool=False
```

**12.** Now, add a field to store the sprite sheet (`atlas`).

```
Field atlas:Image
```

**13.** Add another field for the game font.

```
Field font1:ftFont
```

**14.** To display some text information (the score, the time left, and the final score of one round of play), we need three fields.

```
Field txtScore:ftObject
Field txtTime:ftObject
Field txtFinalScore:ftObject
```

**15.** To display the high-score list, we need an array of `10` objects. Each one reassembles one entry in the list.

```
Field txtHighScore:ftObject[10]
```

**16.** As we want to play back some sound effects, add fields for three sounds.

```
Field sndSelect:ftSound
Field sndExplo:ftSound
Field sndFalse:ftSound
```

**17.** Now, add the game layers.

```
Field layerBackground:ftLayer
Field layerGame:ftLayer
Field layerGFX:ftLayer
Field layerGameOver:ftLayer
Field layerMenu:ftLayer
Field layerScore:ftLayer
Field layerTitle:ftLayer
```

Those were all the fields we need. Now, let's add some constants.

**18.** To control the game, add constants for the various game modes.

```
Const gmTitle:Int = 1
Const gmMenu:Int = 2
Const gmPlay:Int = 4
Const gmGameOver:Int = 5
Const gmScore:Int = 7
```

**19.** In the menu, and in the high-score list screen, we have buttons that can be pressed. To identify them, we need some more constants.

```
Const btnPlay:Int = 11
Const btnScore:Int = 12
Const btnExit:Int = 13
Const btnBack:Int = 14
```

**20.** At some point, we will delete some objects though fantomEngine's timer feature. We need an ID for this.

```
Const triDelete:Int = 21
```

**21.** Of course, we will use some transitions too, so add more constants for showing the menu and removing objects after a transition is finished.

```
Const tmShowMenu:Int = 31
Const tmObjRemove:Int = 32
```

**22.** Finally, add some constants that will store the name of the game, the author, and the version number.

```
Const strTitle:String = "Treasure Chest"
Const strVersion:String = "1.0"
Const strAuthor:String = "YOU"

Method OnCreate:Int()
```

## What just happened?

Phew! A lot of fields and quite a few constants! This is the biggest game in the book and you can see that in the data definition that we just created too.

# First changes to the OnCreate event

To prepare the game for further development, let's modify the OnCreate event the first time (like we always do).

## Time for action – first changes to the OnCreate method

***1.*** First store the size of the canvas in the fields `cw` and `ch`.

```
Method OnCreate:Int()
  SetUpdateRate(60)
  eng = New engine

  cw = eng.canvasWidth
  ch = eng.canvasHeight
```

***2.*** Now, load the sprite sheet.

```
atlas = LoadImage("ts_Tiles.png")
```

***3.*** Then, load the game font file.

```
font1 = eng.LoadFont("ts_font")
```

***4.*** Next, set up the array to store the game grid.

```
    tileMap = Create2DArray(columns,rows)

    Return 0
End
```

### What just happened?

Besides setting up the array, this was business as usual.

# About the OnRender event

If you're wondering whether you need to modify the `OnRender` event, you will be happy to see that you don't need to. It is fine, as it was already defined inside the `baseScript.monkey` file.

# Setting up the game objects

What's next? Let us create some methods that will help us to create the various objects in this game.

## Klick, bang, swoosh... the sound effects!

For Treasure Chest, you will want to add some sound effects too. You will have a sound when you select a menu item, an explosion when gems are removed from the game, and a sound that tells the player that the selected gems don't match.

## Time for action – loading the game sound effects

**1.** Inside the game class, add a new method called LoadSounds.

```
Method LoadSounds:Int()
```

**2.** Load the select, explosion, and false sounds. Then, close the method.

```
    sndSelect = eng.LoadSound("select")
    sndExplo = eng.LoadSound("explosion")
    sndFalse = eng.LoadSound("false")
    Return 0
End
```

## What just happened?

You can now load all the sounds you need in one call, using this method that you just created. If you need more sounds, just add them here. Don't forget to to define a field for any additional sound in the data section.

## Lay your head on me.... the game layers

The whole game user interface is set up in layers. Think about them like very thin sheets of paper that are see-through.

## Time for action – creating layers for the game

To set up the layers, you need to add another method.

**1.** Add the method CreateLayers into the game class.

```
Method CreateLayers:Int()
```

**2.** Store the default layer in the layerBackground field.

```
layerBackground = eng.GetDefaultLayer()
```

**3.** Then, create new layers for all the ones we have defined in the data class.

```
layerGame = eng.CreateLayer()
layerGFX = eng.CreateLayer()
layerGameOver = eng.CreateLayer()
layerMenu = eng.CreateLayer()
layerScore = eng.CreateLayer()
layerTitle = eng.CreateLayer()
```

**4.** Close the method.

```
    Return 0
End
```

## What just happened?

Again, we have implemented a method to create all the layers we need in the game.

# Our beloved play field—the background screen

Now, we will define all the elements of the background screen.

## Time for action – composing the background screen

In the background screen, you will see a grid for all the gems. On the right side of the grid, you will also see the current score displayed, along with the time which is remaining to play this game.

**1.** Insert a new method called `CreateBackgroundScreen` into the game class.

```
Method CreateBackgroundScreen:Int ()
```

**2.** Set the default layer for this method.

```
eng.SetDefaultLayer(layerBackground )
```

**3.** Start two new FOR loops—one for the rows ($x$) and one for the columns ($y$).

```
For Local y:Int = 1 To rows
  For Local x:Int = 1 To columns
```

In the next few pages, you will see the integer value 64 used many times. It is the length of the edge of all sprites that we will load.

**4.** Now, load the grid sprite from the atlas image. The position will be set depending on the $x$ and $y$ values. Close both FOR loops.

```
    Local obj := eng.CreateImage(atlas,0,0,64,64,x*64,y*64)
  Next
Next
```

**5.** Next, add two text objects. One for the score and one for the time.

```
Local tx1 := eng.CreateText(font1,"SCORE:",(columns+1)*64,32)
Local tx2 := eng.CreateText(font1,"TIME:",(columns+1)*64,160)
```

**6.** To display the actual score and time values, we need to add two more text objects, which will be set later in the game, at each frame. After that, close the method.

```
txtScore = eng.CreateText(font1,score,(columns+1)*64,64)
txtTime = eng.CreateText(font1,0,(columns+1)*64,192)
Return 0
End
```

## What just happened?

Another element of the the game is now ready to be created—the background layer. Once you call the method you have just implemented, it will create the background screen for you.

## Give it a name… the title screen

Like all good games, we have a title screen to show too. Again, it's made just of text, but you could easily display an image, too.

## Time for action – creating the title screen

Inside the next method, we will set up the title screen. A colored box, a few text objects, and a timer that will switch the screen automatically to the menu screen, are all we need.

**1.** Add the method `CreateTitleScreen` to the `game` class.

```
Method CreateTitleScreen:Int()
```

**2.** Set the default layer to `layerTitle`.

```
eng.SetDefaultLayer(layerTitle)
```

**3.** Create a dark gray box that is the size of the canvas.

```
Local box := eng.CreateBox(cw,ch,cw/2,ch/2)
box.SetColor(55,55,55)
```

**4.** Add text objects to display the title of the game, its author, and the version number. The title will be scaled by a factor of `2.0`.

```
Local t1 := eng.CreateText(font1, strTitle, cw/2, ch/2-100, 3)
t1.SetScale(2.0)
Local t2 := eng.CreateText(font1, "by "+strAuthor, cw/2, ch/2, 3)
Local t3 := eng.CreateText(font1, "Version "+strVersion, cw/2,
ch/2+50, 3)
```

**5.** To switch the screen automatically to the menu screen, we need to start an object timer. It will be attached to the box object, with the `tmShowMenu` ID and a time value of `3000` milliseconds. After setting it, close the method.

```
eng.CreateObjTimer(b,tmShowMenu,3000)
Return 0
End
```

## What just happened?

You have created a method that will set up the title screen. Because of the timer that is added, it will (once we have added more code later on) switch to the menu screen automatically. The title screen will look like the following screenshot in this game:

## Game over... creating the "game over" screen

At one point of the game, when the time that was allowed is over, it should inform the player that the game is over. Let's create a method for this.

## Time for action – creating the "game over" screen

In the next method, a screen will be created and will display **Game Over** and the score that the player had reached.

**1.** Insert the method `CreateGameOverScreen` into the `game` class.

```
Method CreateGameOverScreen:Int ()
```

**2.** Set the default layer to `layerGameOver`.

```
eng.SetDefaultLayer(layerGameOver)
```

**3.** Create a blue box.

```
Local b := eng.CreateBox(cw/1.5,ch/4,cw/2,ch/2)
b.SetColor(0,0,255)
```

**4.** Add a text object that will display the text GAME OVER.

```
Local tx1 := eng.CreateText(font1,"**** GAME OVER
****",cw/2,ch/2-30,3)
```

**5.** To display the score, add another text object (txtFinalScore).

```
  txtFinalScore = eng.CreateText(font1,"SCORE:
000000",cw/2,ch/2+30,3)
  Return 0
End
```

## What just happened?

When this method is called later on, it will inform the player that the game has ended and show them the score they have attained.

# The menu please... creating the menu screen

Our menu screen that we want to add is made from text buttons. A text button is a text object that has its touch mode activated and a tag set to a given ID constant.

## Buttons ... I need more text buttons!

To set up text buttons easily, we have created a method in *Chapter 4, Game #3, CometCrusher*.

## Time for action – creating text buttons

To create text buttons, we will reuse some code that we have created in a previous chapter.

Copy the CreateTextButton method from *Chapter 4, Game #3, CometCrusher*, into the game class.

```
Method CreateTextButton:ftObject (font:ftFont, txt:String, xp:Int,
yp:Int, id:Int, layer:ftLayer)
  Local but:ftObject = eng.CreateText(font,txt,xp,yp,1)
  but.SetTag(id)
  but.SetTouchMode(2)
  but.SetLayer(layer)
  Return but
End
```

## *What just happened?*

Reusing code is a good thing. Why reinvent the wheel several times. That is why we use the fantomEngine framework in the first place, isn't it?

## The menu screen

Now that we have a method to create text buttons, we can define the menu screen.

## Time for action – creating the menu screen

In the menu screen we create, the game title will also be displayed at the top.

**1.** Insert a new method called CreateMenuScreen into the game class.

```
Method CreateMenuScreen:Int()
```

**2.** Set the the default layer to layerMenu.

```
eng.SetDefaultLayer(layerMenu)
```

**3.** Add a dark-gray-colored box that covers the whole canvas.

```
Local b := eng.CreateBox(cw,ch,cw/2,ch/2)
b.SetColor(55,55,55)
```

**4.** Now, add a text object that will display the game title and scale it by a factor of 2.

```
Local t1 := eng.CreateText(font1, strTitle, cw/2, ch/2-100, 3)
t1.SetScale(2.0)
```

**5.** Now, add three text buttons. We need the buttons Play, Score, and Exit.

```
    Local bt1 := CreateTextButton(font1, "Play", cw/2, (ch/9)*4,
btnPlay, layerMenu)
    Local bt3 := CreateTextButton(font1, "Score", cw/2, (ch/9)*5,
btnScore, layerMenu)
    Local bt6 := CreateTextButton(font1, "Exit", cw/2, (ch/9)*7,
btnExit, layerMenu)
Close of this method.
    Return 0
  End
```

## *What just happened?*

To set up the menu screen, you just need to call the method once in the `OnCreate` event of the game. If you need more menu entries, just add them here. The menu screen will look like the following screenshot of the game:

## What is the score?... creating the high-score screen

What is a good game without the ability to display the highest scores you have reached while playing. For this, we will implement a screen that displays the high scores.

## Time for action – creating the score screen

To display the values of the highest scores, we will utilize the `CreateHighScoreList` method from *Chapter 4, Game #3, CometCrusher*, and make a few changes to it.

**1.** For this, add a method called `CreateScoreScreen` to the `game` class.

```
Method CreateScoreScreen:Int()
```

**2.** Set the score layer as the default layer.

```
eng.SetDefaultLayer(layerScore)
```

**3.** Create a local text object to display the headline.

```
Local txtTitleHightScore:ftObject = eng.CreateText(font1,"H I G H
S C O R E S",cw/2,70.0,1)
```

**4.** Start a FOR loop ranging from `1` to `10`. This will be the factor that controls vertical placement of the list entries.

```
For Local y:Int = 1 To 10
```

**5.** Next, create a local text object that will display the entry number.

```
Local txtScoreNum:ftObject = eng.CreateText(font1,"#"+y,(
cw/4.0)+50.0,80.0 + (ch/20.0)*y)
```

**6.** To display each entry of the list, create text objects that will be stored inside the text array we have defined at the beginning. Then close the FOR loop.

```
txtHighScore[y-1] = eng.CreateText(font1,"0000000",(
cw/4.0)*3.0-50.0,80.0 + (ch/20.0)*y,2)
Next
```

When the list is displayed, you want to provide a button for the user to use to go back to the menu.

**7.** Insert a local text button set with the ID btnBack. Then, close the method.

```
Local bt := CreateTextButton(font1, "Back", cw/2, ch-font1.
Height(), btnBack, layerScore)
Return 0
End
```

## What just happened?

With the last method, you can now create a high-score screen in your game.

## Layer activation

In contrast to the games before, we have a few more layers. To switch every layer off and on each time you need to, it is better to create one method or function that does the dirty job for you.

## Time for action – creating the activate layer method

The next method will activate/deactivate layers, depending on the game mode we give in as the parameter.

**1.** Add a new method called ActivateLayer to the game class. As a parameter, it will take the game mode as an INT value.

```
Method ActivateLayer:Int(mode:Int)
Deactivate ALL layers.
layerBackground.SetActive(False)
layerGame.SetActive(False)
layerGFX.SetActive(False)
layerGameOver.SetActive(False)
layerMenu.SetActive(False)
```

```
layerScore.SetActive(False)
layerTitle.SetActive(False)
```

2. Start a `Select` statement with the variable `mode` as the expression.

```
Select mode
```

3. Check against the `gmPlay` constant. If it's true, activate the background, game, and GFX layers.

```
Case gmPlay
  layerBackground.SetActive(True)
  layerGame.SetActive(True)
  layerGFX.SetActive(True)
```

4. Check against the `gmGameOver` constant. If it's true, activate the background, game, GFX, and the `GameOver` layers.

```
Case gmGameOver
  layerBackground.SetActive(True)
  layerGame.SetActive(True)
  layerGFX.SetActive(True)
  layerGameOver.SetActive(True)
```

5. If the check against the `gmMenu` constant is true, activate the menu layer.

```
Case gmMenu
  layerMenu.SetActive(True)
```

6. Check against the `gmScore` constant and activate the score layer if it's true.

```
Case gmScore
  layerScore.SetActive(True)
```

7. And last but not least, check against the `gmTitle` constant. Again, if it's true, activate the title layer.

```
Case gmTitle
  layerTitle.SetActive(True)
```

8. Close the `Select` statement and the method.

```
  End
  Return 0
End
```

## *What just happened?*

You have created a method that lets you switch layers, depending on the game mode. If you need to add more layers, then don't forget to add a switch for them here, too.

# Finalizing the OnCreate event

We now have methods to create all the static objects of the game. For the dynamic objects, we will have more code to implement, but for now we can finalize the OnCreate method.

## Time for action – finalizing the OnCreate method

The OnCreate method in the game class is the place where all static objects are defined.

1. Inside the OnCreate method of the game class, add calls to the methods you have created previously.

```
font1 = eng.LoadFont("ts_font")
tileMap = Create2DArray(columns,rows)

LoadSounds()
CreateLayers()
CreateBackgroundScreen()
CreateGameOverScreen()
CreateMenuScreen()
CreateScoreScreen()
CreateTitleScreen()
```

2. To display the title screen later on, set the game mode to gmTitle, and active the layers with this mode.

```
    gameMode = gmTitle
    ActivateLayer(gameMode)

    Return 0
End
```

## *What just happened?*

In the OnCreate method, you have added the calls to other methods that will set up all the static objects we need for the game, such as sounds, layers, text objects, buttons, and so on.

If you build and run the game now, you should just see the title screen in its full glory. The switch to the menu screen will be implemented in the engine class, later on.

# Dealing with the high-score list

We have a nice feature in the game, the high-score list. Let's see how we can manage it.

## Loading and saving the list

You have created the high-score screen just recently. So, how do you actually load and save this list, so that it can show the game results over time? Here again, we will make use of code from *Chapter 4, Game #3, CometCrusher*. These two methods are just copied over.

To load/save a high-score list, we will load/save the state of the game.

## Time for action – loading and saving the high-score list

To load and save the state of a game, and so the high-score list, just copy some code from the game CometCrusher.

> **1.** Copy the following code from the LoadHighScore method of *Chapter 4, Game #3, CometCrusher*.
>
> ```
> Method LoadHighScore:Int ()
>   Local state:String = LoadState()
>   If state Then
>     eng.scoreList.LoadFromString(state)
>   Endif
>   Return 0
> End
> ```
>
> **2.** Again, copy the following code from the SaveHighScore method from *Chapter 4, Game #3, CometCrusher*.
>
> ```
> Method SaveHighScore:Int ()
>   Local hs:String = g.eng.scoreList.SaveToString()
>   SaveState(hs)
>   Return 0
> End
> ```

## *What just happened?*

By reusing these two methods, you have saved yourself some valuable time for the future development of this game. It seems small, but when you reuse more and more, the advantage becomes visible.

# Showing the high-score screen

When the player wants to see the high-score screen, the game needs to display the score layer with an updated score list.

## Time for action – showing the high-score list

For this, you need to add a method that will update the list and then show the layer.

**1.** Insert the method ShowScore into the game class.

```
Method ShowScore:Int()
```

**2.** To load the high-score list, make a call to fantomEngine's LoadHighScore method.

```
LoadHighScore()
```

**3.** Start a FOR loop ranging from 1 to the count of score list entries.

```
For Local y:Int = 1 To eng.scoreList.Count()
```

**4.** Set the text for each index in the high-score text object array with the value of the high-score list entry. Then, close the FOR loop.

```
    txtHighScore[y-1].SetText(eng.scoreList.GetValue(y))
Next
```

**5.** Set the game mode to gmScore and activate layers with it using our ActiveLayer method. After this, close the method.

```
    gameMode = gmScore
    ActivateLayer(gameMode)
    Return 0
End
```

## What just happened?

Within the method that you just added, you loaded the high-score list from the game state, filled the value of the list entries into the corresponding text area object, and activated the actual score layer. Later, when you show the high-score list, it will look like the following:

# Managing the tile map

The most prominent part of Treasure Chest is the tile map. In the game, the map is build out of an array that stores the type of gem and image objects that represent the visible part of the game. For sure, it could be handled differently, but we will take this route for now.

## Getting tile map slot IDs

Let's start with two methods that will determine the slot positions of a corresponding gem image object. Remember, its position has to be divided by its width to get the slot position.

## Time for action – getting tile slot IDs

To get tile slot IDs we will create the GetSlotX And GetSlotY methods, as follows:

1.  First add the method `GetSlotX` into the game class with a parameter of the type `ftObject`.

    ```
    Method GetSlotX:Int(obj:ftObject)
    ```

2.  Store the `x` position of the object. It is divided by its width and stored in the local variable `xp` with the type INT.

    ```
    Local xp:Int = obj.GetPosX()/obj.GetWidth()
    ```

3.  Return `xp` and close the method.

    ```
      Return xp
    End
    ```

4.  Next, add the method `GetSlotY` to the `game` class.

    ```
    Method GetSlotY:Int(obj:ftObject)
    ```

5. Store the y position of the object. It is divided by its width and stored in the local variable yp with the type INT.

```
Local yp:Int = obj.GetPosY()/obj.GetHeight()
```

6. Return yp and close this method.

```
   Return yp
End
```

## What just happened?

The two methods that you have added will let you determine the slot positions of a gem inside the tile map.

## Setting tile map slot IDs

To simply set the gem IDs inside the tile map, we will create another method.

## Time for action – setting a tile slot ID

This method will take the slot positions and the gem ID and fill the tile map accordingly.

1. Insert the method SetSlotTile into the game class. The parameters are column, row, and the gem ID. All are of the type INT.

```
Method SetSlotTile:Int(column:Int, row:Int, gem:Int)
```

2. Set the tile map according to the given parameters. Then, close the method.

```
   tileMap[column-1][row-1] = gem
   Return 0
End
```

## What just happened?

The last method allows you to set the slot ID of a tile/gem in the map easily.

## Check/mark the neighboring tiles

Whenever you place or move gems, you need to check if you are allowed to. When you start a new game, you don't want to place a gem when there are already two of the same type next to that new gem. When you move one gem, you only want to allow it if there are two or more of the same type of gem next to it. That is why you need a method that can count them and maybe mark them for further usage

# Time for action – checking neighboring horizontal tiles

We will create two methods for checking the neighboring tiles, as we need to do this for each axis ($x$ and $y$), separately.

**1.** Inside the game class, add a new method called CheckGemsX. As parameters, it will take the column and row, the gem type, and a mark flag.

```
Method CheckGemsX:Int(column:Int, row:Int, gem:Int, mark:Bool = False)
```

**2.** First, add a local found variable of the type INT. It will be set once we find similar gems.

```
Local found:Int = 0
```

**3.** Initialize the slot.

```
tileMap[column-1][row-1] = -1
```

**4.** Check if column is greater than 1. It means there must be gems on the left.

```
If column > 1 Then
```

**5.** Start a FOR loop, stepping backwards from column -1 to the first gem on the left.

```
For Local c:Int = (column-1) To 1 Step -1
```

**6.** If the gem found isn't the same, exit the FOR loop.

```
If tileMap[c-1][row-1] <> gem Then Exit
```

**7.** If the mark flag was set, fill the value 99 into the tile slot. It is used if we want to mark tiles to delete them later.

```
If mark Then
  tileMap[c-1][row-1] = 99
Else
```

**8.** If the flag isn't set, just count the gems by raising found by 1.

```
  found += 1
Endif
```

**9.** Close the FOR loop, and the first IF check.

```
  Next
Endif
```

**10.** Now to the gems on the right. First, check if `column` isn't greater than the field `columns` of the `game` class.

```
If column < columns Then
```

**11.** Next start a FOR loop, ranging from `column+1` to `columns`

```
For Local c:Int = (column+1) To columns
```

**12.** Check if the found gem is the same. If not, exit the FOR loop.

```
If tileMap[c-1][row-1] <> gem Then Exit
```

**13.** If the `mark` flag is set, fill the value `99` into the slot.

```
If mark Then
   tileMap[c-1][row-1] = 99
Else
```

**14.** If not, raise `found` by `1`.

```
   found += 1
Endif
```

**15.** Close the FOR loop and the IF check.

```
   Next
Endif
```

**16.** If the `mark` flag was set, fill the value `99` into the slot of the actual gem, too. You want to delete it also, not only the neighboring tiles.

```
If mark Then
   tileMap[column-1][row-1] = 99
Else
```

**17.** If not, restore the slot with the `gem` parameter.

```
   tileMap[column-1][row-1] = gem
Endif
```

**18.** Return the number of gems we have found, and then close the method.

```
   Return found
End
```

# Time for action – check neighboring vertical tiles

To check the gems vertically, we will use a very similar method.

1.  Just copy the previous method and make the changes according to the marked lines.

```
Method CheckGemsY:Int(column:Int, row:Int, gem:Int,
mark:Bool=False)
  Local found:Int = 0
  tileMap[column-1][row-1] = -1
  'Check gems on the top
  If row > 1 Then
    For Local r:Int = (row-1) To 1 Step -1
      If tileMap[column-1][r-1] <> gem Then Exit
      If mark Then
        tileMap[column-1][r-1] = 99
      Else
        found += 1
      Endif
    Next
  Endif
  'Check gems on the bottom
  If row < rows Then
    For Local r:Int = (row+1) To rows
      If tileMap[column-1][r-1] <> gem Then Exit
      If mark Then
        tileMap[column-1][r-1] = 99
      Else
        found += 1
      Endif
    Next
  Endif
  If mark Then
    tileMap[column-1][row-1] = 99
  Else
    tileMap[column-1][row-1] = gem
  Endif
  Return found
End
```

## What just happened?

You have created two methods that let you count and mark neighboring tiles/gems. We need these to determine the gems that are matching up in a row or column. Marked gems will be removed later on.

## Clearing tiles

Another method we need is one that will delete all the gems that were marked earlier by the two preceding methods we have added.

## Time for action – clearing the tile map

The following method will search through the tile map. If a slot is filled with the value 99 that means the corresponding tile needs to be deleted.

**1.** Insert a method header named `ClearGems` into the `game` class.

```
Method ClearGems:Int()
```

**2.** Start two FOR loops, one for the rows and one for the columns.

```
For Local r:Int = 1 To rows
  For Local c:Int = 1 To columns
```

**3.** Check if the tile map contains the value 99.

```
If tileMap[c-1][r-1] = 99 Then
```

**4.** If yes, initialize the slot.

```
tileMap[c-1][r-1] = -1
```

**5.** Next, perform a touch check. The current number of columns and rows has each to be multiplied by 64 (the image width). The ID is set to 99.

```
layerGame.TouchCheck(c*64.0, r*64.0, 99)
```

I'm sure you wondering why we use a touch check. Later, in the `engine` class, we will check inside the `OnObjectTouch` method for this ID and then remove the object.

**6.** Close the IF check, both FOR loops, and the method.

```
      Endif
    Next
  Next
  Return 0
End
```

# *What just happened?*

You have created a method that will look through the tile map and initialize all slots that need to be deleted and also will take care that the corresponding gem image object will be removed later.

## Counting matching tiles

The next method will be used when two tiles are selected and you need to find out if they can be switched. For this, we need to know how many tiles are the same when both tiles are in their new positions.

## Time for action – counting matching tiles

To count the matching tiles, follow the ensuing steps:

1.  Add the method CountGems into the game class. The parameters are the first and second object.

    ```
    Method CountGems:Int(obj1:ftObject, obj2:ftObject)
    ```

2.  Define four local INT variables that store the x and y positions of the objects.

    ```
    Local x1:Int
    Local y1:Int
    Local x2:Int
    Local y2:Int
    ```

3.  Now define four INT variables that store the number of gems that were found.

    ```
    Local gemCountX1:Int
    Local gemCountY1:Int
    Local gemCountX2:Int
    Local gemCountY2:Int
    ```

4.  Get the slot positions of both objects.

    ```
    x1 = GetSlotX(obj1)
    y1 = GetSlotX(obj1)
    x2 = GetSlotX(obj2)
    y2 = GetSlotY(obj2)
    ```

5.  Retrieve the gem count of the first object. The position is the one of the second object, as that is where the first object is to be moved.

    ```
    gemCountX1 = CheckGemsX(x2, y2, obj1.GetTag())
    gemCountY1 = CheckGemsY(x2, y2, obj1.GetTag())
    ```

**6.** Do the opposite for the second object.

```
gemCountX2 = CheckGemsX(x1, y1, obj2.GetTag())
gemCountY2 = CheckGemsY(x1, y1, obj2.GetTag())
```

**7.** Return the higher of these values.

```
    Return Max(Max(gemCountX1, gemCountY1),Max(gemCountX2,
gemcountY2))
End
```

## What just happened?

The method `CountGems` will let you determine how many matching gems there would be, if two objects switched their locations. We will make use of this data in the `OnObjectTouch` event from the `engine` class.

## The precious one... creating a gem

If gems are deleted, it is only natural to create new ones, in a game like Treasure Chest. For this, we will create a new method.

## Time for action – creating a gem

This method will create the corresponding image object, set the collision properties for the touch check, and return the object.

**1.** Add the method `CreateTile` to the `game` class. The parameters are the x and y coordinates of the image object and its tile ID.

```
Method CreateTile:ftObject(x:Int, y:Int, tile:Int = -100)
```

**2.** Define a local object of the type `ftObject`.

```
Local obj:ftObject
```

**3.** If `tile` is set to `-100`, determine a random value ranging from 0 to 6.

```
If tile = -100 Then tile = Rnd(6)
```

**4.** Set the game layer as the default layer.

```
eng.SetDefaultLayer(layerGame)
```

We have six gem images on the sprite sheet. The `tile` parameter will not only set the object's tag property, but will also set the sprite coordinates.

**5.** If `tile` equals 6, top it to 5.

```
If tile = 6 Then tile = 5
```

**6.** Depending on the `tile` parameter, create an image object from the sprite atlas.

```
If tile < 4 Then
   obj=eng.CreateImage(atlas,tile*64,64,64,64,x*64,y*64)
Elseif tile = 4
   obj=eng.CreateImage(atlas,0,128,64,64,x*64,y*64)
Else
   obj=eng.CreateImage(atlas,64,128,64,64,x*64,y*64)
Endif
```

**7.** Set the object's tag value, the collision radius, and the touch mode to `circle`. Then, close the method.

```
   obj.SetTag(tile)
   obj.SetRadius(30)
   obj.SetTouchMode(2)
   Return obj
End
```

## What just happened?

You have created a method that will create a gem sprite for you. If you add more types of gems, then this method has to be modified.

## Refilling the tile map

Once gems are removed from the grid, you need to fill it up with new gems. These gems will fall from the top of the grid. The grid will be checked for empty slots (ID = -1) from the bottom to the top, and from left to right, in each row. Once an empty slot is found in a row, the method will either find a gem that can fall down or create a new one.

## Time for action – refilling the tile map

**1.** Create a new method called `FillTiles` inside the `game` class.

```
Method FillTiles:Int()
```

**2.** Add two local variables with the type BOOL. They will be used to determine if a row was filled.

```
Local filled:Bool = False
Local filled2:Bool = False
```

**3.** Start two FOR loops for the rows and the columns.

```
For Local r:Int = rows To 1 Step -1
  For Local c:Int = columns To 1 Step -1
```

**4.** Set `filled2` to `False` and check if the tile map is in the initial position (= -1).

```
filled2 = False
If tileMap[c-1][r-1] = -1 Then
```

**5.** If yes, then check if the current row is not the top one.

```
If r > 1 Then
```

**6.** If yes, start another FOR loop going backwards to create a temporary row ranging from the *current row minus one* to *one* (the top row).

```
For Local r2:Int = r-1 To 1 Step -1
```

**7.** Get the current object with a new method of the fantomEngine, called `GetObjAt`.

```
Local obj:ftObject = layerGame.GetObjAt(c*64, r2*64)
```

**8.** If an object was found, check if it is not in transition.

```
If obj <> Null And obj.GetTransitionCount()=0 Then
```

**9.** If it isn't, set `filled` with `True`, as we've now found a gem that needs to be moved to our empty slot.

```
filled = True
```

**10.** Initialize the corresponding slot tile ID of the gem that was found.

```
g.SetSlotTile(g.GetSlotX(obj), g.GetSlotY(obj),-1)
```

**11.** Create a position transition with the current column and row as target. The transition ID is set to 99.

```
obj.CreateTransPos(c*64.0,r*64.0,300,False, 99)
```

**12.** Set `filled2` to `True` and exit the method. Close the IF check and the FOR loop.

```
    filled2 = True
    Exit
    Endif
Next
```

**13.** If `filled2` is `False`, then no gem was found above. Set `filled` to `True`.

```
If filled2 = False Then
  filled = True
```

**14.** Add a new gem tile with the method `CreateTile`.

```
Local newObj:=CreateTile(x,0)
```

**15.** Create a position transition for this new tile, and then close the IF check.

```
  newObj.CreateTransPos(c*64.0,r*64.0,300,False, 99)
Endif
```

**16.** If we are actually in row `1`, then set `filled` to `True` and directly add a new gem tile.

```
Else
  filled = True
  Local newObj:=CreateTile(c,0)
```

**17.** Again, create a position transition for this new gem.

```
newObj.CreateTransPos(c*64.0,1*64.0,300,False,99)
```

**18.** Close the last two IF checks and the FOR loop.

```
    Endif
  Endif
Next
```

**19.** If `filled` is set to `True`, then exit the method.

```
If filled = True Then Exit
```

**20.** Close the top FOR loop and close the method.

```
  Next
  Return 0
End
```

## What just happened?

Wow, what a method! But it will do the dirty job of iterating through the tile map and filling it with new tiles.

# Methods for the update process

Now that we have the methods that manage the tile map, we can think about detailing the `OnUpdate` event of the game class. For this, we need some more methods that will help us during this state of the game.

# Starting a new game

It is always good practice to have the start of a new game or level done by a function or method. Sometimes, a lot of variables have to be set, and so let us do that here too.

## Time for action – creating a StartNewGame method

This method will do various things, from cleaning up the layers to initializing the tile map to setting the end time.

1.  Start a new method called `StartNewGame`, inside the `game` class.

    ```
    Method StartNewGame:Int()
    ```

2.  Define a local `tile` variable with the type INT.

    ```
    Local tile:Int = 0
    ```

3.  Seed the random number generator with the current value of `Millisecs` and set the game score to `0`.

    ```
    Seed = Millisecs()
    score = 0
    ```

4.  Set the game mode to `gmPlay` and activate layers with it.

    ```
    gameMode = gmPlay
    ActivateLayer(gameMode)
    ```

5.  To create the objects, set the default layer to `layerGame` and remove all objects form the game layer and the GFX layer.

    ```
    eng.SetDefaultLayer(layerGame)
    layerGame.RemoveAllObjects()
    layerGFX.RemoveAllObjects()
    ```

6.  Create the tile selector and make it invisible.

    ```
    selector = eng.CreateImage(atlas,64,0,64,64,0,0)
    selector.SetVisible(False)
    ```

7.  Start two FOR loops, one for the rows and and one for the columns.

    ```
    For Local y:Int = 1 To rows
      For Local x:Int = 1 To columns
    ```

8.  Initialize the tile map by setting the value to -1. Then, close the FOR loops.

    ```
        tileMap[x-1][y-1] = -1
      Next
    Next
    ```

**9.** Again, start two FOR loops for `rows` and `columns`.

```
For Local y:Int = 1 To rows
    For Local x:Int = 1 To columns
```

**10.** Add a `Repeat` statement.

```
Repeat
```

**11.** Set the value of `tile` with a random number ranging from `0` to `6`. Set the maximum allowable value to `5`.

```
tile = Rnd(6)
If tile = 6 Then tile = 5
```

**12.** Insert an `Until` statement, which will check gems horizontally and vertically to make sure that more than one gem doesn't have the same ID. This ensures that three matching tiles are not already in a row.

```
Until (CheckGemsX(x,y,tile)<2 And CheckGemsY(x,y, tile)<2)
```

**13.** Set the tile map with the new `tile` value.

```
tileMap[x-1][y-1] = tile
```

**14.** Depending on the `tile` value, create a new gem tile.

```
Local obj:=CreateTile(x,y,tile)
```

**15.** Close both FOR loops, and then set the field `justStarted` to `True`.

```
    Next
Next
justStarted = True
```

**16.** Set the game ending time to the current value of `Millisecs` + `gameTime`. Then, close the method.

```
    endTime = Millisecs()+(gameTime)
    Return 0
End
```

## *What just happened?*

The method `StartNewGame` will just do that—start a new game. Of course, it will also clean up every setting that was done before so you can start a new game afresh.

# Give me some information... displaying info

While someone is playing the game, they want to know how much time is left. Basically, it is a countdown in minutes and seconds. There is no out-of-the-box functionality in Monkey that will provide such a string, so let's create one.

## Time for action – updating the text info

We will build the functionality to update text info into a method that will update not only the time left, but also the game's score value.

1.  Add a new method called `UpdateInfoText` in the `game` class.

    ```
    Method UpdateInfoText:Int()
    ```

2.  Set the text property of `txtScore` with the score value.

    ```
    txtScore.SetText(score)
    ```

3.  Calculate the number of seconds left by subtracting the current millisecond value from the end time, after adding `750` (to make it more accurate), and then dividing everything by `1000`, to get seconds.

    ```
    seconds = (endTime-Millisecs()+750)/1000
    ```

4.  Determine the number of minutes left using the value of `seconds`.

    ```
    minutes = seconds/60
    ```

5.  Subtract the result of *minutes times 60* to get the seconds left.

    ```
    seconds -= (minutes*60)
    ```

6.  Depending on how many seconds are left, set the text property of `txtTime`.

    ```
    If seconds > 9 Then
      txtTime.SetText(minutes+":"+seconds)
    Else
      txtTime.SetText(minutes+":0"+seconds)
    Endif
    ```

7.  Close this method.

    ```
        Return 0
      End
    End
    ```

## *What just happened?*

The method `UpdateInfoText` will update the game's score text object and also calculate the time left in minutes and seconds. During the game, the updated info text objects will look like this:

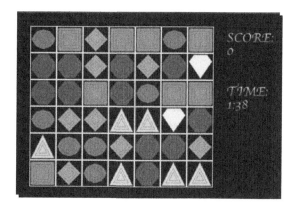

## Showing the "game over" screen

The 'game over' screen in Treasure Chest is a very simple one. It will display a little box with the text **Game Over** and your score.

## Time for action – showing the "game over" screen

We will display **Game Over** by following the ensuing steps:

1.  Create a new method called `ShowGameOver` inside the `game` class.

    ```
    Method ShowGameOver:Int()
    ```

2.  Set the game mode to `gmGameOver` and activate layers with it.

    ```
    gameMode = gmGameOver
    ActivateLayer(gameMode)
    ```

3.  Set the final score text object with the `score` value. Then, close the method.

    ```
      txtFinalScore.SetText("SCORE: "+score)
      Return 0
    End
    ```

## What just happened?

This method will take care of showing the 'game over' screen.

## Showing the menu screen

Usually, you don't need an extra method to show a layer, but if you do this in multiple places in your code, it makes sense to add a method for it and just call it. It helps in reducing the length of your code by removing redundant lines.

## Time for action – showing the menu

The menu screen is shown using the following steps:

1. Add the method ShowMenu into the game class.

```
Method ShowMenu:Int()
```

2. Set the game mode to gmMenu and activate layers with it. Then, close the method.

```
gameMode = gmMenu
ActivateLayer(gameMode)
Return 0
End
```

## What just happened?

We created a simple method to display the menu layer.

# Bring me up-to-date—detailing the OnUpdate event

Finally, we are getting to the update stage, and you can see more things.

## Time for action – detailing the OnUpdate method

The OnUpdate method of the game class is responsible for calculating the delta time since the last frame and updating the game, depending on which mode it is in.

1. Start a Select statement on the game mode.

```
Method OnUpdate:Int()
  Local d:Float = Float(eng.CalcDeltaTime())/60.0
  If isSuspended = False Then
    eng.Update(Float(d))

    Select gameMode
```

**2.** Check for the constant `gmPlay`.

```
Case gmPlay
```

**3.** Start a touch check on the game layer to determine which gems are selected.

```
If eng.TouchHit(0) Then
    eng.TouchCheck(layerGame)
Endif
```

**4.** Check if there are no gems moving.

```
If layerGame.GetObjTransCount()= 0 Then
```

**5.** Fill up empty slots with new gems.

```
FillTiles()
```

**6.** Check if gems line up and clear them. Then, close the IF check.

```
    ClearGems()
Endif
```

**7.** If the *N* key is pressed, reset the grid calling `StartNewGame`.

```
If KeyHit(KEY_N) Then StartNewGame()
```

**8.** If the *Esc* key is pressed, show the menu layer.

```
If KeyHit(KEY_ESCAPE) Then ShowMenu()
```

**9.** Update all the info text objects.

```
UpdateInfoText()
```

**10.** Check for the `gmGameOver` constant.

```
Case gmGameOver
```

**11.** If there was a 'touch hit', or if the *Esc* key was pressed, activate the menu layer.

```
If eng.TouchHit(0) Or KeyHit(KEY_ESCAPE) Then
    gameMode=gmMenu
    ActivateLayer(gameMode)
Endif
```

**12.** Next, check for the `gmScore` constant. If there is a 'touch hit', then conduct a 'touch check' on the score layer.

```
Case gmScore
    If eng.TouchHit(0) Then eng.TouchCheck(layerScore)
```

**13.** Now, check for the `gmMenu` constant. Again, if there is a 'touch hit', then conduct a touch check on the menu layer.

```
Case gmMenu
    If eng.TouchHit(0) Then eng.TouchCheck(layerMenu)
```

**14.** And, finally, check for the `gmTitle` constant. If the *Esc* key is pressed, activate the menu layer.

```
        Case gmTitle
          If KeyHit(KEY_ESCAPE) Then
            gameMode=gmMenu
            ActivateLayer(gameMode)
          Endif
      End

    Endif
    Return 0
End
```

## What just happened?

Now, the update phase is set in stone. When you build and run the app, you can now press *Esc* in the title screen and it will switch to the menu screen. From there, you will be able to show the score layer and also start a new game.

To remind you what the menu screen looks like in the game, have a look at the following screenshot :

# Vroom... vroom—the engine class

Now it is time to bring some life into the game—the actual game play. Also, we will produce some eye candy, meaning some particles. And we will make some noise too.

# Eye candy—particle effects

Whenever a gem is removed, you want to enhance the graphical effect by displaying a particle effect or something similar. Particles are usually some animated graphics that change over time and then disappear.

## Time for action – spawning an explosion

**1.** Add the method `SpawnExplosion` to the `engine` class. The parameters are the number of particles and their position.

```
Method SpawnExplosion:Int(amount:Int, xp:Int, yp:Int)
```

**2.** Set the default layer to `g.layerGFX`.

```
SetDefaultLayer(g.layerGFX)
```

**3.** Start a FOR loop as a counter ranging from `1` to `amount`.

```
For Local i:Int = 1 To amount
```

**4.** Create a new particle object.

```
Local explo:ftObject = CreateImage(g.atlas, 128, 0,32,32, xp, yp)
```

**5.** Set its scale, angle, spin, and speed randomly.

```
explo.SetScale(Rnd(2,12)/10)
explo.SetAngle(Rnd(0,359))
explo.SetSpin(Rnd(-4,4))
explo.SetSpeed(Rnd(1,2))
```

**6.** Play the explosion sound.

```
g.sndExplo.Play()
```

**7.** Create an object timer, so that the particles will be removed after a random time. The timer ID is `g.tmObjRemove`.

```
CreateObjTimer(explo, g.tmObjRemove, Rnd(100,2000))
```

**8.** Close the FOR statement and the method.

```
  Next
  Return 0
End
```

## What just happened?

This new method will spawn some particles that will be deleted via a timer.

## Tick tock... acting on object timer events

Treasure Chest has two situations where a timer is set, and we need to act on it:

- When the title screen is shown
- When a particle is spawned

# Time for action – acting on object timer events

To act on timer events, fantomEngine provides the `OnObjectTimer` method in the `engine` class. We need to modify it.

1.  Modify the `OnObjectTimer` method in the `engine` class by adding a `Select` statement on `timerId`.

    ```
    Method OnObjectTimer:Int(timerId:Int, obj:ftObject)

        Select timerId
    ```

2.  Check for the constant `g.tmShowMenu`. Here, we deal with the automatic switch from the title screen to the menu screen.

    ```
    Case g.tmShowMenu
    ```

3.  Check if the game mode is `g.gmTitle`, and then activate the menu layer.

    ```
    If g.gameMode = g.gmTitle Then
      g.gameMode = g.gmMenu
      g.ActivateLayer(g.gameMode)
    Endif
    ```

4.  Check for the constant `g.tmObjRemove`. Here, we deal with deleting the particle objects. After that, close the `Select` statement.

    ```
        Case g.tmObjRemove
           obj.Remove()
       End

       Return 0
    End
    ```

## What just happened?

The `OnObjectTimer` method will take care of the title screen's switch to the menu screen and the removing of particles.

## Touch me—acting on Touch checks

The text objects in the menu and the score screen and also the gems in the grid are touchable and we make touch checks in various places in the game. To act on this, you need to modify the `OnObjectTouch` method in the `engine` class.

## Time for action – enhancing the OnObjectTouch method

The `OnObjectTouch` method is updated as follows:

**1.** First add two FLOAT variables at the start which will store the difference factor regarding objects positions.

```
Method OnObjectTouch:Int(obj:ftObject, touchId:Int)

    Local xdiff:Float
    Local ydiff:Float
```

**2.** Check if game mode is equal to the constant `g.gmMenu`.

```
If g.gameMode = g.gmMenu Then
```

**3.** Start the `Select` statement on the object's `Tag` property.

```
Select obj.GetTag()
```

**4.** Check against the constant `g.btnPlay` (the play button). If yes, then start a new game.

```
Case g.btnPlay
  g.StartNewGame()
```

**5.** Check against the constant `g.btnScore` (the score button). If yes, then show the high-score screen.

```
Case g.btnScore
  g.ShowScore
```

**6.** Check against the constant `g.btnExit` (the exit button). If yes, then exit the app.

```
Case g.btnExit
  g.eng.ExitApp(True)
```

**7.** Close the `Select` statement. After that, play the `g.sndSelect` sound and close the IF statement.

```
   End
   g.sndSelect.Play()
Endif
```

**8.** Now comes the part where we check if a gem was selected and if it can move.

**9.** Start an IF check. Check that the game mode is set to `g.gmPlay`, that there are no transitions in the game layer, that the touch ID is not `99`, and that `justStarted` is not `True`.

```
   If g.gameMode = g.gmPlay And g.layerGame.GetObjTransCount() =
0 And touchId <> 99 And g.justStarted = False Then
```

**10.** Check if the first tile was selected before.

```
      If g.firstTile <> Null Then
Get the X/Y distance of the first tile and the current one
         xdiff = g.firstTile.GetPosX() - obj.GetPosX()
         ydiff = g.firstTile.GetPosY() - obj.GetPosY()
```

**11.** Check if the tile is the neighboring one. We do this by comparing the absolute differences between the $x$ and $y$ positions.

```
If ((Abs(xdiff)<80.0) And (Abs(ydiff)<2.0)) Or ((Abs(ydiff)<80.0)
And (Abs(xdiff)<2.0)) Then
```

**12.** Set the second tile to the current object.

```
   g.secondTile = obj
```

**13.** Now, check if there are at least two neighboring tiles of the same kind.

```
   If (g.CountGems(g.firstTile, g.secondTile)>1) Or (g.CountGems(g.
secondTile, g.firstTile)>1) Then
```

**14.** Initialize both tile slots

```
   g.SetSlotTile(g.GetSlotX(g.secondTile), g.GetSlotY(g.
secondTile),-1)
   g.SetSlotTile(g.GetSlotX(g.firstTile), g.GetSlotY(g.
firstTile),-1)
```

**15.** Transform these tiles to their opposite coordinates and close the IF check.

```
   g.firstTile.CreateTransPos(g.secondTile.GetPosX(),g.secondTile.
GetPosY(),300,False,99)
   g.secondTile.CreateTransPos(g.firstTile.GetPosX(),g.firstTile.
GetPosY(),300,False,99)
   Endif
```

**16.** Initialize the first and second tile objects.

```
g.secondTile = Null
g.firstTile = Null
```

**17.** Place the tile selector outside the map so it can't be detected by the touch check.

```
   g.selector.SetPos(0, 0)
   g.selector.SetVisible(False)
Else
```

**18.** There are no neighboring tiles, so initialize the first tile and make the selector invisible.

```
g.firstTile = Null
g.selector.SetPos(0, 0)
g.selector.SetVisible(False)
```

**19.** Play the `g.sndFalse` sound.

```
   g.sndFalse.Play()
   Endif
Else
```

**20.** The first tile was selected, so make the selector visible and set it to the position of the current tile. After that, close the two IF checks.

```
   g.firstTile = obj
   g.selector.SetPos(obj.GetPosX(), obj.GetPosY())
   g.selector.SetVisible(True)
   Endif
Endif
```

**21.** If the game mode is `g.gmPlay` and the touch ID is `99`, then raise the value of `score` by `100`, spawn an explosion, and remove the tile.

```
If g.gameMode = g.gmPlay And touchId = 99 Then
   g.score += 100
   SpawnExplosion(7,obj.GetPosX(), obj.GetPosY())
   obj.Remove()
Endif
```

**22.** Tell the game that the first frame was displayed. This is important because it somehow will set the selector wrong.

```
g.justStarted = False
```

**23.** Check if the `Back` button was selected.

```
If obj.GetTag() = g.btnBack Then g.ShowMenu()

Return 0
End
```

## What just happened?

Now that we have handled the touch events, all buttons are functional, and you can start a new game. You can also select the first two tiles. We still need to handle the transition and the winning conditions of the game, so let's go further.

# We've reached our parking position... a transition is done

After both the selected gems have moved, something has to happen. That would be setting the slot IDs for the new gems and also checking if matching gems can be removed.

## Time for action – detailing the OnObjectTransition method

The `OnObjectTransition` method is detailed as follows:

**1.** Modify the `OnObjectTransition` method of the `engine` class. Insert a local pair of position variables and a pair of counting variables.

```
Method OnObjectTransition:Int(transId:Int, obj:ftObject)

Local xp:Int
Local yp:Int
 Local cntX:Int
Local cntY:Int
```

**2.** Check if the transition ID is equal to `99`, and if so, get the `x` and `y` positions of the slot from the calling object.

```
If transId = 99 Then
  xp = g.GetSlotX(obj)
  yp = g.GetSlotY(obj)
```

**3.** Now, set the slot tile with the tag value of the object.

```
g.SetSlotTile(xp, yp, obj.GetTag())
```

**4.** Determine the count. How many gems match at the given row and column of the object?

```
cntX = g.CheckGemsX(xp, yp, obj.GetTag())
cntY = g.CheckGemsY(xp, yp, obj.GetTag())
```

**5.** If there is more than one matching gem, call `CheckGems` again, but this time with an additional `True` flag to mark the gems or have them removed.

```
    If cntX>1 Then  g.CheckGemsX(xp, yp, obj.GetTag(), True)
    If cntY>1 Then  g.CheckGemsY(xp, yp, obj.GetTag(), True)
  Endif


  Return 0
End
```

# What's the situation?... layer update events

At one point of the game you need to check if the game has ended. We do this by comparing the current value of milliseconds to the end time that was set when the game started.

## Time for action – acting on layer update events

**1.** Modify the `OnLayerUpdate` method in the `engine` class.

```
Method OnLayerUpdate:Int(layer:ftLayer)
```

**2.** Check if the game mode is equal to `g.gmPlay`.

```
If g.gameMode = g.gmPlay Then
```

**3.** Check if the end time is equal to or smaller than the current `Millisecs` value. If yes, that means the game time ran out and you must show the 'game over' screen.

```
If g.endTime <= Millisecs() Then
  g.ShowGameOver()
```

**4.** Add the last score to the score list, and save the high-score list.

```
g.eng.scoreList.AddScore(g.score,"---")
g.SaveHighScore()
```

**5.** Close the last two IF checks.

```
    Endif
  Endif


  Return 0
  End
End
```

## What just happened?

Because we now act on the fact that the time ran out, we can finally play the full game. If everything builds well, you could see this:

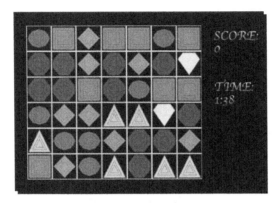

## Have a go hero – enhancing Treasure Chest

Again, there are things that were left out of the game. For example, an option screen, or a way to remove gems, sounds, effects, and other things, too. Also, you could add some bonus gems that give you extra time. You see, the possibilities are many. Have fun digging through the code, and create YOUR version of Treasure Chest.

# Summary

In this chapter, we developed the final game for this book. Here's what we covered in the chapter:

- ◆ We learned how to set up 2D arrays
- ◆ We learned how to store the tile map and how to do this with arrays
- ◆ We learned how to connect the tile map to the image objects

In the next chapter, will look at how you can make some pocket money with your apps. So, stay tuned and motivated for the last and final chapter!

# 10
# Make Some Money for Bananas

*Most game developers today have heard stories from other developers who have become rich overnight by publishing games and apps in well-known mobile app stores.*

*They read about people who made lots of money with simple games and were enchanted by the so-called gold rush in mobile app development still going around.*

*But let's face it, every one dreams of this. And somehow people think it is very easy to make big money there. In the early days of the app stores, it was much easier because the competition wasn't that big. Nowadays, the app stores are loaded with apps and games. A lot of them are similar. Even if you have created the most awesome game, you can't be sure that people will notice it in the mass of new releases every day and week. So, you need a lot of luck. You need a good app and you need to publish it at the right place and time, and of course, to the right audience.*

This chapter will concentrate on two methods that will help you make more money with your Monkey games. They are as follows:

- ◆ Sell your app for a one-time fee inside a marketplace
- ◆ Display advertisements in the app

Giving your game away for free and displaying ads has become very popular these days, and so we will look into this more closely. Some people say that the classic way of selling apps will become a method of the past sooner or later. But you as a developer have to make a choice when you release an app or game. You can definitely release it for free and just enjoy the feedback from users. But everyone likes to have a little extra pocket money for a pizza or a movie, right?

So, let's go and get the money rolling for some bananas!

# Which markets exist for your game?

The short answer is many! The long answer is it depends on the platform your game is running on. Let's look at the platforms that Monkey supports at the moment:

## iOS

When you build apps for the mobile iDevices of Apple, the only place where you sell these and publish these apps is the iTunes App Store. You need to sign up for an iOS developer account to be able to publish your apps to a device for testing, and also for publishing them on the iTunes App Store.

## OSX

Here you have several choices. You can publish an app on your own web space, or sell it through a publisher. Another possibility is the (OSX) App Store from Apple. Again, you have to sign up for an OSX developer account to do this.

## Android

As time goes by, more and more options to publish and sell your apps will become available. Besides Android Market from Google, where you need to sign up for an account, there are also markets such as Amazon or, now, Barnes and Noble, where you can try to publish your app. Of course, you can distribute your app on your own website too.

## XNA

As a Windows phone app, you can sell it through the Windows Phone Marketplace. If you target the XBOX 360, then there is XBOX Life. You can also sell it as a normal Windows XNA application from your own web space.

## HTML5/FLASH

Here, the whole Web is your place. Google opened the Chrome Web Store to publish HTML5 and FLASH apps, and so hundreds of possibilities exist.

# Existing methods of making money

There are quite a few ways to make money from your game. Some of them are described in the following text.

# Selling your game at a fixed price

First of all, the classical way is to sell your application at a fixed price. The customer pays once and then plays the game as long and as many times he/she wants.

The problem for you as a developer, in this case, is that you will lose a lot of sales due to piracy of the game. This problem even exists in the app stores and markets these days.

# Subscriptions

This is another method that is used for commercial games and for free games too. People pay a monthly/yearly subscription fee to be able to play the game or to get access to better features in the game. The subscription model was successfully introduced by *World of Warcraft* and other such games.

# Advertisement

One method is to give out your app/game for free. To make money, you can display advertisements inside the app. This can be a rotating banner ad located at the edge of the canvas or a full-screen ad interrupting the game at one point. Displaying a full-screen ad will block the player from proceeding further for a while and is often seen as an interruption to their game play. As you can imagine, most players have a negative opinion about this.

No matter what kind of ads you use, one way to earn money from this is when people actually click/tap on these ads. Another way is by just displaying ads for as much time as possible. With the latter method, it isn't necessary for the customer to interact with the ad, but it needs more ad impressions to be displayed to bring in some serious money. In this chapter, we will implement ads that generate money in both ways.

Releasing an app for free with ads also almost erases the piracy problem, as everyone can download the app for free. However, be aware that on open platforms such as Android, people are already using **Ad-blockers**. Also, your app needs to have online access to display advertisements.

# In-App purchases

The last common method here is In-App purchases. These are extra features of a game that are available once the user purchases the **In-App** item. There could be extra levels, more weapons, removal of advertisements, and so on. You can implement this in a free app or in a commercial one; it is your choice.

# Implementing advertising in your app

In this section, we will learn how to add advertisement into our apps with banner ads.

Generally, Monkey doesn't support ads out of the box. There is also no third-party module that you could use. But don't be afraid; unless you want to switch between different ad providers through your monkey code, or control the ads through your monkey code, it is pretty straightforward to implement ads inside the exported iOS and Android projects.

## Which ad providers exist?

The answer to this question is very, very short—many!

Before you choose an ad provider, you should do some research on the Internet, about how much they pay, when they pay, whether they are reliable, and stuff like that. Try to find more information from other developers. Anyway, some ad providers and services are listed as follows. (This list doesn't provide the complete list of ad providers!)

- iAd (Apple's native ad platform)
- AdMob (Google's own ad service)
- Greystripe
- MobFox
- Mobclix
- InMobi and many more

This book will not show you how to implement every service. The way to implement ads into your app is very similar, and once you understand one way, it shouldn't be too difficult to implement a different service on your own. First, you will get some information about how to implement AdMob and then we will concentrate on implementing MobFox.

## Implementing AdMob

If you haven't found the AdMob website already, here is the link to it:
`http://www.admob.com/`.

Signing up there is a piece of cake, and you can get AdMob running in your game very easily. The Monkey community already used it and there are two posted topics that will get you going very easily.

## iOS

If you follow the instructions at `http://www.monkeycoder.co.nz/Community/posts.php?topic=1246#11122` closely and also study the example from the AdMob website, you should have AdMob-based ads running in your game in no time.

## Android

The same logic applies for AdMob ads in Android apps (`http://www.monkeycoder.co.nz/Community/posts.php?topic=1121#18854`). It is very easy to implement. One thing you have to note is that, through this method, you have no control to hide/show ads at will, at the moment. So, you need to design your game to have the ads displayed at all times. And why not? You want to make money with it, so showing the ads all the time will help you in this cause.

# Implementing MobFox in iOS

MobFox is known for being a well-paying ad provider for the European and US market. The good thing is that they natively support a backfill option. At the moment, this is InMobi. **Backfilling** means that whenever MobFox can't provide an ad, they will use your backfill settings to show an ad from your backfill provider. InMobi is very strong in the Asian market, and so many countries and continents are covered through MobFox/InMobi.

## Signing up at MobFox

The MobFox website is located at `http://www.mobfox.com/`.

Just sign up for a publisher account there and enter your personal and payment details. After this, you are ready to implement ads into your game.

## Creating the ID for an iOS app in MobFox

To be able to display ads in your iOS-based game, you need to create a new app in your MobFox account.

# Time for action – creating a new MobFox app ID

To create a new account, follow the ensuing steps:

1. Click on the button **New Site or App** under **Sites & Apps**, on the:

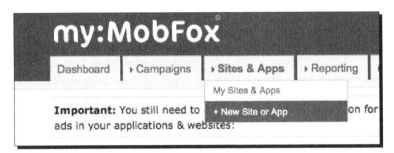

2. Choose **iPhone Application**, as we want to implement an ad on this platform.

3. Click on **Continue**.

**4.** Next, enter your app details. Give it a name, if you have one the app store URL, (or your website URL) and if not, add a little description.

**5.** Click on **Continue**, again.

**6.** It is important to set the correct category, as MobFox will check if your app is in the correct one and might not activate the ads for your app if the category is not properly set. Choose **Entertainment** for a game.

**7.** The last step we need to take of is to make a note of the **Publisher Site ID**. We need this ID to be entered inside the XCODE code later, so that ads can be displayed.

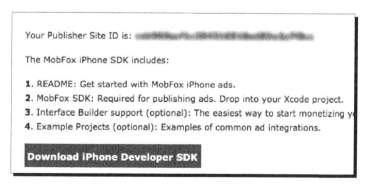

**8.** Now, download the iPhone Developer SDK from MobFox, if you haven't done this already.

## What just happened?

You created a new MobFox app ID for your iOS-based game. The first step is done. Now, you need to add a few details to your XCODE project.

## Implementing MobFox into your XCODE project

If you haven't built an iOS project already, do it now. For this chapter, we will use the game *Chain Reaction*. Please export an XCODE project and use it as a base for the following changes.

## Time for action – adding the MobFox framework to the XCODE project

To add the MobFox framework to the XCODE project, follow the ensuing steps:

**1.** Open your XCODE project from the **ios | build** folder by double-clicking on the project file name:

**2.** This will open your iOS build inside XCODE. Now, it is time to add MobFox to the project.

**3.** Right-click on the project header under **Groups & Files**.

**4.** Choose **Add**, and then choose **Existing Files...**:

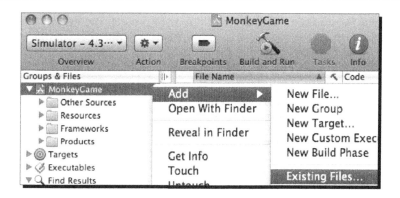

5. Select the **SDK** folder from your unzipped MobFox SDK.

6. Click on **Add**:

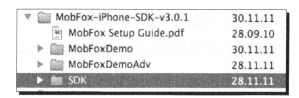

7. Next, check the **Copy Items into destination group's folder** checkbox, select the **Recursively create groups for any added folder** radio button, and then click on **Add** again:

8. Now, you have added the MobFox SDK to your project. The header files are there; make sure that the `MobFox.framework` file is included in the project:

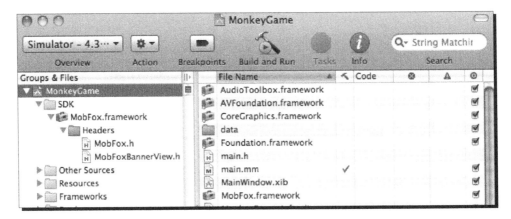

9. Now, perform a build in XCODE. Usually, you will get some warnings from your Monkey code, but that is OK. It should still build.

## What just happened?

You added the MobFox framework to your XCODE project. Nothing will be shown at the moment if you let your app run, but that will be the next step.

## Displaying MobFox ads in the app

To display ads inside the app, you need to change the project files at some point. There isn't much change, but this needs to be done to have MobFox display its ads.

## Time for action – modifying the code to display ads

First, you need to open the `main.h` header file and make some changes to it. We dive here into Object-C/C++ code, so be confused if the code looks different from the native Monkey code:

1. Add an `import` statement for the `MobFox/MobFox.h` file:

```
#include <OpenAL/alc.h>
#import <MobFox/MobFox.h>
// ***** MonkeyView *****
@interface MonkeyView : UIView{
```

**2.** Next, add the `MobFoxBannerViewDelegate` to the Monkey view controller:

```
// ***** MonkeyViewController *****

@interface MonkeyViewController : UIViewController
  <MobFoxBannerViewDelegate> {
@public
}
@end
```

**3.** Next, we need to modify the `main.m` file, the heart of your Monkey code. Insert the `viewDidLoad` method into the `MonkeyViewController` implementation and call its `super` implementation. Place the method right under the `shouldAutorotateToInterfaceOrientation` method, which controls how the app will be able to rotate natively:

```
@implementation MonkeyViewController

- (BOOL)shouldAutorotateToInterfaceOrientation:(UIInterfaceOrientat
ion)interfaceOrientation{

//..........
}

- (void)viewDidLoad {
    [super viewDidLoad];
```

**4.** Now, create a new MobFox banner view:

```
   MobFoxBannerView *bannerView = [[MobFoxBannerView alloc]
initWithFrame:
```

The frame for creating the banner will be at the bottom of the screen. So, at the beginning, the ad is hidden in the off-screen area. You can't use the view sizes, as the view in Monkey is very small by default:

```
CGRectMake(0, [[UIScreen mainScreen] bounds].size.height, 320,
50)];
```

**5.** Set the banner's delegate to self. This will trigger loading an ad:

```
   bannerView.delegate = self;
```

**6.** Set the background color of the banner view:

```
   bannerView.backgroundColor = [UIColor darkGrayColor];
```

**7.** Set `refreshAnimation` for the banner view to the `CurlDown` animation type:

```
bannerView.refreshAnimation = UIViewAnimationTransitionCurlDown;
```

**8.** Add the banner subview to the Monkey view. Then, close the method:

```
[self.view addSubview:bannerView];
}
```

This method creates a new banner view, but you still need to let MobFox know your MobFox publisher ID. This is done inside the `publisherIdForMobFoxBannerView` method:

**9.** First, add a pragma compiler switch for MobFox Delegate:

```
#pragma mark MobFox Delegate
```

**10.** Insert the `publisherIdForMobFoxBannerView` method, with `NSString` as a return value and `banner` as a parameter:

```
- (NSString *)publisherIdForMobFoxBannerView:(MobFoxBannerView *)
banner
{
```

**11.** Return the publisher ID that you got when you created the app on the MobFox website. Close the method:

```
return @"InsertYourIdHere";
}
```

The banner was created in the off-screen area. When it receives an ad from MobFox, it should slide into the visible area. This is done with the next method.

**12.** For this ad, use the `mobfoxBannerViewDidLoadMobFoxAd` method. The parameter is `banner`:

```
- (void)mobfoxBannerViewDidLoadMobFoxAd:(MobFoxBannerView *)banner
{
```

**13.** So that you can see in the debugger that an ad was loaded, output some text that lets you know about it:

```
NSLog(@"MobFox: did load ad");
```

**14.** You want the banner to slide into the view, so begin a new animation:

```
[UIView beginAnimations:@"MobFox" context:nil];
[UIView setAnimationDuration:1];
```

**15.** Set the frame of the banner to its final visible destination. Here, the bound size property works, for some reason. The height of the banner is 50 pixels, so we place it accordingly:

```
banner.frame = CGRectMake(0, self.view.bounds.size.height - 50,
320, 50);
```

**16.** Next, commit the animation and close the method:

```
//banner.frame = CGRectMake(0, 0, 320, 50);
[UIView commitAnimations];
}
```

Once an ad is received, the banner view will slide into the visible screen area. But sometimes, ads are not available. It could be that MobFox doesn't serve an ad, or the device has no connection to the Internet. For this, we need a method to slide the banner view outside the screen area.

**17.** Add the method `didFailToReceiveAdWithError` with `error` as a parameter.

```
- (void)mobfoxBannerView:(MobFoxBannerView *)banner didFailToRecei
veAdWithError:(NSError *)error
{
```

**18.** Output a message with the error so you can retrieve this in the debugger:

```
NSLog(@"MobFox: did fail to load ad: %@", [error
localizedDescription]);
```

**19.** Start a new UIView animation:

```
[UIView beginAnimations:@"MobFox" context:nil];
[UIView setAnimationDuration:1];
```

**20.** Create a target frame for the banner outside the view bounds, and commit the animation:

```
banner.frame = CGRectMake(0, self.view.bounds.size.height, 320,
50);
[UIView commitAnimations];
```

**21.** Close this method:

```
}

@end
```

**22.** You have now added all the methods that are needed to display ads in your app. If you try to build the game now, you will see some errors showing up. This is because a Monkey project is natively a C++ project. However, we are using Object-C here, and so need to let the linker know about it. For this, you need to change the linker flags, as follows:

❑ Double-click on the project name to bring up the project info.

❑ Inside the **Build** tab, search for other linker flags.

❑ Add the **-ObjC** entry to it.

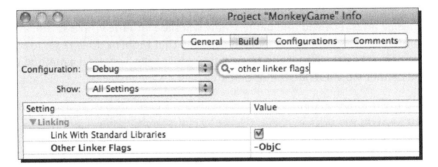

❑ Make sure you add this flag to the debug and release configuration.

## What just happened?

You have added all the needed methods to your XCODE project to display MobFox ads inside your game. If you now build and run the project inside the simulator, you should see a test banner ad:

## Activating real ads

After you have finished the implementation, two more steps have to be taken to display real ads in your game. First, change the URL link to your app inside the app store once you know it.

Second, when the application is going live, request the activation of ads from MobFox. This can be done from your MobFox account, inside the list of apps.

# Implementing MobFox in Android

You will see that MobFox is much easier to implement inside your Android project, as compared to iOS.

## Creating the ID for an Android app in MobFox

To be able to display ads in your Android-based game, create a new app in your MobFox account.

## Time for action – creating a new MobFox app ID

You can create a new MobFox app ID as follows:

1. Again, create a new app inside your MobFox account.

2. Select **Android Application**.

3. Click on **Continue**:

**4.** Now, enter your app details, just like you did for the iOS application:

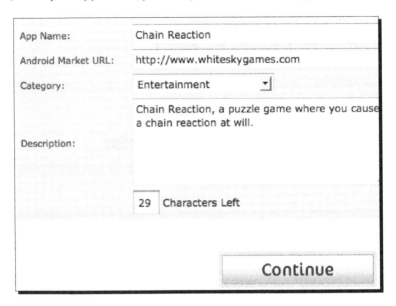

**5.** Click on **Continue**.

**6.** Finally, write down the publisher ID for later use. You can always retrieve it from the **options** dialog of your app, inside your MobFox account:

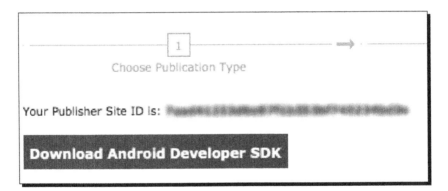

**7.** Download the Android Developer SDK from the MobFox website.

**8.** Unzip it to a location of your choice.

## *What just happened?*

You just have created a new MobFox app ID for your Android-based game. The first step is done; now, you need make a few changes to your Android project.

## Implement MobFox into your Android project

Of course, you need an Android project build before you can make the changes. If you didn't build it, then do that now.

## Time for action – modifying the project to display ads in Android

We need to add the MobFox SDK to the Android project now.

1. With your file explorer, locate the MobFox SDK folder where you have unzipped the JAR file:

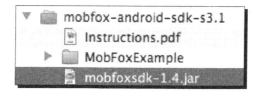

2. Copy the `mobfoxsdk.jar` file from the MobFox SDK folder.

3. Paste the copied library into the `libs` folder of the Monkey build folder. If you copied it correctly, it should look like the following screenshot:

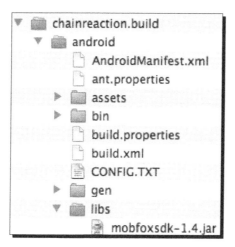

**4.** Now, browse within your file explorer to the `templates` folder in the Monkey build folder. It will look like the following screenshot:

The two interesting files here are `AndroidManifest.xml` and `res/layout/main.xml`. As they are both located inside the `templates` folder, both are used as a base for these files whenever you rebuild the app from inside Monk. Make the next changes here and not in the regular files.

**5.** Next, open the `templates/AndroidManifest.xml` file with a text editor.

**6.** Add two permissions—one for using the Internet and one for reading the phone state. MobFox needs this to retrieve device information and get the ad. Also, change the minimum SDK version to `4`:

```
<?xml version="1.0" encoding="utf-8"?>
<manifest xmlns:android="http://schemas.android.com/apk/res/
android"

  package="${APP_PACKAGE}"

  android:versionCode="1"
  android:versionName="1.0"
  android:installLocation="auto">

  <uses-sdk
    android:minSdkVersion="4"
    android:targetSdkVersion="7" />

  <uses-feature android:glEsVersion="0x00010001" />

  <uses-permission android:name="android.permission.INTERNET"></
uses-permission>
    <uses-permission android:name="android.permission.READ_PHONE_
STATE"></uses-permission>
```

**7.** Now add the activity for `mobfox InAppWebView`:

```xml
    <application android:label="${APP_LABEL}" android:icon="@
drawable/icon">
      <activity
        android:name="MonkeyGame"
        android:label="${APP_LABEL}"
        android:screenOrientation="${SCREEN_ORIENTATION}"
        android:configChanges="keyboardHidden|orientation"
        android:theme="@android:style/Theme.NoTitleBar.Fullscreen">
        <intent-filter>
          <action android:name="android.intent.action.MAIN" />
          <category android:name="android.intent.category.LAUNCHER"
/>
        </intent-filter>
      </activity>
        <activity android:name="com.mobfox.sdk.InAppWebView"/>
    </application>
</manifest>
```

**8.** Next, you need to change the `templates/res/layout/main.xml` file.

**9.** Open the `main.xml` file with a text editor.

**10.** Change the linear layout to a relative one.

**11.** You need to change the last line in the file, accordingly:

```xml
<?xml version="1.0" encoding="utf-8"?>
<RelativeLayout
  xmlns:android="http://schemas.android.com/apk/res/android"
  android:layout_width="fill_parent"
  android:layout_height="fill_parent"
  android:orientation="vertical" >

  <view class="${APP_PACKAGE}.MonkeyGame$MonkeyView"
      android:id="@+id/monkeyview"
    android:keepScreenOn="true"
      android:layout_width="fill_parent"
    android:layout_height="fill_parent"
    />
</RelativeLayout>
```

**12.** Now add `mobFoxView`:

```
<view class="${APP_PACKAGE}.MonkeyGame$MonkeyView"
    android:id="@+id/monkeyview"
  android:keepScreenOn="true"
    android:layout_width="fill_parent"
  android:layout_height="fill_parent"
  />
  <com.mobfox.sdk.MobFoxView
      android:id="@+id/mobFoxView"
      android:layout_width="fill_parent"
      android:layout_height="50dp"
      publisherId="InsertYourPublisherIdHere"
      android:layout_centerHorizontal="true"
      android:layout_alignParentBottom="true"
  />
</RelativeLayout>
```

## What just happened?

We have added the required permissions and changed the minimum SDK level of our project. We have also modified the layout definition. When you rebuild the project now, from within Monk, and install the game on your Android device, you should have a test banner sliding into view, from the bottom of the screen. It should look like the following screenshot:

## Adding a backfill through InMobi

The great thing about MobFox is that you can add an InMobi backfill. Whenever MobFox can't serve an ad, it will try to get one from your provided InMobi settings and display this instead. All you need to do for this is to create an app inside InMobi and set the app ID inside the backfill options in MobFox. Let's do that now, for the Android app.

### Signing up at InMobi

The InMobi website is located at `http://www.inmobi.com`.

Just sign up for an account there; it is very straightforward and fast.

## Create an Android app in InMobi

To get the app ID you need for MobFox, you need to create a new app inside InMobi.

## Time for action – creating an app ID in InMobi

Like with MobFox, you need to register a new app inside your InMobi account.

**1.** Navigate to the **Publisher** dashboard of your InMobi account.

**2.** Click on **My Sites/Apps**:

**3.** Next, register a new Android App:

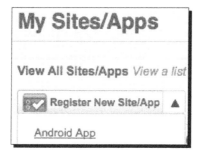

**4.** If you know the Android Market link already, then enter these details. If not, then just enter the name of your app.

**5.** Click on **Save**:

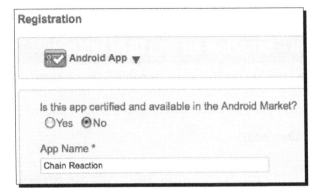

**6.** Now you will see the **App/Site ID** of the Android app.

**7.** Write this code down, which you need to enter soon in your MobFox account:

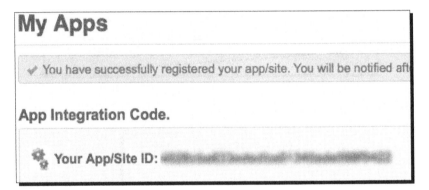

## What just happened?

You created a new InMobi app ID. This ID will be used for the backfill options in your MobFox account.

## Setting the backfill option in MobFox

Now, we need to set the backfill option for the Android app in MobFox.

# Time for action – add a backfill in MobFox

1. For this go back into your MobFox account and open the **Sites & Apps** page.

2. Locate the app you want to add the backfill to and click on the little **BackFill** label.

| Chain Reaction | Android Application | ● | Request Activation | BackFill | |

3. Next, activate the backfill for this app.

4. Select **InMobi** as the backfill option.

5. Enter your app ID inside the filed for **InMobi Site ID**.

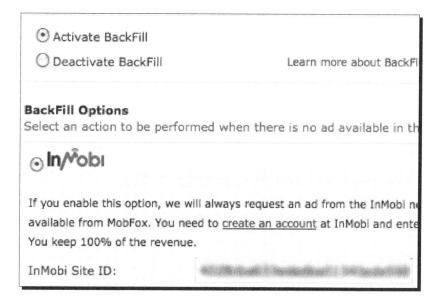

6. Click on **Save** so the option will be activated.

## What just happened?

You have set the InMobi backfill option in your MobFox app settings. For iOS, the process is very similar; you just need to create an iOS app in InMobi.

# Publishing in the Android market

Before you can publish your app/game in Google's Android market, you need to do some homework, first. Here is a list of things you need to do:

- Create the app icons
- Change the app label and package name
- Set the version code and name
- Rename the app package
- Remove the debug key from the package
- Create a private key to sign the app
- Sign the package with your new private key
- Zipalign your app package

Let's go through each task one by one.

## Create app icons

The good thing is that we have learned about this before in *Chapter 5, Game #4, Chain Reaction*. If you've forgotten about it, then just take your time to read it up again.

## Change the app label and the package name

Again, this is something we have done together at the end of *Chapter 5, Game #4, Chain Reaction*. If you are not familiar with it, have a look there again.

## Setting the version code and name

Inside the `android/templates/AndroidManifest.xml` file, there are two lines that you need to change, once you work on updates of your app:

```
android:versionCode="1"
android:versionName="1.0"
```

The `versionCode` value is just an integer that should be raised by one with every version you release. It actually will indicate if your user will become notified that there is an update for your app. So, don't forget to raise this number each time you create the final build of your next app version. `versionName` is information the user can see on the device and maybe in the market too.

# Rename the app package

When you build the app, the name of the package is always set to `monkeygame-debug.apk`. The file is located inside the `android/bin/` folder. Just rename it to your liking, say something like *awesomegame.apk* or *myfirsthitgame.apk*. Of course, a more meaningful app name would be better.

# Remove the debug key from the package

Every time you build your app through Monk, the resulting `.apk` file is signed with the default debug key, even when you create a release build. You need to delete it from the package, so that you can resign it. For this, you need a tool such as WinRAR. Open the `.apk` file with it (do not extract it) and remove the `META-INF` folder. That is the place where the debug key is stored.

# Create a private key to sign the app with

To create a new private key for your app, please read up Google's instructions at `http://developer.android.com/guide/publishing/app-signing.html`, first.

To create a new keystore for you app, just open your terminal (OSX) or your console (Windows) and type the following command:

```
keytool -genkey -v -keystore yourKeystoreName.keystore -alias
        alias_name -keyalg RSA -keysize 2048 -validity 10000
```

It will start the `keytool` utility, where you have to answer a few questions. If you set a password, make sure that you remember it!

# Sign the package with your new private key

Next, sign the `.apk` package with your new private key. While still in the console or terminal, type in the following command:

```
jarsigner -verbose -keystore yourKeystoreName.keystore

        my_application.apk alias_name
```

Depending on your folder names, you might have to use the whole path of your keystore in it.

## Zipalign your app package

To make sure that your package it properly aligned, bitwise, you need to run Zipalign on it.

For this, type the following command inside your terminal or console:

```
"/pathToYourAndroidSDK/tools/zipalign" -v 4
    "pathToYourAPK/my_application.apk"
    "pathToYourAPK/my_application_final.apk"
```

Now, you have a signed and align package file that you could upload to the Android Market. All you need now is a Google developer account, and then you can upload your app there.

To sign up there, go to `http://developer.android.com/index.html` and click on the **Publish** button. It is very easy to publish your app there, and you will figure it out in no time.

# Publishing in Apple's App Store

To publish in the App Store, you need to have a developer account there. As preparation, you will need to perform some tasks, such as these:

- ◆ Add the app icons
- ◆ Change the name and the app package
- ◆ Set the distribution code sign profile
- ◆ Create a package to submit

## Add the app icons

When you build your iOS app from Monk, there is no icon added to the Xcode project. There are several icon sizes, which can or have to be added to the project. Please refer to the detailed explanations inside the iTunesConnect Developer Guide. For example, it will tell you that, for an iPhone app, you need an icon with the size of 57x57 pixels (`icon.png`), and for the iPad, one with a size of 72x72 pixels (`icon-72.png`).

The default project settings of a Monkey Xcode project will create a universal app. This means it will run on an iPhone and on an iPad. So, you need to provide both icons. Create them in your favorite graphics application. Then, you need to add them to the project.

# Time for action – adding an icon to the Xcode project

Adding an icon for your app is done inside XCODE.

1. Start Xcode and open your Monkey project.

2. With your right mouse button, select the **Resources** group.

3. Then select **Add | Existing Files...**:

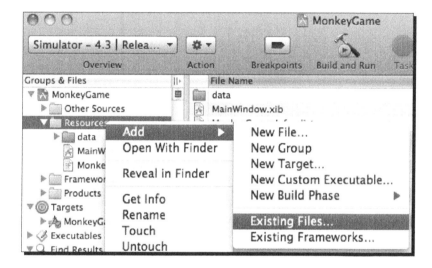

4. Select the icon file that you want to add and click on **Add**.

5. Now choose if you want to copy the icon into the destination group's folder, or just add a reference to it.

6. Click on **Add** to add the icon to the project:

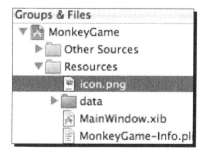

# What just happened?

You added an icon for your project. The resource section in the project should look similar to the one shown in the following screenshot:

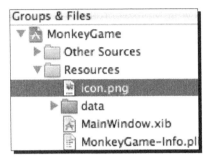

Change the name of the app package. When you build an Xcode project from Monk, it will always have the same name—*MonkeyGame*. You could rename the whole Xcode project, but then you would not be able to update it through a new build in Monk. It's better to set the product name in the target info settings.

## Time for action – setting the product name in the target settings

To set the product name, you have to change a property inside the target info settings.

1. Double-click on the entry **MonkeyGame** in the **Target** section:

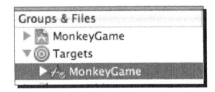

2. This will bring up the **Target "MonkeyGame" Info** dialog.

3. Select the **Build** tab and search for **product name**.

4. Now, with a double-click on the **Value** field, set your product name:

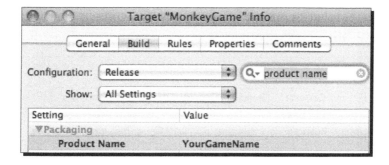

Make sure you do this in all configurations that you want to distribute to the app store.

## What just happened?

You have set the product name of your app. When you build your app in Xcode, it will create a `.app` file that is named after your product name.

## Set the distribution code signing profile

To be able to set the distribution code signing profile, you need to have one created in your provisioning portal and then put it in your key chain. The last step is easily done through dropping it in the Xcode Organizer on your device. But, for details about all this, refer to the iOS developer documentation.

Before you can actually create a distributable app, you need to let Xcode know which code-signing profile it should use to sign the app with.

## Time for action – setting the distribution code signing profile

To set the distribution profile, you need to set it inside the project info settings.

*1.* Double-click on the **MonkeyGame** entry in the **Groups & Files** list:

*2.* This brings up the **Project "MonkeyGame" Info** dialog.

*3.* Search for **code signing identity**.

4. Change the value for **Any iOS** to your distribution profile by selecting it from the provided list:

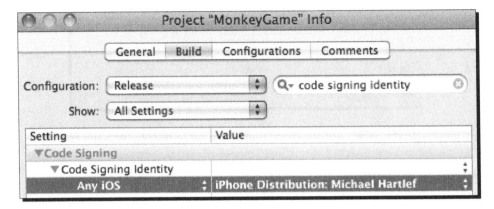

If you can't see your profile inside the list, then it wasn't installed properly. Reinstall it and then restart Xcode.

## What just happened?

You have set the distribution code signing profile. Xcode is set now, so you can create an app for distribution.

## Create a package to submit

Creating a distributable app is very easy.

## Time for action – creating the app package

Again, this done in XCODE and with your project. Please open the project in XCODE, if it isn't opened already.

1. Select the configuration you want to submit. Usually it is **Release-iphoneos**.

2. Build the project.

3. If no error showed up, you should now see the app under the product name you have set in the `build/Release-iphoneos` folder:

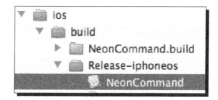

4.  The final step is to create a ZIP archive of this app.

5.  Right-click on the app name and select **Compress "YourAppName"**.

6.  This will create the archive you need to upload to the app store.

### *What just happened?*

You have done it! You have created the distributable app package, which you can upload into the app store. How to do this is explained in the iTunesConnect Developer Guide, which you can find in your developer account.

# Summary

In this last chapter, you have read about how to make money with your app or game. You have learned the following:

*   Which markets you could publish your game in

*   The methods that exist to monetize your game

*   How to implement MobFox ads inside your game

*   How to use InMobi as a backfill for MobFox

*   How to sign an app for publishing in the Android Market

*   How to create a distributable app for the Apple App Store

That's it! You have finished this book. It was quite a journey and an adventure, but now you are able to create exciting games with Monkey and can also make some money with your apps. Be aware: success doesn't come over night, and sometimes, never at all because, there is always some luck involved in the process. Just keep going and try to learn from your previous projects and from over developers. Game development is a great hobby, and for a lot of developers, also what they spend their working life with. It is up to you! Choose your path!

It would be great to hear your feedback about the book. Either to the publisher of this book or on my website at `http://www.whiteskygames.com`.

Good luck and a lot of success with your journey into game development!

# Index

**Thank you for buying**
**Monkey Game Development: Beginner's Guide**

## About Packt Publishing

Packt, pronounced 'packed', published its first book "Mastering phpMyAdmin for Effective MySQL Management" in April 2004 and subsequently continued to specialize in publishing highly focused books on specific technologies and solutions.

Our books and publications share the experiences of your fellow IT professionals in adapting and customizing today's systems, applications, and frameworks. Our solution-based books give you the knowledge and power to customize the software and technologies you're using to get the job done. Packt books are more specific and less general than the IT books you have seen in the past. Our unique business model allows us to bring you more focused information, giving you more of what you need to know, and less of what you don't.

Packt is a modern, yet unique publishing company, which focuses on producing quality, cutting-edge books for communities of developers, administrators, and newbies alike. For more information, please visit our website: www.PacktPub.com.

## Writing for Packt

We welcome all inquiries from people who are interested in authoring. Book proposals should be sent to author@packtpub.com. If your book idea is still at an early stage and you would like to discuss it first before writing a formal book proposal, contact us; one of our commissioning editors will get in touch with you.

We're not just looking for published authors; if you have strong technical skills but no writing experience, our experienced editors can help you develop a writing career, or simply get some additional reward for your expertise.

## PhoneGap Beginner's Guide

ISBN: 978-1-84951-536-8          Paperback: 328 pages

Build cross-platform mobile applications with the
PhoneGap open source development framework

1.  Learn how to use the PhoneGap mobile
    application framework

2.  Develop cross-platform code for iOS, Android,
    BlackBerry, and more

3.  Write robust and extensible JavaScript code

4.  Master new HTML5 and CSS3 APIs

5.  Full of practical tutorials to get you writing code
    right away

## jQuery Mobile First Look

ISBN: 978-1-84951-590-0          Paperback: 216 pages

Discover the endless possibilities offered by jQuery mobile
for rapid mobile web development

1.  Easily create your mobile web applications from
    scratch with jQuery Mobile

2.  Learn the important elements of the framework and
    mobile web development best practices

3.  Customize elements and widgets to match your
    desired style

4.  Step-by-step instructions on how to use jQuery
    Mobile

Please check **www.PacktPub.com** for information on our titles

# Sencha Touch Mobile JavaScript Framework

ISBN: 978-1-84951-510-8        Paperback: 316 pages

Build web applications for Apple iOS Google Android touchscreen devices with this first HTML5 mobile framework

1. # Learn to develop web applications that look and feel native on Apple iOS and Google Android touchscreen devices using Sencha Touch through examples

2. Design resolution-independent and graphical representations like buttons, icons, and tabs of unparalleled flexibility

3. Add custom events like tap, double tap, swipe, tap and hold, pinch, and rotate

# iPhone User Interface Cookbook

ISBN: 978-1-84969-114-7        Paperback: 262 pages

A concise dissection of Apple's iOS user interface design principles

1. Learn how to build an intuitive interface for your future iOS application

2. Avoid app rejection with detailed insight into how to best abide by Apple's interface guidelines

3. Written for designers new to iOS, who may be unfamiliar with Objective-C or coding an interface

4. Chapters cover a variety of subjects, from standard interface elements to optimizing custom game interfaces

Please check **www.PacktPub.com** for information on our titles

CPSIA information can be obtained at www.ICGtesting.com
Printed in the USA
LVOW03s2020161213

365577LV00009B/116/P